T0303862

The Intimate Supply Chain

Leveraging the Supply Chain to Manage the Customer Experience

DAVID FREDERICK ROSS

CRC Press
Taylor & Francis Group
Boca Raton   London   New York

CRC Press is an imprint of the
Taylor & Francis Group, an **informa** business

Auerbach Publications
Taylor & Francis Group
6000 Broken Sound Parkway NW, Suite 300
Boca Raton, FL 33487-2742

© 2008 by Taylor & Francis Group, LLC
Auerbach is an imprint of Taylor & Francis Group, an Informa business

No claim to original U.S. Government works
Printed in the United States of America on acid-free paper
10 9 8 7 6 5 4 3 2 1

International Standard Book Number-13: 978-1-4200-6497-1 (Hardcover)

Library of Congress Cataloging-in-Publication Data

Ross, David Frederick, 1948-
     The intimate supply chain : leveraging the supply chain to manage the customer experience / David F. Ross.
          p. cm.
     Includes bibliographical references and index.
     ISBN 978-1-4200-6497-1 (hbk. : alk. paper)
     1. Business logistics. 2. Customer relations. I. Title.

HD38.5.R6752 2008
658.7--dc22   2008013049

Visit the Taylor & Francis Web site at
http://www.taylorandfrancis.com

and the Auerbach Web site at
http://www.auerbach-publications.com

Contents

Preface

The genesis of this book can be traced to a personal experience I encountered at a certain gas station at the Oakland Airport in 2006. After a difficult week at a client site, I pulled into one of many national brand gas stations that lined the road on the way to the rental car return. The station seemed to be clean, modern, with a mini-mart attached; I expected an experience just like I have had with hundreds of gas stations across the United States. Trouble began, however, when I inserted my credit card (VISA) into the payment slot on the pump to start the process of filling up the car to avoid those irksome high refueling charges. After twenty years on the road, my card was rejected and I was instructed to pay inside.

As I marched to a big glass window, I met a fellow traveler from New York who was having the same problem. "What's the story here?" I asked. "Beat's me," he said. As we stood at the big glass window, a clerk was busily doing something around the service desk, doing her best it seemed to ignore us. My temper was beginning to boil and I took my fist and pounded on the glass. That got her attention. I politely let my newfound comrade go first. "How much do you want?" she asked. The guy said all he wanted was to fill up the car before returning the vehicle. "How much do you want?" the clerk demanded again. "I don't know," he said, "I just want to fill it up." "I have to have an exact dollar amount and you have to prepay," she demanded. The guy threw a $50 bill into the slot. "When you are done I will pay you back the difference," she said.

As my comrade steamed off to fill his tank, my turn was next. I got the same absurd routine. I held up the credit card to the glass. "Listen, lady," I said, "this is a guaranteed payment card." It was like talking to a wall. "You have got to tell me how much you want!" "I don't know!" I said, "I just want to fill up the tank." In the end she wound up charging my card for the proverbial $50. "Come back when you're done," she said, "and I will issue you a credit for the balance." I went back to my car and pumped about $20 worth into the tank.

At this particular time I happened to be reading Womack and Jones's successor to *Lean Thinking* (1996) entitled *Lean Solutions* (2005). The following paragraph seemed to repeat itself again and again in my mind as I stood at the pump.

> But curiously, despite a growing variety of better products with fewer defects at lower cost available from a growing range of sales channels, the experiences of consumers seem to be deteriorating. In recent years, we've frequently found ourselves discussing this phenomenon with managers. They report that when they are wearing their producer hats in the office or at the factory, things seem to be getting better. But when they go home and put on their consumer hats, things seem to be getting worse.[1]

I had just spent a week with a client discussing how SCM (supply chain management) and ERP (enterprise resource planning) toolsets were going to make their lives better, more efficient, more capable of producing awesome products and services. And here I was, at the end of a pump, becoming more and more frustrated, not with the gas and the amazing supply chain that had gotten it there, but with the unbelievable failure of a complex channel community to provide a satisfying experience *to me* at the pump, which in the end is the whole point of lean, adaptive, demand-driven networks.

With these thoughts running through my mind I made my way back into the station for the credit on my $50 charge. When I got into the station, I now found myself behind a long line of other consumers who were being subjected to the same negative buying experience. As I inched my way to the counter my blood pressure was at the bursting point. I gave the clerk my card and asked for my credit. With Womack and Jones's words blazing in my mind I also asked for the manager. I asked her how she could possibly run a business that went out of its way to virtually punish every customer that walked in, not to mention the costs of doing every transaction (remember I was at a location where virtually everyone coming in was returning rental cars) twice. "Company policy!" was the answer. I told her that such a policy only benefited the company, made customers' lives miserable, and perpetuated an unbelievably wasteful business practice. She just repeated, "Company policy." I thought I had better get out before the police came, but I left with a parting shot—"I will never, ever buy anything from this company again!"—and you know, I haven't.

As I sat back in my seat for the long plane ride to Chicago, I began to seriously think about what had happened at that service station. Could I have been wrong, all those decades, preaching to management about how the endpoint of everything was in managing the process, about squeezing out costs, removing redundancies, reengineering organizations, accelerating development times, and, of course, turning out brilliant products that would cause customers to stand in line and pay exorbitant prices for a chance to be one of the lucky ones to get them?

And what about this business of how companies like Wal-Mart, Target, IKEA, Whole Foods Market, and other mass marketers, who now seem to be capturing the ever-dwindling supply of consumer dollars, did not really have to care about the customer experience as long as they could compete on price and convenience? It was becoming apparent, the more I thought about it, that such a view was purely an abstraction. People simply did not make their buying decisions by subjecting each purchase they made to a crude calculus of lowest price. Often they were willing to spend more with suppliers that just made them feel better, more emotionally and psychologically engaged in the buying experience.

The more I look around, the more important this requirement for suppliers to be *intimate* with their customers' wants and needs seems to be becoming. It is even cracking the formidable foundations of Wal-Mart. In a November 2007 *Wall Street Journal* article it was declared that the Wal-Mart era is coming to a close. The reason: rival retailers have "lured Americans away from Wal-Mart's low-price promise by offering greater convenience, higher quality, or better service."[2] As Wal-Mart struggles to overhaul its down-market, politically incorrect image, competitors have been stealing customers by pitching themselves as more upscale, more focused on providing exciting experiences that appeal to customers' desire for quality and individualized attention. Even in a commodity buying situation where products *are* interchangeable, it has become increasingly clear that customers, both business and consumer, will choose those suppliers that enable them to have a meaningful experience, that seek to go out of their way to build effective long-term relationships that addict customers and drive sustainable profits.

Such companies are all around us—Starbuck's, Toyota, Dell Computer, Apple Computer, Sony, Cold Water Creek, and others—that have gotten the message and are rapidly distancing themselves from the pack. And that message, according to Peppers and Rogers, is that "the customer experience is now the battleground for competitive advantage."[3] In a word, today's customers have come to measure value, based not only on the products/services, but equally on the experiences they receive when they interact with a supplier. Price, quality, and features are important, but so are the perceptions and sense of engagement customers come away with that demonstrate a supplier's value to them—their feelings of assurance and peace of mind aroused when dealing with the supplier's people and systems, and the enjoyment they get when using the goods because of their emotional value.

It has also become apparent that the supply chain is becoming more important than ever to support this need for customer intimacy. Assembling the components to continuously deliver such value to the customer in today's global business environment simply cannot be done by companies acting alone. More than ever, businesses are depending on their membership in effective supply chain communities to drive *customer-centered strategies*. Lean, adaptive, demand-driven networks provide market leaders with new ways to be customer-driven, gain greater visibility to channel demand and supply events, pursue new levels of operations excellence, attain new mechanisms for fulfillment and replenishment agility, and explore fresh opportunities for supply chain collaboration. But today's customer requires their suppliers and their channel networks to advance to the next step: they must be intimate with their individual needs and desires. Customer intimacy opens up an entirely new region of supply chain management by seeking to manage the customer's *experience* with a company and its products. Customer intimacy seeks to build rich relations with customers at every network touchpoint by delivering information, service, innovative products, and interactions that result in compelling experiences that build loyalty and add value to the network community.

The mission of this book is to provide a window into the concepts, techniques, and practical application of *intimate supply chain management*. Each chapter of this book attempts to explore how the convergence of today's global economic environment and the powerful role exercised by the customer is dramatically reconstructing the philosophy and practice of SCM. The first chapter focuses on identifying customers and understanding what they expect from the supply chains with which they do business. Today's customers are seen as exerting an ever-expanding influence over supplier selection and the conditions of the buying process. They are demanding that their suppliers be sensitive to their need for highly configurable, customized solutions designed to fit their unique wants and needs. In addition, customers are demanding that suppliers be *intimate* with the type of buying experience they prefer. Increasingly customers are determining *value* not as the acquisition of the envelope of goods and services available, but as arising from the opportunity for them to be engaged in emotionally and psychologically fulfilling experiences that enable them to be involved in authentic relationships with their suppliers and their brands. Customer intimacy requires companies to understand that the richness of the customer experience grows organically and is the culmination of a variety of touchpoints, often with a global footprint.

Chapter 2 is concerned with how today's global economy has altered forever the business environment and dictated new rules of competitiveness. In the past, marketing objectives centered on expanding a business's strengths in branding, processes, and service: performance was determined by increasing the value the customer provided *to the firm*. Over the past decade or so this paradigm has been shattered by the emergence of a global economy driven by product proliferation, low cost, and outsourcing. Instead of simply competing through brand loyalty and processing advantages, companies must now provide a level of intimacy and completeness of experience that their customers simply cannot find with any other supplier. For most customers, finding products and fulfilling needs are simply a mouse-click away; companies must now be able to offer a total experience that optimizes value *from the perspective of the customer*.

Exploring how SCM can assist companies to grow and prosper in the new global economy is the subject of Chapter 3. From its inception, the supply chain has been viewed purely as a pipeline for the flow of information and products from suppliers to the customer. In today's customer-centered supply channels, such a definition of SCM has become increasingly insufficient. As customers' demands for individualized, unique goods and services expand, supply chains are expected to provide not only the highest quality products and services, but also an outstanding buying experience that provides superior value at each channel network touchpoint. To accommodate this new responsibility, Chapter 3 introduces a new view of the supply chain by dividing it into three interactive yet separate channels: the *demand channel*, the *process value chain*, and the *value delivery network*. The balance of the chapter then proceeds to discuss the components of the first two channels.

Chapter 4 continues the discussion of the new view of SCM by investigating the third and final channel component, the *value delivery network*. While the role of the *process value chain* is to produce the products and services required by the *demand channel*, it is the responsibility of a supply chain's *value delivery network* to ensure their timely and cost-effective distribution to channel intermediaries and end customers. Delivery networks can be simple, such as producer direct to the end customer, or complex and composed of combinations of tiers of partnerships and alliances. Decisions related to channel management and operating mechanics directly impact the ability of supply chain constituents to activate the types of value relationships they wish to pursue with their customers.

Chapter 5 continues the redefinition of SCM by tracing it from its foundations in logistics to the utilization of new channel management models. After providing a redefinition of SCM based on an examination of its six competencies (customer management, collaboration, operations excellence, partner management, channel alignment, and use of integrative technologies), the discussion moves to a consideration of the variations emerging in the science of SCM. Three distinct approaches are identified: *lean supply chain management, adaptive supply chain management*, and *demand-driven supply network management*. The second part of the chapter is focused on detailing the concept and practices associated with the *lean* supply chain. Six core competencies are identified: demand management, use of process Kanban tools, process standardization, channel partnership, communication, and lean SCM implementation. The chapter concludes with a short review of how best-in-class lean supply chains have an edge in ensuring channel costs and delivery mechanisms and are capable of delivering the value customers want from their suppliers.

Although lean supply chains are necessary to ensure cost effectiveness and the removal of channel redundancies, the speed of change and the growing presence of supply chain risk have driven companies to move beyond lean to embrace the concept of *adaptive, demand-driven supply chain management*. Chapter 6 focuses on detailing the theory and practice of these two new approaches to SCM. The *adaptive supply chain* can be defined as a virtual networked community capable of sensing change as it occurs anywhere in the supply chain. Adaptive supply chains are *demand-driven*, composed of networked federations of suppliers that provide *supply flexibility*, centered on providing visibility to channel events that increases *delivery velocities*, and possessed of *agile organizations* capable of rapidly adapting resources, competencies, and outsourced partners to dampen risk and grow market share. A *demand-driven supply network* (DDSN) is defined as a system of technologies and business processes that senses and responds to real-time demand across a network of customers, suppliers, and employees. Instead of a product focus, a DDSN requires supply chains to be customer-centered by deploying demand-sensing strategies and demand-shaping processes that open new opportunities to work with the customer.

Although the new approaches to SCM introduced in the first six chapters are critical to operating successful supply channels, competitive advantage today will go to those supply chains that are not only lean, adaptive, and demand-driven, but which also cultivate intimacy with the customer. Chapter 7 is concerned with a full investigation of the concept of the *intimate supply chain*. Fundamental to the discussion is the concept of *customer experience management* (CEM). The application of CEM to the supply chain opens up an entirely new region of SCM by seeking to manage the customer's *experience* with a company and its products. CEM understands that the *quality* of a customer's interactions with a supplier is as important as the quality of the actual products and services received. Customer intimacy utilizes CEM in an effort to build rich relations with customers at every network touch-point by delivering information, service, innovative products, and interactions that result in compelling experiences that build loyalty and add value to the network community.

Chapter 8 continues exploring how CEM principles cannot only support, but actually lead the way in translating customer engagement strategies into higher lifetime value by leveraging the tremendous capabilities found in the supply chain. A critical theme of the book is that companies cannot hope to provide the necessary level of customer winning value without the enabling power of their supply network partners. Leveraging a supply chain, however, is a complex task and will require the leadership of a dominant player or channel steward to manage channel direction, actual channel design, and alignment of channel value propositions with customer expectations. The goal is to ensure each participant in the channel community possesses a lean, agile, demand-driven organization flexible enough to continuously enable them to identify new sources of value and exciting experiences that attract and nurture customers into engaging, long-term relationships.

Investigating how technologies can assist companies to assess the success of their customer intimacy initiatives is the subject of the final chapter. Three components are identified. The first is concerned with exactly identifying each customer or customer group along with the nature of their relationship with the business. The second component entails the deployment of technology toolsets such as *customer relationship management* (CRM), *enterprise resource planning* (ERP), and other computerized applications. These business systems enable companies to compile extensive databases and the means for data extraction and summarization necessary for the identification of performance metrics that reveal short-term profitability as well as measure long-term customer equity. The chapter concludes by detailing an array of *best practices* that ensure companies and their supply chains are focused on customer intimacy.

Endnotes

1. James P. Womack and Daniel T. Jones, *Lean Solutions: How Companies and Customers Can Create Value and Wealth Together* (New York: Free Press, 2005), 3.
2. msn.com, articles.moneycentral.msn.com/Investing/Extra/TheEndOfTheWalMart Era.aspx (November 8, 2007).
3. Peppers & Rogers Group, "Turning Customer Experience into Competitive Edge: Nikon's Journey to Leadership," *Carlson Marketing White Paper,* (Norwalk, CT: Carlson Marketing, 2006), 2.

Acknowledgments

The concept of *customer intimacy* is a new management science that has arisen in response to today's changing global environment and the expectations of an increasingly demanding customer. Marketing and *customer relationship management* (CRM) thinkers, such as Bernd H. Schmitt, Paul Greenberg, and John I. Todor and consulting firm *Right Now Technologies,* provided the groundwork upon which the *intimate supply chain* was built. In addition, I would like to thank my friends at Lawson Software for the help and support they provided. I also would like to express my sincere thanks to the many students, professionals, and companies that I have worked with over the past several years who have contributed their ideas and experience.

The author would especially like to thank the executive and editorial staff at CRC Press and the Taylor & Francis Group for so eagerly welcoming the project. I would especially like to thank Ray O'Connell at CRC for his trust in the book development and manuscript preparation. The author would also like to thank the entire staff at the University of Chicago Library for their help. Finally, I would like to express my thanks to my wife Colleen and my son Jonathan for their support, encouragement, and understanding over the many months during which this book was written.

About the Author

A distinguished educator and consultant, David F. Ross, PhD, CFPIM, has spent over thirty-two years in the fields of supply chain and manufacturing management. During the first twelve years he held corporate and operations management positions at such companies as McMaster-Carr Supply Company and Illinois Tool Works. For the past twenty years he has been in the Enterprise Business System (ERP) industry with companies such as Computer Sciences Corporation, SSA, DataWorks, Intentia, and currently, Lawson Software. Of those years, six were spent in ERP consulting. For the past fourteen years he has focused on ERP education program development, internal professional development, e-learning tools development, and education administration deployment. For the past nine years Dr. Ross has been responsible for all Lawson M3 U.S. education and training for customers and internal professional development (david.ross@us.lawson.com).

Dr. Ross holds a PhD from the University of Chicago and is recognized as a CFPIM (Certified Fellow in Production and Inventory Management) by APICS (Association for Operations Management). He is active in the Chicago APICS chapter certification education program and has taught the CPIM curriculum for many years. He has been a frequent speaker at a variety of conferences such as APICS, BrainStorm, Beverage Technology, Logistics & Supply Chain Summit, and others, and is a sought-after expert by industry media and analysts. He also has taught operations management at Northeastern Illinois University and Oakton Community College in Des Plaines, Illinois.

The Intimate Supply Chain is Dr. Ross's fourth book in the field of distribution and supply chain management. His first book, *Distribution Planning and Control* (1996), is used by many universities in their logistics management curricula and is a foundation book for APICS's Certified in Production and Inventory Management

(CPIM) program. A second edition was published in January 2004 and is on APICS's best seller list. His second book, *Competing through Supply Chain Management* (1998), was one of the first critical texts on the science of supply chain management. His third book, *Introduction to e-Supply Chain Management* (2003), merged the concepts of e-business and supply chain management, and has been adopted as a cornerstone text for APICS's Certified Supply Chain Professional (CSCP) program.

Chapter 1

The Revolution in Customer Management

Becoming Intimate with Today's Customer

As far back as the turn of the twentieth century, business strategists have been wrestling with the theory and practice of integrating the customer with the distribution channel. Writing in 1915, supply channel pioneer Arch W. Shaw described distribution as composed of two separate yet interconnected functions: *demand creation* and *physical supply*. Demand creation consists in the communication of the *value* to be found in the array of products and services that fulfills the wants and needs of the customer. Regardless of the demand, however, even the best goods and services would possess no value to the customer if they were not available at the desired time, place, and cost. It was distribution's role to solve this basic problem of creating exchange value by ensuring that the flow of the output of production was matched to the customer's requirements as efficiently and as quickly as possible. Shaw felt that finding a solution "was the most pressing problem of the business man today" and "in this great task he must enlist the trained minds of the economist and the psychologist. He must introduce the laboratory point of view."[1]

Although the science and practice of marketing, production, and channel management are today infinitely more refined and robust than they were in the early 1900s, Shaw's comments have lost none of their pertinence. Regardless of

1

the industry, the ability to anticipate, understand, even engineer the wants and needs of the customer, and then construct fulfillment processes that possess the immediacy and agility necessary to provide the optimal product/service solution has never been more compelling and unforgiving. In the past companies sought to create and deliver standardized, mass-marketed products to a captive customer who had relatively little alternative purchase choice. Today's customer simply will not tolerate goods and services that not only do not meet stringent requirements for quality and configurability, but also do not provide an intimate buying experience at the lowest cost with the minimum in effort and time expended.

This opening chapter seeks to discuss the dramatic changes occurring in the "voice" of the customer and how their demands for superlative service and value are requiring the retooling of supply chains on a global dimension. It seems a cliché to state the obvious, that "customers are the most important assets of a company" and that competitive leadership goes to those companies that are "customer-oriented." Despite the almost universal agreement on the importance of the customer, companies often find themselves pursuing customer service strategies that are centered purely on internal measurements of product and departmental profitability, and are out of touch with what customers actually want and need. The destructive nature of such centripetal objectives has only become more perilous as companies and their supply chains struggle to survive in an increasingly global marketplace.

1.1 What's Going on with Today's Customer?

The supply chains that will survive and thrive in the twenty-first century will be those that understand that the customer, the marketplace, and the competition have dramatically changed and will continue to evolve into radically new forms presenting exciting new challenges. Formerly, it was the producer and the distributor who determined product and service content, pricing, methods of transaction, fulfillment, and information transfer. In contrast, today's customers are exerting an ever-expanding influence over product development and the terms of order management, demanding to be treated as individuals, and requiring that their supply partners provide them with configurable, solutions-oriented bundles of products, services, and information custom designed to meet a specific want or need.

Furthermore, customer demands for superior products and services have been heightened by their ability to source from "world-class" companies across global marketplaces. Through the ubiquitous power of the Internet, buyers can now access goods and information at any time, from anywhere on earth. Today's customer is simply demanding more control over the buying experience; easy-to-use order management tools that empower them to design their own solutions; flawless and speedy fulfillment; robust information content; ease of search, ordering, and self-service follow-up; and effortless methods for financial settlement.

Finally, customers are increasingly demanding unique, individualized buying experiences that enhance existing relationships as well as provide fresh, exciting sources of value. The more emotionally and psychologically satisfied customers are with the goods and services they purchase, the deeper their sense of engagement and loyalty to their favorite companies and their brands. Simply, today's customer perceives the value arising from the range of experiences they receive to be far greater than the actual possession of the goods themselves. In an environment where both business customers and consumers have access to virtually any product they require from a wide variety of channel formats, increasingly they are striving for connection and solutions to the complexity and change found everywhere in their lives. Satisfying this desire for positive, satisfying engagement, in turn, grows relationship value and customer equity for firms and their supporting supply chains.

The transposition of power from the producer/distributor to the customer has placed not just some but all companies in a life-and-death struggle to continuously develop adaptive business models that enable them to attract and build sustainable customer loyalty. But before they can build the type of flexible organizations and supply chains necessary to be more customer centric, companies need first to define exactly who the customer is, and secondly, what the increasing power of the customer means to all facets of the supply chain, from product design and production to fulfillment and financial settlement.

1.1.1 Who Is the Customer?

All businesses, whether product or services oriented, have a single, all-encompassing objective: *retaining and making more profitable existing customers and utilizing whatever means possible to acquire new customers.* Realizing this objective in today's fiercely competitive marketplace is easier said than done. Until just recently, the approach of most companies was, after much marketing analysis, to develop product and service mixes that *they* felt best fit each of their major market segments, devise the necessary pricing and promotional schemes to ensure brand loyalty, and reset distribution channels to ensure timely fulfillment.

Recently, however, companies have begun to realize that competitive differentiation lies much deeper than simply matters of global size, the array of available products/services, organizational agility and "leanness," or even the robustness of supply chain networks. In fact, what makes companies successful is that they are *customer-centered.* Today's leading company sees itself not as an aggregate of brands, sales territories, and productive resources, but rather as a *"portfolio of customers"*[2] organized for the sole purpose of enhancing customer equity by conceiving, communicating, and executing superior value for its customers.

Who exactly are a company's customers? While the term *customer* at first glance may appear to be intuitive, in reality there are several types of customers in the demand channel. As illustrated in Figure 1.1, customers can be defined as:

Product/Service Flow

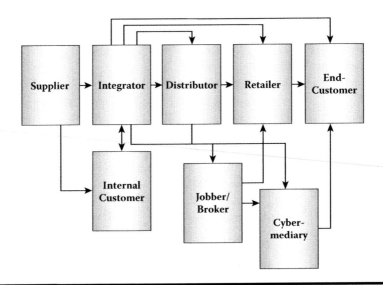

Figure 1.1 Types of customers.

- *Integrators.* This type of customer normally buys raw materials and finished components from primary suppliers for the purpose of consuming them in the production of finished goods. Integrators stand at a pivotal point in the distribution process and, depending upon marketing strategies, can sell to several types of downstream buyers.
- *Internal customers.* This type of customer pulls or has products pushed to them from supply sources that are *internal* to the enterprise. The source of supply could be either the parent integrator or an upstream internal stocking point. The demand from an internal customer is accorded the same value as demand from an external customer. Internal customers consume the product received, distribute it to downstream stocking points, sell it to external partners in the supply chain, or sell it to end-customers.
- *Distributors.* This type of customer normally acquires products in bulk in a finished or semifinished state from either an integrator or another intermediary higher up in the supply channel. These products are then processed to a finished state or sold as is to their downstream channel intermediaries for resale or to be consumed by other integrators. A key function of the distributor is to perform finished good differentiation at the end of the postponement process.
- *Jobbers or brokers.* This category of customer differs from a distributor in two important regards: they rarely take ownership of inventory and they offer a very limited range of services. For the most part, their function is to

act as middlemen, who for a commission, facilitate the buying and selling of products between suppliers and customers.

■ *Cybermediaries.* The application of the Internet has spawned a radically new type of customer that, while occupying a position in the supply chain, may never actually own or physically inventory products. This type of customer can take the form of a buying exchange or a virtual supplier that leverages Internet technologies to perform matching of products and buyers, and coordinates marketing and transaction processes for network partners. Examples of cybermediaries are Amazon.com and e-Bay.

■ *Retailers.* Retailers are normally considered as occupying a position at the terminal point in the distribution process. The function of retailing is to acquire and deliver finished products and services directly to end-consumers for their personal, nonbusiness use.

■ *End-Customers.* The end-customer is the endpoint of the supply chain process. End-customers normally buy products for private, nonmanufacturing use. In today's environment end-customers have the ability to leverage traditional sources of supply, such as retailers or distributors, as well as radically new sources, such as cybermediaries accessible through the Internet, when searching for solutions to their needs.

It is quite useful to separate this array of customers into two groups: *business customers* and *consumers*. In general, the first grouping consists of supply chain participants—suppliers, integrators, distributors, and retailers. For the most part, these customers are characterized as consumers of goods and services for the purpose of value-added processing or movement to the end-customer based on derived demand. The second grouping consists of individual consumers resident at the termination of the supply chain process who employ goods and services for their personal use.

Managing the buying experiences of these two customer groups is very different. The business customer buys goods and services for company use, usually buys a narrow range of goods in large quantities based on derived demand, and is dependent on close relationships with a narrow range of suppliers who customize processes to fit their specific demands. As such, company buyers judge the value of their experiences by the ease of the purchasing and payment process; personal connection with supplier sales staffs; cost, quality, and utility of the products received; and willingness of the supplier to work with them in a constructive manner that provides a win-win situation for both.

The experiences demanded by consumers are quite different. They are susceptible to marketing and advertising targeted at a mass market and are heavily influenced by product design, brand loyalty, and lifestyle contexts when making a buying decision. Although many consumer decisions are driven by practical necessity, they just as easily can be driven by impulse, emotion, and irrational predilections. Intimacy with business customers means knowing about their business plans, product life cycles, and supply channel relationships. In contrast, intimacy with the customer means knowing about their emotional needs, appealing to their intuition, and meeting the psychological desires for experiences that just make them feel better. Of course these two customer groupings do merge and can be considered as members of the same supply chain ecosystem. In today's closely interdependent supply networks, failure at any point will immediately cascade down to the end-customer to be matched by the return flow of complaints, excess costs, and possible loss of business to the very sources of the supply chain.

When considered as an archetype, a *customer* can be defined as any entity in the supply chain that creates demand for products and services. Determining just what this definition means hinges on the depth of vertical channel integration. A supply chain strategy could consist of three possible categories.[3] In a *vertically integrated* channel the producer performs all value chain activities, beginning with receipt of customer demand, continuing with product configuration, and concluding with product delivery and after-sales services. In this model the producer is directly connected to the end-customer without the use of sell-side channel partners. The benefits of such a strategy center on retaining direct control of product distribution, pricing and promotions, marketing information, after-sales services, and degree of customer intimacy. The disadvantages center on absorbing responsibility for managing complex channels of distribution and channel transaction management, and performing product sorting (conversion of production quantities into the assortments and lot sizes demanded by the marketplace), and specialization functions (performance of channel tasks such as postponement, exchange, or warehousing).

In the second category of delivery channel strategy, *third party delegated*, the producer relies on channel partners to perform all customer delivery functions. In this model the producer rarely has direct contact with the end-customer. The advantages of this strategy are that channel intermediaries assume responsibility for all critical channel functions, such as intensity of market penetration, selling and promoting, buying and building product assortments, bulk breaking, value-added processing, transportation, warehousing, sequencing, merchandizing, and marketing information management. Disadvantages center on loss of control of pricing, branding, margins, and immediacy of the timeliness and accuracy of marketplace feedback. In addition, in delegated channels producers are dependent on the quality of sell-side channel partner intimacy with the customer, and risk the potential of debilitating power struggles with channel intermediaries over costs and pricing.

The final category of channel strategy is termed a *hybrid selling model.* In this option the producer selectively performs some of the delivery functions while surrendering control of the remaining activities to sell-side channel partners. The advantages of this model are significant. Producers will be able to offer the best delivery and price option to end-customers while utilizing channel partners to optimize marketing, selling, fulfillment, and service capabilities. However, this medium does pose several problems. Suppliers cannot directly control their partners' operations and they must recognize their limited ability to dictate partner practices, policies, pricing, and promotional activities. Furthermore, supply channels are often nonexclusive with the result that partners can concurrently offer the products/services of a competitor. And finally, the use of any intermediary risks loss of control over customer intimacy or even loss of the producer's brand identity.

Regardless of the channel system that emerges, companies need to be very clear as to who is the targeted customer or customer group. Performing such a task is not an easy one, especially as the number of channel intermediaries grows. Often players in the supply chain can get confused with regard to who the end-customer in the demand chain really is. As Rangan points out, "a channel intermediary is rarely a customer. Firms servicing business customers, for example, usually have difficulty in keying in on their end users because they often view the entity they are selling to as the customer."[4] Keeping focused requires that one always view the product from the vantage point of where the end-customer perceives value to reside. For example, a food processor should view the value of their product as it appears to the end-customer, not how it is sold to distributors or retailers. The company that provides the product packaging, on the other hand, sees channel intermediaries involved in bulk-breaking as the true customer and not the consumer who is buying the food and not the packaging.

1.1.2 What Do Customers Want?

While the content and orientation varies greatly, it can be said that what customers want from their suppliers are complete solutions to their wants and needs that create superior value at the lowest cost with the minimum in effort and time expended. What is customer value? Since the beginnings of trade in ancient times, exchange value has been considered as possessing two components. In the first, value can be described as the exchange of the physical worth or usefulness found in a good or service for the comparable worth or usefulness found in another desired good or service. The most basic form of this exchange process is barter. Secondly, value can be described in abstract terms as the exchange of goods or services based on concepts such as desirability, need, or caprice. In this type of exchange, value always involves a tradeoff between the actual or perceived benefit received and the effort and cost to obtain it. The strength of the attributes associated with a transaction, such as availability, service, quality, image, and price, experienced by the customer determine the level of satisfaction received.[5]

In the past, companies have sought to provide value to their customers by seeking control over the content of their customer relationships—for the most part, profitably managing the customer centered on the efficient execution of the exchange transaction. The goal was to determine how more goods could be sold to each customer, how the cost of serving the customer could be reduced, and how effectively productive and distributive functions could be optimized within the boundaries of acceptable customer service. Concepts of brand and mass marketing were defined around the standardization of products and services, a product-centric approach to the marketplace, product-driven pricing and discounting, mass distribution, and an assumed uniformity of customer wants and needs. In managing the customer, companies were driven by five essential marketing concepts.[6]

1. The *production concept* held that customers would remain loyal to companies that always had products available, delivered on a timely basis, and were low in cost. The goal of the organization was, therefore, to ensure high production efficiencies and as complex a distributive supply chain as possible.

2. The *product concept* held that customers would axiomatically purchase those products that possessed superior quality, the highest performance, the most desirable features, or other intangibles. Following this concept too closely can result in a form of "marketing myopia," where products are designed, built, and distributed without really discovering what customers truly want or need. Offering only one kind of color for an automobile as long as it is black is an example of the dangers of this concept taken to the extreme.

3. The *selling concept* held that customers were primarily passive in their approach to the marketplace and that, if not properly motivated and provided with attractive incentives, would purchase indiscriminately from any supplier based on subjective criteria such as caprice, fashion, or convenience. To ensure customer loyalty marketing needed to continuously devise effective sales, promotions, and advertising campaigns that kept the customer focused on the company's unique product/service value story. The selling concept focuses on the need of the seller to generate revenues from the product/service mix.

4. The *marketing concept* held that the essential function of the organization was to continuously refocus the company's value propositions to ensure satisfaction of targeted customer segment wants and needs, redeploy the product/service mix to satisfy changing market demand, coordinate all organizational customer-focused activities, and produce profits through the creation of satisfied customers. The marketing concept centers on the needs of the buyer and how the entire organization can be focused on identifying and delivering total customer value.

5. The *societal marketing concept* held that a company's prime responsibility was to ensure that customers received complete satisfaction of their product/service needs and desires without doing damage to societal or environmental values. The goal of this concept is to ensure an ethical approach to marketing that balances customer demands, company profitability, and the well-being of the general public.

Although the above five marketing concepts constitute the core strategy followed by many companies today, they all suffer from a common assumption: *they all view the customer as a fairly passive agent in the buying process whose prime role is to provide a steady stream of profits to the organization.* While the customer may have unique wants and needs, which these concepts are supposed to help marketers to uncover, they have usually distracted companies from their primary goal—understanding the total customer experience. Normally they degenerate into a strategy where the role of the supplier is focused on defining the most broadly based mix of products/services that appeals to the greatest number of customers, calculate the pricing and transactional parameters, determine the measurements surrounding acceptable delivery and service response, and detail the boundaries of their customer relations. In short, the above marketing approaches are fundamentally oriented around developing and managing the product and selling and distribution.

Recently, this assumption has been seriously called into question. There can be little doubt that customers still consider the exchange process as providing them with goods and services that possess "value" or that meet a particular desire or need. However, instead of a passive recipient of standardized goods and services, today's customer has become an active driver in the structuring of the exchange event itself as well as in the design, manufacture, and distribution of products and services. The customer is increasingly demanding a say in issues relating to pricing, the use of technology, order management, delivery, reverse logistics, and the need for collaborative relationships with their suppliers. Past marketing strategies focused on the value garnered by the supplier and were driven by such attributes as optimizing economies of scale and scope, mass production and distribution, and cost efficiencies regardless of actual customer wants and needs. Today's customers, on the other hand, want their suppliers to orient their businesses around what adds value to them, not what adds value to the supplier. In the next section we will see what has caused this dramatic transformation in the power of the customer and the role of the supplier.

1.2 Dimensions of Customer Management

The groundwork of past marketing approaches rested on the assumption that unearthing the products and services customers wanted could be accomplished by searching through customer transactions, categorizing them into groups based on specific value filters generic to the industry, and then designing a product/service mix strategy that would best appeal to each customer segment that was identified. It was then the role of marketing to design promotional, pricing, and distribution initiatives that would support the customer strategy. Finally, it was the producer's role to execute production and inventory management strategies that satisfied expected channel demand while optimizing productive resources. In the end, despite declarations boasting of a "customer-centered" marketing strategy, such initiatives really focused on determining the value customers would have on enterprise goals, such as product-line revenue generation and divisional/territorial profitability.

Today, as marketplace power continues to shift to the customer, this model has become increasingly obsolete. While revolutions in communications and computerized tools have provided the mechanism, the real driver of this transformation as been the ability of each customer to assert their *uniqueness*. Rather than being placed within an aggregate market segment serviced by standardized products and supporting services that the company wants to sell, today's customer is demanding that their suppliers instead understand and provide solutions that they want to buy. That they be, in short, *intimate* with what product/service solutions each of their customers wants and how they are to be serviced without telling the supplier how they are to do it. Rather than marketing a product/service to as wide a group of customers as possible, companies are being required to continuously devise value propositions that offer unique solutions that are capable of evolving with the competitive needs of each individual customer.

The "individualization" of the customer is perhaps no more evident at the dawn of the twenty-first century than in the empowerment provided by the Internet revolution. The ubiquitous presence of the Internet enables a range of *customer-centric* drivers previously thought unthinkable. To begin with, the Internet provides customers with an enormous variety of choices and unprecedented access to information. For example, the Internet requires suppliers to provide all-around 24/7/365 business coverage. Also, advances in connectivity have opened markets across the globe, thereby enabling customers to search virtually anywhere for just the right product/service solution at the right price. Customers now assume they can view marketing materials, catalogs, and price lists, configure orders as well as comparison shop, negotiate contracts and execute aggregate buys, participate in online auctions, receive a variety of information from correspondence to training, and review delivery and financial statuses online and in real-time by using the Internet. To be successful, companies are realizing that survival means structuring an organization that is continuously reinventing itself to be able to "treat different customers differently"[7] rather than anchoring hopes on even the most seemingly unassailable product or service in the search for competitive advantage.

And while technology has enabled customers to exert their power to freely roam the marketplace in search of suppliers capable of providing unique, configured solutions that are at the same time convenient, easy to transact, cost effective, and minimize time and effort, it has also enabled businesses to focus on each individual customer. As pointed out above, however, such a capability often requires a veritable revolution in the way companies and their supply chains have traditionally approached the customer. As Peppers and Rogers have so effectively summarized:

> Instead of focusing on one product or service at a time, in order to sell that product to as many customers as possible, you must focus on one customer at a time and try to sell that customer as may products and services as possible—over the entire lifetime of the customer's patronage. Rather than try to figure out what *all* your customers need, in other words, you now have to figure out what *each* of your customers need, one customer at a time.[8]

Until very recently, most companies focused their energies on the revenue-generating value of their products and services, regardless of who was doing the buying. Nowadays, globalization and the facilitating power of the Internet have forever reversed past marketing paradigms. The ability of the customer to easily choose (and change) who they buy from has forced all companies to shift their strategic focus from *what* they are selling to *who* they are selling to.

1.2.1 Defining the Content of Customer Wants and Needs

For the most part, marketing strategies focus on how companies can leverage their portfolio of products and services to retain their existing customer base, acquire new customers, and expand their margins. Creating strategies that successfully accomplish these objectives, however, begin not by engineering the value packages a firm can offer the marketplace, but rather by understanding what constitutes value to the customer. When considered from this perspective, being customer-centered can be said to consist of effectively performing the following five critical elements (Figure 1.2).

1.2.1.1 Value Dimension

Businesses have long known how customers provide value *to them*—by increasing current-period and future cash flows. The goal is simple. When customers have a good experience with suppliers they are likely, on the basis of that experience, to buy

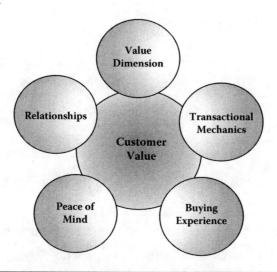

Figure 1.2 Elements of customer value.

from those suppliers again and again. Similar to the way an investment increases in value over time as interest compounds, so the value of a customer likewise increases as each positive experience increases the probability that the customer will not only continue to buy, but to buy more often.

Understanding what provides value *to* the customer, however, is decidedly a much different thing. In contrast to creating marketing and product strategies based only on the goal of increasing the lifetime value of their customer portfolio, companies that are truly customer centric are focused on increasing value *to* the customer, by viewing the business and its offerings through the eyes of the customer. Why do customers buy from you and not your competitors? What special solutions do you provide that the customer simply cannot find elsewhere? What additional product/service composites can you offer that will not only lock in but increase the value customers feel they receive from you?

Case Study 1.1

 **Valuing The Customer**

A decade ago, Pella Corp., a maker of windows and doors, assumed its customers would buy whatever products it made. According to IT Director Rick Hassman "We got caught up in belief that our windows would sell themselves." With sales on the decline, management quickly decided that such thinking needed to be abandoned in favor of an aggressive initiative focused on customer service.

The goal was to provide customers with more options in price, color, and size by enabling a make-to-order environment. Instead of holding inventory, everything is built to customer specification.

Pella's journey from product-centricity to customer-centricity typifies what all product manufacturers must go through

sooner or later. Over the last few years, manufacturers have begun to realize that product advantage is very difficult to sustain. Whether companies want to admit it, it's all too easy for competitors to copy and improve upon a company's most innovative designs, match quality advantages, and beat prices.

What can't be duplicated, says Jim Shepard, senior VP for AMR Research, is the unique relationship companies have with their customers. "The real value is the customer relationship. As long as you sustain that, you'll succeed."

Source: Paul, Lauren Gibbons, "Valuing the Customer," *Managing Automation*, February, 2006, pp. 30–32.

Basically, what customers value from their suppliers depends on the envelope of perceived solutions and benefits attained from available products and services, as well as the cost to acquire them. The issue of what provides value to the customer can be a complex one indeed and should not be confused with the cost to the supplier. A widget that costs pennies to make may provide significant value to the customer who will pay many times its cost because it is wanted or needed. In general, the contents of what provides value to the customer can be decomposed into three regions.[9]

a. *Economic value.* Customers receive economic value when they can leverage a product or service to generate additional value beyond the initial cost. This is particularly the case involving business-to-business commerce. Negatively, value can also be acquired when the customer applies the product/service to reduce associated costs, the savings of which exceed the original cost of the purchase.

b. *Solution value.* The acquisition of a product or service can provide benefit to the customer by providing access to certain desired functions, features, or attributes. Value in this region is found in the capability of the feature to provide a desired level of performance or capability. While such value may in some cases be difficult to quantify (e.g., owning a Lexus versus a Mercedes), in other cases it may be possible to calculate the cost of certain features against alternatives to determine those with the optimum tradeoff (e.g., selecting a compact car versus an SUV when gas mileage is the dominant value).

c. *Psychological.* There can be no doubt that intangible factors can have a significant impact on customers' perceptions of product/service value. Psychological preferences are often subliminal (e.g., brand loyalty or image), and lead customers to believe they are receiving value beyond direct economic or solution-driven benefits. Normally focusing on the concept of *brand,* customers feel they receive increased benefits and reduced risk when they buy from a known supplier. Brand becomes increasingly more important as the differentiation between product/service feature, function, and cost erodes through market and technological maturity.

1.2.1.2 Relationships

Despite all the talk of their supposed fickleness, today's customer is searching more than ever to build intimate relationships with their supply chains. Classically, companies focused on *brand* as the medium by which they could lock in customers. Brand loyalty was the bond that enabled company and customer to consciously (and unconsciously) solidify expectations about specific products and services while defining the boundaries of issues relating to such values as quality, price, and delivery.

While the marketing power of branding has lost none of its strength, it has been altered in today's marketplace in a fundamental way. Although customers will choose to bypass cheaper alternatives to purchase brands such as Toyota,

Nordstrom, or Starbucks, increasingly the value of brand loyalty is being transferred from the feature–function envelope surrounding the product or service itself to the depth of the expected value of the solution provided by the buyer's past experience. For companies this means that their interaction with the customer must spawn a relationship that is enriching and develops over time with each successfully executed transaction. At bottom, relationships make customers feel that they will consistently receive an expected level of value, that they are in control of their purchasing experience, and that they are confident that the product/service will provide the solution they seek.

Finally, customers understand that their loyalty to a brand is two-sided: companies can be assured that continuous attention to providing value to the customer will increase brand equity; customers, on the other hand, can count on a brand to provide a buying experience that competing brands simply cannot duplicate. The accumulated experience of a customer gives them confidence in what they buy and who they are buying from. Relationships affirm customers' feelings that their dialogue with their suppliers, exercised through the actual purchasing transaction, provides them with an unmistakable sense of empowerment as well as a partnership that will be replicated over and over again.

1.2.1.3 Peace of Mind

When it is said that in the exchange process customers expect to receive value from their supply chains, it is important to note that the value they seek extends beyond the receipt of a product or service at a particular price or quality. While the possession of goods and services provides value to the customer in and of itself, it is nevertheless *extrinsic* to the customer. If every transaction was an isolated event and there was no connection in the customer's mind among any series of buying events, then the simple acquisition of goods would constitute the totality of the purchasing experience.

Inherent in every transaction, however, are values that are *intrinsic* to the simple possession of a product, and these values provide an emotion for the customer, an expectation that can be broadly called "peace of mind." Stated simply, in every transaction, all customers are keenly aware of a range of expected values that provide a sense of well-being and affirmation when they buy a particular good or service. Whether it is a simple convenience commodity or a complex, expensive product, customers will often decide on a certain brand because they feel they can count on a wide array of associated attributes that provide a "field of comfort" surrounding and permeating both the product and the buying experience, which extends beyond the product or service in itself.

Peace of mind can actually be broken down into two interconnected components: *conformance* and *assurance*. Conformance is concerned with how effectively the product/service consistently matches the expected specification without the customer continuously verifying the contents of the goods or measuring the results once applied to the want or need. Possible dimensions of conformance extend to such attributes as:

- *Performance* or the capability of the product/service to consistently perform as it has in the past or will perform according to new features.
- *Reliability* or the capability of the product/service to always perform within a previously identified and acceptable range without failure.
- *Durability* or the expectation that a product/service will continue to provide value in terms of both its technical and economic dimensions.
- *Aesthetics* or how the physical appearance or the harmonious complexity of a product makes customers feel.
- *Value/price tradeoff* or whether the customer feels the price of a product/service is worth the value received.

While conformance focuses on the *physical* attributes customers have come to expect from a particular brand or service, assurance is focused more on the confidence or trust, often subliminal, that dealing with a tried-and-true product or supplier brings to a transaction. Possible dimensions of assurance are:

- *Acceptability of risk* or freedom from worry about the efficacy of the value or usefulness of a product or service.
- *Tangibles* or the image of quality (state-of-the-art or highly qualified personnel) or permanence (facilities or a strong history) a customer receives from a supplier. Tangibles give the customer a sense of confidence the products/services they are receiving are truly "world class."
- *Responsiveness* or the consistency and promptness with which customers expect their post-transaction service needs will be met.
- *Competence* or the knowledge that the supplier possesses the required skills and knowledge, which extends from the design of the product/service all the way through post-sales support.
- *Courtesy* or the consistent level of politeness, respect, consideration, and professionalism customers have come to expect from their top suppliers.
- *Credibility* or the high standards of honesty, trustworthiness, and believability customers feel when dealing with their suppliers.
- *Security* or the knowledge that sensitive data customers share with their suppliers will be kept in confidence and will not be compromised.
- *Access* or the degree of ease by which customers can order and communicate with their suppliers, the availability of goods and services within a desired time limit, and the speed by which products and services are delivered to the customer.

In a world of instant access to suppliers and products from across the globe, peace of mind can be easily overlooked as a critical determinant of customer acquisition strategies. Peace of mind permits customers to eliminate the anxiety, worry, and hassle associated with satisfying their requirements. Peace of mind enables customers to be assured that they can trust their suppliers to protect and nurture the special intimacy they share with their partners.

1.2.1.4 Transactional Mechanics

Today's customer has come to expect a buying experience that places them in control of the transaction, provides easy access to customized products and services tailored to meet their individual needs, and allows them to feel secure in the knowledge that the relationships they have built with their supply partners will ensure that their best interests are scrupulously guarded and used to engender for them richer sources of value. Customers expect their suppliers to provide a robust array of mechanisms that facilitate their sourcing needs while resonating with their demands for personalized service. The following can be found among these mechanisms:

1.2.1.4.1 Customer-Centric Value Chains

Past supply chains were constrained by a series of one-to-one relationships whereby goods and information flows were restricted to chained channel dyads, such as supplier–manufacturer or distributor–retailer. Performance values were constructed around the pursuit of cost efficiencies that stressed acceptable service; fixed, one-size-fits-all product lines; and disjointed, dysfunctional flows of goods and data that resulted in time delays, mismatches of supply and demand, and costly channel inventory buffers.

Satisfying today's customer, on the other hand, requires entire supply chains to deconstruct their traditional networks and reassemble them into customer-focused webs that can provide any-to-any connections capable of driving procurement webs, manufacturing webs, even leveraging concurrent channel strategies. Customers require that every node in the supply chain be capable of linking in real time with every channel resource to provide the best and fastest solution to their needs. Customer buying decisions should trigger targeted marketing, sourcing, and customized product/services activities and assign the fulfillment task to the channel partner best able to satisfy it.

1.2.1.4.2 Agile and Scalable Suppliers

Intimate customer management requires supply chains that can provide unique product/service solutions that are low in cost and capable of rapid change as the needs of the customer evolve through time. Customization and configurability require suppliers to structure nimble organizations based on flexible production, distribution, and information processing. Such lean, scalable supply chains seek to build customer value through the real-time synchronization of product/service transfer, use of outsourcing to support internal weaknesses, and deployment of technologies to ensure vital marketplace information capture.

1.2.1.4.3 Fast Flow Fulfillment

If anything can be said about today's customers it is that they expect products and services to be delivered as quickly and completely as possible. Satisfying this expectation requires that suppliers streamline and fast flow all points along the demand fulfillment cycle (Figure 1.3). The process begins with effective *marketing*. Customers want their suppliers to be intimate with their long- and short-term buying behaviors and to be able to present to them tailored options to address specific needs. The goal is to have suppliers pre-engineer product/service selections that provide targeted value to customers without forcing them to spend needless time searching through alternatives that inhibit them from quickly finding the solutions they need. In such an environment, customers not only expect, but welcome cross-selling opportunities.

Perhaps the most critical result of effective marketing is the development of *product/service catalogs* that are configured to meet the exact needs of the customer. These catalogs should allow customers to quickly focus in on the goods/services envelope they want with the minimum effort in navigation and search. This factor is especially crucial when it comes to catalogs available through the Internet.

Once the desired products/services have been identified, the process of tendering an order should be as simple and seamless as possible. Effective *order management* today should begin by providing customers with online access to critical

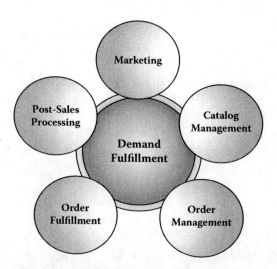

Figure 1.3   Components of demand fulfillment.

product, pricing, and fulfillment information. As the order process begins, customers should be presented with online tools to comparison shop, search for desired quality and service specifications, view product/service aggregations, participate in online auctions, design their own product/service solutions through configuration capabilities, and access related product/service mixes.

While it can be said that the order management process is the prime mover that sets the ordering transaction in motion, it is *order fulfillment* that provides for the speedy and accurate transfer of goods, services, and order information to the customer. No matter how dazzling the order placement function, inaccurate, unresponsive fulfillment simply adds cost to the customer. Among the key elements of effective fulfillment are very short cycle times, availability of products and services, dependability of fulfillment to meet published services standards, convenience, and quality and performance.

Finally, fast flow fulfillment requires effective *post-sales processing*. This area contains two dynamics: customer service management and financial settlement. Customers today understand post-sales service to mean more than returning information about the goods and services they have purchased. Most customers perceive service as an extended part of the purchase and, as such, it increases the value they receive from their supplier. Another element of service customers are demanding is fast flow and convenient payment. Increasingly, companies are acquiring electronic payment systems that enable trading partners to receive bills, authorize payment through credit and purchase cards, match payments to purchase orders, and download statement information directly into customers' systems.

1.2.1.4.4 Networking

In the past, customers were faced with an almost insurmountable information barrier that disabled them from working directly with their suppliers: the inability to leverage information systems that permitted continuous peer-to-peer networking. With breakthroughs in computer technologies, it is now possible to connect different computers and their databases together in a network. The advantage of networked systems is that buyer and supplier can now communicate information directly without regard to time or distance. Networking empowers customers to cut across functional barriers within their own and their suppliers' organizations and interweave common and specialized knowledge to provide unique solutions to their sourcing requirements.

1.2.1.4.5 Digitizing Sourcing

The rise of Internet technologies has dramatically and forever altered the traditional landscape of customer management. Today's web-enabled applications are providing radically new approaches to generating value for customers while facilitating the sales process, enhancing customer service capabilities, and restructuring companies into highly integrated, customer-centric organizations. On the surface of things, the Internet has enabled customers to utilize applications that provide simple, self-directed tools for browsing and locating solutions to product/service needs from anywhere on the globe. Web-enabled tools have made it easy for customers to execute order entry and pricing negotiations, engage in bidirectional communications that increase personalization of the transaction, and source directly from suppliers, thereby bypassing costly channel intermediaries. Finally, today's order management technologies permit customers to be self-directed with access to 24/7 service, real-time information, online support, digital documentation and training, and web page customization that provides them with personalized methods of influencing their suppliers' value propositions in order to dramatically increase individual value.

1.2.1.5 Managing the Customer Experience

In a global business environment marked by a veritable explosion in the number of new products, ease of customization, and instantaneous communication, the role of the customer and what they want from their suppliers has dramatically changed from what it was even at the beginning of the new century. More than ever, customers have the power to make their own decisions about what they buy, how much they are going pay, how it is going to be delivered, and whom they are buying from. In a word, customers have come to measure value based not only on the products/services, but equally on the *experiences* they have when they interact with a supplier. In turn, today's best companies are succeeding by unearthing and nurturing a special intimacy with their customers aimed at capturing unmistakable competitive advantage and new levels of profitability.

Although the term has been around for a quarter century, this rediscovered customer management concept is termed *customer experience management* (CEM), and it has been defined as "the customer's perception of interactions with a brand, from marketing communications to sales and service processes to the use of the product or service."[10] CEM is about understanding the content of and effectively managing customer interactions while building brand equity and long-term profitability. Although the hard elements of customer interaction, such as transaction management, information transfer, and brand identification reinforcement are critical, they constitute only part of the customer relationship story. Of equal importance are the perceptions and interactions customers come away with from a buying experience that demonstrate a supplier's value to them, their feelings of assurance and peace of mind aroused when dealing with the supplier's people and systems, and the emotional content of the products and services they receive.

The realization is that it is the merging of superior products and services with high-quality supplier–customer interaction that is at the core of the intimate supply chain. As globalization and the Internet proliferate goods and services and expand the reach of competitors, even companies with apparently unassailable competitive advantage are finding it difficult to maintain market leadership based on products, price, or the strength of their supply chains alone. Value today is measured in the eyes of the customer rather than what value the customer provides to the business. This means that every touchpoint, not only inside the firm but also out in the supply channel wherever the customer interacts with partners, products, or services, must be shaped to provide customers with an overwhelming buying experience, a veritable *wow* experience.

As will be discussed later in this book, CEM has often been confused with *customer relationship management* (CRM). While CRM is also concerned with enhancing the experience of individual customers so that they will remain customers for life, there is a significant difference between CRM and CEM. To begin with, CRM is clearly focused on determining customers' value *to* the organization, while CEM's concern is to understand the depth of the value customers receive *from* the organization. At heart CRM is a technical and information mapping tool used to assist a company's marketing team in identifying, capturing, and retaining customers. CEM, on the other hand, attempts to look at the business from the customer's point of view to ensure the portfolio of product and services resonates with the type of experiences they expect.

In fact, as the power of the customer to determine the marketplace continues to expand, the very idea that a supplier can actually "manage" the customer's experience at all has begun to supplant all previous marketing concepts. As product/service sourcing continues to move from performing services to self-service, customers are increasingly taking charge of their own buying experiences rather than having them managed for them. In fact, the best companies can do today is simply ensure that every touchpoint in the customer experience, from products and services, to pricing, promotions, and after-sales service, is carefully tailored to add value and expand the positive experience of the customer.

In their analysis of what today's customer really wants from their suppliers, Womack and Jones have come up with an effective short list or what they call the *Principles of Lean Consumption* to guide companies in shaping marketing objectives. The new manifesto of winning and retaining customers consists of the following six points.[11]

1. Customers want suppliers to provide them with a complete solution to their problems. A partial solution (one where the customer must search for other providers to complete the solution) is no solution.
2. The solution should be attained and implemented with as little cost, time, and effort on the part of the customer as possible.
3. All of the components necessary to provide the solution need to be available exactly when they are needed.
4. Suppliers need to provide a complete solution *where* the customer expects to find it without having to merge disconnected sources.

5. The components of the solution must be available *when* the customer wants it.
6. Bundle the product/service envelope so that the solution can be acquired by the customer with a minimum number of decisions and with ease of effort.

The key point is that today it is the satisfaction gained through ease of sourcing and completeness of the *solution* and not the *product/service* that constitutes the key value for the customer. This means that individual companies and supply chains that are focused inward, on attempting to manage the marketplace rather than critically examining customers and their individual experiences, can never really provide the encompassing solutions those customers so deeply value. An intimate supply chain, on the other hand, is continuously searching to identify just who its best customers really are and adapting its business to provide the optimal value propositions desired by its most profitable customers.

1.3 Summary and Transition

Perhaps at no time in history has the power of the customer to influence the content and process of managing sourcing and the buying experience been as dominant as it is in today's marketplace. In the past, it was the producer and the distributor who determined products and services, pricing, methods of transaction, fulfillment, and information transfer. In contrast, the proliferation of products, ever-shortening product life cycles, price and quality pressures brought about by the expansion of the global economy, the enabling power of the Internet, and the establishment of an on-demand culture has changed forever the customer's buying expectations. Today's customer is exerting an ever-expanding influence over the nature of products, services, and delivery; they require suppliers to be sensitive to their need for highly configurable, customized solutions that are designed to fit their unique wants and needs.

Supply chains can consist of several types of customers, from producers and agents to distributors, retailers, and end-customers. Although the type of demand (whether independent, derived, or dependent) may occur at different points in the delivery channel, all customers want complete solutions to their wants and needs that create superior value at the lowest cost with the minimum in effort and time expended. Realizing this objective requires today's supply chain to shift from selling products and services to as many customers as possible, to a focus on figuring out what *each* customer wants and needs, one customer at a time. This strategy can only be activated by constructing solutions delivery systems that are responsive to individual customer needs. They must be, in short, *intimate* with the type of buying experience each customer expects and capable of evolving with the competitive needs of each individual customer.

Becoming intimate with the customer means more than just product and service positioning; it means understanding what constitutes value to each customer.

When considered from this perspective, being customer-centered can be said to consist in performing five critical elements well. The first is value. What customers value depends on the envelope of perceived solutions and benefits attained from the portfolio of available products and services. The content of value can be seen as purely economic, solution based, or psychological. Secondly, customers value relationships that enable them to feel that they will consistently receive an expected level of value, that they are in control of their buying experience, and that they are confident that the product/service received will provide the solution they seek.

Another important element customers value is the sense of well-being, affirmation, and peace of mind they receive when buying a particular good or service they feel conforms to their expectations. Such assurance kindles confidence that dealing with a trusted brand or supplier brings to a transaction. The fourth element can be found in the availability of transactional mechanics that enable customers to easily order, configure, and manage their sourcing needs while resonating with their demands for personal service. Finally, companies must expand their concept of customer management to include CEM. Simply, customers have come to value the *experiences* they receive when they interact with a supplier as much as the goods they acquire. The merger of superior products and services with high-quality supplier–customer interaction stands at the very core of the intimate supply chain.

To be truly on the road to customer intimacy means that business strategists must expand their view of what brings satisfaction to their customers and see it from a global perspective. Rather than a short-term focus that fails to extend beyond the most recent transaction, companies must understand that the richness of the customer experience grows organically and is the culmination of thousands of touchpoints, often with a global footprint. Because the depth of today's customer experience spans businesses and is distributed over many geographies, we must turn in the next chapter to an exploration of how globalization is driving what customers perceive as an order-winning experience.

Endnotes

1. Arch W. Shaw, *Some Problems in Market Distribution* (Cambridge, MA: Harvard University Press, 1915), 41–44.
2. This phrase was coined by Larry Seldin and Geoffrey Colvin in their book *Angel Customers and Demon Customers* (New York: Portfolio, 2003), 7.
3. Further discussion relating to channel systems in V. Katuri Rangan, *Transforming Your Go-to-Market Strategy: The Three Disciplines of Channel Management* (Boston, MA: Harvard Business School Press, 2006), 90–91; David F. Ross, *Distribution Planning and Control: Managing in the Era of Supply Chain Management* (Norwell, MA: Kluwer Academic Press, 2004), 75–93; and Chris Selland, *Sell-Side Channel Management*, Aberdeen Group White Paper (Boston, MA: Aberdeen Group, September 2004).

4. Rangan, 76. Mentzer and Moon have attempted to explain the distinction in supply chain demand by calling the amount of product consumed by the end-use customer *independent demand*. Whether it is a customer buying in a retail store, online, or a business buying goods expended in its own operations, this type of demand determines the true supply chain product demand. The channel entity that serves the end-use customer directly experiences independent demand. All channel nodes supporting this end-use supplier experience *derived demand*. That is, these channel intermediaries see demand secondhand and as an aggregate from the customer-touching supplier. Derived demand, unlike customer demand, is expressed in inventory storage points in the channel and guided by the order fulfillment and purchasing policies of upstream channel suppliers. John T. Mentzer and Mark A. Moon, "Understand Demand," *Supply Chain Management Review* 8 (4): May/June 2004, 38–45.

5. See the discussion in William C. Johnson and Art Weinstein, *Superior Customer Value in the New Economy: Concepts and Cases* (Boca Raton, FL: CRC Press, 2004), 5–7.

6. See Philip Kotler, *Marketing Management*, 11th ed. (Upper Saddle River, NJ; Prentice Hall, 2003), 17–27.

7. This phrase is found in Don Peppers and Martha Rogers, *Return on Customer: Creating Maximum Value from Your Scarcest Resource* (New York: Currency/Doubleday, 2005), 72.

8. Ibid., 73.

9. These points have been summarized from Sunil Gupta and Donald R. Lehmann, *Managing Customers as Investments: The Strategic Value of Customers in the Long Run* (Upper Saddle River, NJ: Wharton School Publishing, 2005), 115–121.

10. Bob Thompson, *Customer Experience Management: Accelerating Business Performance*, Customer Think Corporation Burlingame, CA (June 2006), 2.

11. James P. Womack and Daniel T. Jones, *Lean Solutions: How Companies and Customers Can Create Value and Wealth Together* (New York: Free Press, 2005), 9–17.

Chapter 2

Learning to Grow and Prosper in a Global Economy

Realities of Supply Chain Management in the Twenty-First Century

There can be little doubt that we are in an age of profound, exciting, yet unsettling change in the life of peoples and nations. Not since the dawn of the Industrial Revolution in the latter half of the eighteenth century have economies, institutions, beliefs, and values been subject to such a sudden, qualitative, and fundamental transformation as is occurring today. The genius of the Industrial Revolution rested upon the ability of a few highly developed countries to converge technology, physical productive assets, capital, and social organization to burst through the bounds previously imposed on productive resources by famine, war, plague, and occasional sociopolitical collapse. Henceforward, the emerging industrialized nations were characterized by an irreversible capability for sustained, rapid, and almost limitless production of goods and services, which advanced the standard of living of their peoples and dramatically enhanced their political power.

Today, no one would seriously argue that the Industrial Revolution has lost its steam. In fact, industrialism and its mechanisms of capitalism, free trade, and mass consumption have expanded dramatically over the intervening two hundred years, reaching just about every corner of the earth, overwhelming the vestiges of the old agrarian social contract, and sweeping away alternative economic and political systems. If anything, the virtual explosion of free-market industrialization in countries formerly driven by centralized economies (particularly India, China, and the former Soviet Republics) has unleashed enormous productive resources that hold the promise as well as pose the threat to transform centuries-old economic and political structures.

As the twenty-first century began, it had become evident that the Industrial Revolution had entered a new stage—we are now living in a *global economy*. The transition began in the late 1980s with talk among economists and the business public alike that the more industrialized nations were in the process of rapid migration from an industrial to a service economy. In this new postindustrial world, old industrial giants were looking to emerging nations as rich sources for cost-effective production and a seaway into local economies. By the first years of the new century, enabled by radical breakthroughs in transportation and computerized technologies like the Internet, it was evident that the world had indeed shrunk: skills, ideas, and processes could now be integrated across companies, distances, and political borders with an immediacy previously thought impossible. As one current bestselling book has declared, "The World is Flat!"[1] Instead of a fractured world of winners and losers, nations across the earth were increasingly becoming nodes in a massive global supply chain for manufacture and services with the creation of wealth the only target.

This chapter seeks to explore how globalization has presented supply chain strategists with a variety of radically new challenges. On the supply side, globalization is altering forever the rules of competition, driving companies into outsourcing and offshoring of production and distribution, forcing once monolithic, proprietary organizations into collaborative partnerships, and necessitating the construction of value streams that span the globe. Globalization has also intensified the need for businesses to enhance the customer's experience. If the goal is to know and provide each customer with a unique experience and a superior level of personal value, the capability of supply chains must correspondingly be expanded to deliver value across international borders separated by global space and time.

2.1 Basis of Globalization—A Primer

The importance of international trade has grown dramatically as a critical component of business strategy and activity since the 1970s. For example, during the intervening thirty years, American imports and exports have grown exponentially as evidenced by Table 2.1. Although the trade deficit had expanded to almost $758.5 billion in 2006, the United States has benefited enormously from global trade. Foreign capital finances the U.S. account deficit, effectively allowing savings-poor Americans to live

Table 2.1   U.S. Imports and Exports (Goods & Services), 1965–2006

Year	Exports	Imports	Balance
1965	35,285	30621	4,664
1970	56,640	54,386	2,254
1975	132,585	120,181	12,404
1980	271,834	291,241	−19,407
1990	535,233	616,097	−80,864
1995	794,387	890,771	−96,384
2002	974,721	1,395,789	−421,067
2004	1,157,250	1,769,341	−612,092
2006	1,445,703	2,204,225	−758,522

Source: U.S. Census Bureau, U.S. Department of Commerce

Note: All figures are in millions of U.S. dollars.

beyond their means. Free trade boosts U.S. output by $1 trillion dollars annually. According to the Peterson Institute for International Economics, this value is equivalent to ten thousand dollars annually per U.S. household. This explosion in global trade is the result of a number of trends, such as continued world economic growth and the connective power of information technology, which are expected to accelerate the expansion of the global economy as the twenty-first century proceeds.

Broadly speaking, this explosion in globalization can be traced to four macroeconomic factors: (1) the maturing of the economies of today's industrialized nations, (2) the growth of global competition, particularly from emerging nations, (3) the application of information technology, and (4) the expansion of the principle of the comparative advantage of nations.

2.1.1   Declining Self-Sufficiency of Nations

The maturing of the economies of the industrialized nations of the world has fundamentally altered conventional thinking about global trade and the role of the supply chain. By the late 1980s it had become clearly evident that the economies of the United States and the Western block of nations were passing from a long era of rapid expansion to one of maturity. Although it is true that at the beginning of the new millennium the United States and the Group of Eight (G8) countries still occupied a position of global economic hegemony, it was also clear that nations once described as Third World were experiencing a period of unprecedented economic growth. Not only were these emerging nations serving as sources of low-cost labor and new markets, they were also rapidly becoming economic powerhouses on their own. In the 1970s and 1980s nations like Japan and Korea had captured the electronics market and dominated banking and manufacturing; by 2007 China had become the world's manufacturer and Toyota had dethroned, in a convincing fashion, the once might U.S. auto industry.

Fueling this global economic growth is the realization that nations can no longer be self-sufficient; that even the wealthiest of the old industrialized nations are now dependent on other countries for raw materials, commodities, and energy. Often components assembled in foreign lands, critical for the cost-effective domestic production of finished goods, can be purchased much cheaper from factories located in Asia or Latin America. Finally, there can be no denying that certain imported products are here to stay. China's growing capacities in the production of high-labor content, low-cost commodities, machine tools, and textiles can only be expected to expand; Japanese leadership in microelectronics and the automobile market are testimony of the impact of foreign products on American purchasing habits.

This growing interconnectedness of nations, rich and poor, is without a doubt the single greatest challenge to today's supply chain. The challenge comes from two directions. First, the global nature of business has accelerated the power of the customer. As discussed in the first chapter, customers today have the power to source from companies located anywhere on the globe. This means that supply chains must be capable of identifying demand as it occurs anywhere in the value chain network and then determine how the required products and services can be dynamically positioned at the right place, at the right time, at the lowest cost to deliver the "perfect order."

Configuring supply channels to realize this objective constitutes SCM's second challenge. Most companies today have leveraged *lean* techniques and integrated ERP systems to achieve relatively high levels of customer service, cost control, and financial management of their domestic operations. Mastering global trade, however, has proven to be another matter indeed. Managing cross-border supply chains, tackling the complexities and manual processes associated with contracting, ordering, shipping, and financial settlement, continuously evolving customs and regulatory issues, and the ever-present possibility of global supply chain disruption, have added new dimensions of complexity, cost, time, and risk to business management.

The globalization of trade and industry is not just a fad: companies that do not find ways of achieving worldwide integration and coordination of economic activities, financial management, and networked information transfer are doomed to fall behind their competitors in the race to provide the most value to the customer. A winning global strategy is one that will:

1. Use globalization as a mechanism to expand worldwide, gain new customers previously beyond the reach of domestic operations, leverage foreign industries to remove costs and redundancies, tap into new sources of development talent and products, and spread the possible impact of risk to global partners.
2. Ensure the optimal utilization of product life cycles and processes by selling to as wide a geographically dispersed customer base as possible. Such a strategy seeks to amortize product development, production, inventory, and

distribution costs as quickly as possible by expanding beyond the domestic marketplace.

3. Provide a channel whereby companies can leverage foreign markets to provide new sources of profit and brand penetration unavailable to competitors.

4. Bypass government restrictions and import tariffs by establishing companies inside foreign countries. In addition, a local presence inside developing nations enables companies to compete on an equal footing with indigenous businesses while providing a future outpost before outside competitors arrive.

5. Profit from economies of scale, scope, and low cost to be found in other nations. Besides just production and logistics cost savings, global companies can also profit from local economic incentives, lower tax rates, and countertrade opportunities.

6. Ensure participation in the global trade movement. The economic value of international trade is vastly outpacing the growth to be found in any one nation. Between 1951 and 2000, global trade grew 2,000% (or a compounded 6.2% per year) while the world economy grew 700% (or 4% per year compounded).[2] Assuming continued progress integrating national economies, the World Bank estimates that by 2030 total global trade is expected to almost triple to $27 trillion. Trade as a percentage of total output will rise from about one-quarter to more than one-third.[3]

2.1.2 Growth of Global Competition

While it can be said that the explosion in global trade can be attributed to many factors, perhaps the most important (with the exception of a few rogue countries such as North Korea) is the widespread economic development occurring today in all nations. Part of this development can be traced to the expanding global perspective of multinational companies. Eager to tap into vast reservoirs of cheap labor, low taxes, and favorable local governmental incentives as well as to be on the ground floor for the opening of new marketplaces, multinationals have dramatically increased their investment in foreign countries with an eye on partnering locally and building long-term supplier and customer relationships. For example, Intel, Microsoft, Google, and AMD, all announced large investments at the beginning of 2006 in India targeted at building infrastructure for complex, high-value products. As of mid-2006, Wal-Mart had 60 stores in China, employing over 32,000 people and located in 30 cities. Developing countries, such as Brazil, China, and India, who enjoy lower operating costs, are seeking to catapult their economies to "world-class" status by courting foreign investment alongside domestic companies with leadership in textiles, apparel, and electronics.

In addition, many nations have come to realize that deregulation and opening avenues of global trade, reducing tariffs, and fostering free trade are necessary to their continued expansion. This has become particularly evident with the end of centralized economies in Russia, India, and the former Eastern European block. While varying in degree and application, this expanding orientation of the world's countries toward a market-driven economy can only be expected to accelerate global competition. Assisting in this development has been the rise of supranational trading blocks in the Americas, Europe, and Asia. Trade organizations such as the WTO (World Trade Organization), Asean, the European Union, Mecosur, NAFTA (North American Free Trade Agreement), and CAFTA (Central America Free Trade Agreement) have been formed to promote the emergence of economic regions, the development of distribution channel infrastructures, the speed of communications, and the promotion of national security.

Beyond the initiatives of global corporations, efforts directed at national deregulation, and the formation of regional trading blocks, globalization is increasingly being driven by individuals residing in both advanced and developing nations, who are using tools like the Internet to network within and collaborate with each other in the search for new opportunities. The sheer size of global competition has dramatically increased. In 1985 the "global economy" consisted of North America, Western Europe, Japan, East Asia, Africa, and Latin America and comprised some 2.5 billion people. Today, with the end of the Cold War and the shift of countries like China, India, and the Soviet Union from economies driven by autarky to forms of market capitalism, the global economy expanded almost overnight to encompass 6 billion people.[4]

Although it is true that only a small minority of the people across the globe are education- and infrastructure-equipped to compete on an equal footing, there can be no denying that availability of what is becoming a global labor pool has already begun to undermine long-established patterns of employment and the availability of skills traditionally found only in the First World marketplace. In fact, regardless of their stage of development, the educational and performance requirements of workforces everywhere are moving toward homogeneity and interchangeability. Assisted by technology, knowledge resources today can easily span geographies, where tools like the Internet have the capability to network repositories of individual skills from anywhere on the globe. According to La Londe, "This, in turn, leads to the development of organized global knowledge markets, all competing for the best available knowledge resources."[5]

At the risk of becoming irrelevant, companies everywhere on the globe must be careful to develop plans that integrate the massive new numbers of companies and pools of talent exploding everywhere across the globe into their competitive plans. Clear strategies must be formed that ensure, for example, that companies are not embarking on a campaign that winds up going head-to-head with a lower-cost competitor somewhere else on the globe. Similarly, companies must be careful to protect core competencies and sources of innovation when they develop sourcing dependencies with suppliers and workers on the other side of the earth.

Case Study 2.1

 **Developing The Supply Chain**

Critical to global trade success is the importance of partnering with local businesses to build supply chain expertise in developing nations.

Astec Power, a worldwide supplier of power supplies to OEMs in the computer and telecom industries, has been careful to develop its Chinese partners. The Carlsbad, California firm involves its Asian partners in the innovation, product design, and distribution process. To ensure quality, Astec has created a supplier development program where 50 Astec engineers work with suppliers to continuously drive improvement.

According to George Foo, Astec V.P. of operations, the investment has resulted in the company winning "millions of dollars in new business by investing in local supply chain professionals and in development of market intelligence."

In another example, the Walt Disney Co. has determined that to make the new Hong Kong Disneyland a success, local partnering is critical. Overall the company intends to hire and operate locally to become part of the region's cultural fabric.

An essential part is leveraging local resources to keep the supply chain invisible, increase speed, and decrease the risk of disruption. The company intends to send its Hong Kong employees to other Disney facilities around the world for six months to learn the business. The goal is to ensure growth plans don't move faster than supply chain and organizational expertise allow.

Source: Kuehn, Kurt, "Five Universal Business Plan Challenges Driving Supply Chain Alignment in the 21st Century," *Supply & Demand Chain Executive*, December 2005/January, 2006, pp. 50–53.

2.1.3 Technology and Management in the Global Economy

There can be little doubt that the explosion in today's information technology tools is fueling the growth of globalization. In little over a decade, breakthroughs in Internet technologies, communications linkages, and software architectures have enabled companies across the globe to not only accelerate the speed and productivity of business functions, but also to activate opportunities for supply chains to network their information repositories and special competencies. The activation of such opportunities, in turn, provides for the structuring of new forms of organization capable of closer integration with each other and deeper intimacy with the customer.

Internally, today's information technologies enable companies to efficiently manage transactions, collect, analyze, and generate information about customers, processes, products, services, and markets, and link business functions through real-time databases and applications permitting timely and effective decision making. *Externally,* information technologies enable supply chain strategists to architect value-chain networks that are collaborative, agile, scalable, fast flow, and web-enabled. The goal is to present customers anywhere in the supply chain a single, integrated response to their wants and needs by creating a unique network of value-creating relationships. Connectivity and synchronization at this level require the elimination of channel information silos and the construction of collaborative, channelwide communication and information enablers directed at a single objective: *total customer satisfaction.*

Employing this power requires both planners and technologists to rethink their use of the computer. Actualizing the supply chain networking potential of today's information systems will require enterprises to move beyond traditional paradigms that utilize computerization purely as a means to plan and control internal business processes. In fact, connectivity enablers, like the Internet, now permit companies to escape the narrow boundaries of their own information environments to network with a universe of geographically dispersed trading partners and create a level of real-time strategies, operations, and planning systems previously thought unattainable. Today's boundary-spanning technology tools enable companies to harness the explosion of data that continuously emanates from every point in the supply chain galaxy, integrate it with internal business systems, perform sophisticated analysis of the information, make visible an accurate picture of individual enterprise and supply chain partner performance, and build revolutionary capabilities and competencies for the generation of new sources of products and services, whole new businesses and marketplaces, and radically new forms of competitive advantage.

At the core of today's technologies can be found two fundamental principles. The first is the availability of a technical infrastructure that links computer systems and people. The word commonly used for this process is *integration.* Integration calls for the elimination of the ideological, strategic, and performance barriers that separate functions within an organization, between supply chain nodes, and between supply chains and customers. Organizationally, integration means leveraging information tools to bring business functions together by facilitating ever-closer coordination in the execution of joint business processes. Integration focuses on activating the creative thinking within and between enterprises. Integration attempts to bring into alignment the challenges and opportunities offered by information technologies and the cultures and capabilities of the modern organization.

The second principle at the core of today's technologies is *networking.* In the past, computer system architectures permitted only hierarchical communication. As each processor completed its tasks, the output was then available for the next processing task, which, in turn, passed its output to the next downstream processor. As illustrated in Figure 2.1, with the advent of service-oriented architectures (SOA) and Internet browsers, the process of communicating information has shifted from processing hierarchies to connecting dispersed computers and their databases together in a network. The advantage of networked systems is that people can now communicate information directly to other people in the network. This peer-to-peer networking enables companies to leverage the capabilities, skills,

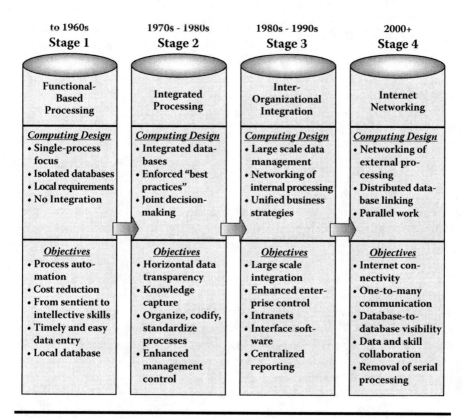

Figure 2.1 Technology evolution.

and experience of people by integrating and directing their talents around focused tasks. What is more, networking provides businesses with the ability to assemble virtual resource teams from across the value chain consisting of the best talent with access to the most relevant data and capable of articulating and executing customer-winning value in any form in the shortest time and at the lowest cost.

What is so important about integration and networking? Integration enables companies to become more agile and more flexible so that they can quickly identify shifts in demand and then be capable of engineering supporting changes to capacities and inventories along the entire supply chain. Networking, on the other hand, enables company resources to work in parallel across internal business functions and across resources separated by global space and time. Together, integration and networking provide whole supply chains with the capability to unify an increasingly fragmented and dynamic global network, focus and coordinate multiple cross-functional, cross-enterprise task teams, and structure businesses and value chains to activate continuous learning.

Harnessing and meaningfully directing integrated, networked computing is one of today's most critical challenges. Globalization is in the process of altering our fundamental business assumptions, values, and attitudes about the meaning of work, the source and use of knowledge, and the awakening and formulation of our creative visions. As one futurist put it over a decade ago, today's technology tools are not concerned with activating a single person's or company's capabilities in isolation, "but with how we *empower, energize, and enable* one another. It presupposes an integrative environment."[6]

2.1.4 The Comparative Advantage of Nations

It can be said that the concept of trade in goods, services, and ideas is at the very core of civilization. In poetry, philosophy, and economics it has long been proclaimed that no man and, for that matter, no society is an island, self-sufficient and autonomous. Neither the composite skills of a single individual nor the commonwealth of a particular state can provide the fullness and potentiality available when individuals and nations exchange the fruits of their special productive competencies. In pre-industrial history, trade arose when one society found that surpluses of food, raw materials, or handicrafts could be traded for other commodities in scarce supply, which neighboring societies happened to have in abundance. With the dawn of the Industrial Revolution and the ensuing changes in the nature and availability of products, size of the marketplace, and capabilities of distribution, the need for trade correspondingly grew exponentially. In fact, as national economies expanded their industrial output, the need for materials they did not possess in abundance, products they did not produce in sufficient quantities or not at all, and outlets for their own surplus manufacture, made trade with other nations a critical component of business strategy.

The logic that trade was advantageous for a community of nations was a fundamental precept in the early writings of what the nineteenth century termed *political economy*. Adam Smith wrote in *The Wealth of Nations*, "If a foreign country can supply us with a commodity cheaper than we ourselves can make it, better buy it of them with some part of the produce of our own industry, employed in a way in which we have some advantage."[7] The concept is simple and intuitive. If a nation can acquire relatively expensive products from another nation that can produce them in greater quantities at a lesser cost, and if in turn it can provide goods it has in abundance at a lower cost than can be produced in the trading nation, both nations will gain through trade. Since the law of variation in human competencies, sociopolitical development, and physical resources guarantees the uneven creation and production of goods and services, trade not only provides the ability for all nations to enjoy the collective productive output of human ingenuity, it also furthers the growth of wealth in individual nations. Distribution is the mechanism by which trade is executed, and the more robust and the more sophisticated the capabilities of distribution, the easier the labors of nations can contribute to the acceleration of standards of living across the entire globe.

Case Study 2.2

Indian Outsourcers

With the collapse of the Internet bubble, the U.S. IT community saw thousands of jobs outsourced to low-cost programming factories in India. Just a few short years later, however, those same Indian firms have themselves seen their costs escalate and have been turning to even lower cost knowledgeable workers in China.

For example, Tata Consultancy Services (TCS) and Microsoft joined together to invest $14.6 in mid 2006 to found TCS China. The reason: the lower cost of Chinese workers. The monthly salary for programmers in high-tech hot spots like Beijing, Shanghai, and Shenzhen was between $600 and $960. That's about half the pay for a similar position in India, where tech salaries are rising at about 15% per year.

U.S. firms also are by-passing India for China. Mavent, a developer of mortgage compliance software, chose Chinese developers after deciding India's sources were getting too expensive and were suffering from too much staff turnover. According to Mavent's VP of product development, their Chinese partners are saving 60% on development costs compared with U.S. prices.

Today, Indian services vendors like Satyam, Infosys, and Wipro have all opened offices in China. Accenture, EDS, and IBM likewise have also opened operations in an attempt to leverage China's growing comparative advantage in programming services.

Source: McDougall, Paul, "Indian Outsources Acquire a Taste for Chinese Fusion" *Information Week*, July 31/Aug 7, 2006, p. 36.

2.1.4.1 Theory of the Comparative Advantage of Nations

While the above description of exchange between nations seems obvious, there is, however, a subtle twist in the mechanics of how the basis of the exchange process works. To begin with, the existence of trade assumes that the availability of raw materials, productive competencies, technical capabilities, and power to drive productive resources are not equally available everywhere on the earth. In addition, it assumes that whether by circumstance of climate, physical geography, population size, and openness of politics and culture, the economic life of nations has and will continue to evolve along different paths. Together, these two fundamental assumptions guarantee that even if two nations produce the same product, only one of the two will have an economic advantage in the production of that product. This phenomenon of trade between nations was formalized by the English economist David Ricardo (1772–1823) and is known as the principle of the *comparative advantage of nations*.

The Ricardian model conceives of international trade as founded on the twin concepts of *absolute* and *comparative* advantage. An *absolute advantage* in trade can be said to exist when a nation produces goods not produced in other nations, or can produce certain goods dramatically cheaper or with higher productivity relative to other nations so that it possesses a monopoly. Beneficial trade for that nation occurs when it exchanges those goods for other goods produced by nations for which they in turn have an absolute advantage. When trade occurs between nations possessing absolute advantage in certain products, each can be said to benefit by exchanging the productive value each possesses.

In reality, however, there are few products in which a nation has an absolute advantage. Even in handicrafts, nations often produce similar products with minimal variation in form, fit, and function. In such cases, Ricardian theory holds that if all nations are to benefit from the production of each other, each nation must choose goods in which they enjoy a special advantage, and those goods should be the ones in which they have a *comparative advantage*. To identify a nation's comparative advantage goods requires comparison, not of actual productive/resource costs, but of the *opportunity* cost of producing those goods in each nation.

Ricardo uses an example of two countries, England and Portugal, that both produce the same two goods, cloth and wine. If England is more productive in the manufacture of cloth than wine and Portugal is more productive in the making of wine than cloth, then England can be said to have a comparative advantage in cloth production and Portugal in the production of wine. England's opportunity cost advantage in cloth occurs because it would cost England less to transfer resources from the production of wine to produce more cloth than it would cost Portugal to transfer resources from wine to cloth production. This means that even if it cost less in Portugal to produce both products, England would still have a comparative advantage in the production of cloth. From another perspective, if Portugal is twice as productive in the manufacture of cloth and three times as productive in the making of wine than England, Portugal should specialize in and trade the good (wine) in which it is "most best" at producing while England should specialize in and trade the good (cloth) in which it is "least worse" at producing.

The utility of comparative advantage can be seen in its impact on pricing, production levels, consumption levels, wages, incomes, employment levels, and standards of living in each trading nation. If there was no trade and two nations produced similar goods, the product that each enjoyed as a competitive advantage would have a lower price than the same good would have in the other country. When trade began between these two nations, the relatively cheaper prices for comparative advantaged goods would stimulate trade as well as increase production in the advantaged nation due to the potential for increased profits. In general, trade for its advantaged good would rise, while the cost for acquiring its disadvantaged good would fall. As such, the profit available from trade would drive nations to specialize in the advantaged good while the law of diminishing profits would result in the simultaneous phasing out of local industries producing the disadvantaged good.

It is interesting to note that as imports of advantaged goods from another nation rise, the apparent superiority of productive resources, workforces, technologies, or even lower cost in disadvantaged home industries serves less and less a competitive advantage. The more trade between nations becomes free and unencumbered by governmental protection and tariffs, the less chance disadvantaged industries in all nations have of survival. Paradoxically, this means that the technology advantage possessed by highly industrialized nations like the United States and the low-cost labor advantages of less-developed nations like India and China does not guarantee the survival, much less paramountcy, of disadvantaged industries. Industries in any nation forced to compete with the advantaged products of a trading nation are doomed to increasing unprofitability and ultimate closure.

2.1.4.2 Applying the Theory of Comparative Advantage

The Ricardian concept of the comparative advantage of nations, while logically ines-capable, is often assailed as based on assumptions about how nations and industries behave that are untenable in the real world. For example, most nations today have tariffs and restrictions on industries and trade that seek to favor disadvantaged local industries. Further, the theory of competitive advantage assumes that industries exist in an environment of perfect competition, when in reality, governments or long-standing market dominance has weighted the power in favor of certain local businesses. However, all economic theories are based upon certain assumptions that may appear initially counterintuitive, oversimplistic, or incapable of withstanding the actual conditions of the real world. While they do not provide foolproof pro-cesses by which economic structures can be confidently built, they do nevertheless provide useable constructs that can guide effective thinking by exposing the general principles of the economic mechanisms propelling men and nations.

Despite the criticisms that can be leveled at the Ricardian theory, the model does provide a number of critical insights that more than ever are driving the eco-nomic life of nations in the twenty-first century. Without a doubt, the most dra-matic development in economic life today is the emergence of China, India, and other Third World nations. In fact, the great debate that has been raging ever since the turn of the new century is whether the lowering of trade barriers and the use of outsourcing, supply-chaining, and offshoring is really advantageous for more developed nations like the United States or does it represent an undermining force slowly diminishing long-standing and hard-fought-for economic standards and life values. And in today's world Ricardian theory seems so much more insidious where products are not the only things moving to the nations with low-cost compara-tive advantage; so are jobs consisting of specialized knowledge or those of a purely service nature.

While the merits of this debate can be almost endlessly discussed in favor of one side or another, it does appear that the economic realities of comparative advantage are slowly winning out. For starters, access to cheap, high-quality products have immeasurably helped to fuel the economic prosperity all nations seem to be enjoy-ing as the second half of the decade proceeds. Former iron curtain nations gripped by autarky are seeing their standards of living rise, their peoples embracing the market economy, and their political systems relaxing barriers to personal freedoms. Furthermore, the comparative advantage of nations has further spurred on innovation. Instead of conceiving of the global economic system as fixed and immutable (the so-called *lump of labor* theory), today's business environment is constantly expanding, creating new jobs, new opportunities, and new wealth, not only in the G8 industrialized nations, but in emerging industrial, technological, and financial powerhouses like China, India, and Dubai.

A more detailed look at China provides direct evidence of the ubiquity of Ricardian theory. In the popular view, China's almost limitless reservoir of cheap labor provides Chinese companies with an overwhelming comparative advantage in labor-intensive industries. Median monthly wages (160 hours) in the United States, for example, are $2,160 and just $120.80 in China. Beyond the labor content, China's manufacturing base is also much more cost-effective and characterized by heavy investment in capital equipment and information technology (some 25 to 30 percent more than U.S. plants) that will enable it to widen its global lead and solidify its objective of becoming the "world's factory."

While China's exploding economic growth in manufacturing does indeed make it difficult for the manufacturing sectors of its trading partners to compete on an equal footing, Ricardian comparative advantage, however, is providing new opportunities for other nations. Economic benefit is indeed moving in both directions. In the most direct sense, China's growing dominance has forced foreign manufacturers to abandon noncompetitive industries at home while encouraging production of goods they are "most best" or "least worse" at producing.

In a larger sense, Chinese success is driving a whole new range of opportunities that simply did not exist during the days of the Cold War. For example, U.S. manufacturing companies' investment in China increased by 40% in the two years from 2004 to 2006. These investments included R&D (research and development) centers, warehouses, distribution facilities, sales offices, and factories. Such investments have enabled U.S. companies to make money in China. According to a Deloitte study, in 1999 just 10% of U.S. companies operating in China had margins above their global average. By 2004, the percentage had risen to 42%.[8]

China has also become the United States' third largest importer behind Canada and Mexico and the fastest growing export partner. While the Chinese trade deficit reached $232.6 billion at the end of 2006, Chinese consumers' desire for U.S. goods, whether made locally or imported, has also grown dramatically. For example, exports to China in 1985 were $3.9 billion. Exports stood at $16.1 billion in 2000, $34.7 billion in 2004, and ended 2006 at $55.2 billion or 3.8% of all U.S. foreign trade.[9] When it is considered that China possesses the world's largest consumer market (a population of 1.3 billion with a rapidly rising middle class), U.S. firms have the ability to leverage their comparative advantages to avail themselves of new opportunities for collaboration and partnership.

Case Study 2.3

Retooling China

So much press has been given to the dramatic rise of China that the dark-side of its head-long plunge into the global economy tends to be overlooked. In just two decades the Northeast region of the country (Dongbei) has gone from economic powerhouse to industrial dinosaur. Once the center of Maoist China's heavy industrial might and one of its richest regions, the area constituting what is commonly known as Manchuria, has today fallen on hard times so reminiscent of other "rust belts" across the globe.

Much of the scenario sounds all too familiar to U.S. steel, machine tools, and now automotive industrial workers. As China struggles to stay the course towards a marketing economy, Dongbei's economy is disintegrating amid the closure of thousands of state-run factories, millions of laid-off workers, a growing gap between rich and poor, rampant corruption, potentially deadly human and environmental disasters, and the specter of social unrest.

While industrial workers in the developed nations feel their jobs have been outsourced to developing nations, the truth is that China's revitalization has cost 31 million Chinese their jobs between 1998 and 2003. And, as found everywhere, those Chinese workers in their 40s and 50s, trained solely to perform tasks in the old state-owned factory system, are the hardest hit and least employable. Privatization and investment in modern software and manufacturing plants has signaled in China an end to the old state-run factory system mind-set of complacency and entitlement at all levels in society.

There is something eerily similar to the old social safety nets and guaranteed employment of the socialist-era state-owned factories in China and the womb-to-tomb approach to employees found in the struggling U.S. steel, mining, and automotive industries that are at the forefront of out-sourcing and obsolescence today.

See Larmer, Brook, "The Manchurian Mandate," *National Geographic*, Vol 210, No 3, Sept. 2006, pp. 42–73.

2.1.4.3 Realities of the Marketplace and Ricardian Theory

Companies in the United States must guard against taking the seemingly iron law of Ricardian theory too far. G8 countries cannot simply count on an indefinite leadership in the high end of product development creativity, design, and innovation, while leaving the less skilled, lower-paying tasks of repetitively producing low-margin products and services to developing nations. For example, Japanese historical comparative advantage in the production of small, inexpensive automobiles would dictate that they would continuously focus on increasing their dominance in that market, while leaving the higher-end and more lucrative trucks and luxury cars to America's Big Three auto industry who had, in turn, a seemingly perpetual lock in that segment of the market. The significant troubles besetting Ford and GM in the mid-2000s are in good measure due to their inability to change their thinking about products and customers centered on a false belief in the immutability of Ricardian theory.

Competitive enterprises must understand more than ever that in the twenty-first century capabilities are not static and that all competitive advantage is temporary. Reposing a company's future or, for that matter, an entire nation's economy on the belief that competitors will not attempt to develop capabilities that seemingly are in conflict with their natural comparative advantages (for example, low cost vs. innovation) is a serious mistake. No matter how deeply imbedded in a company a core competency, be it a product, service, brand, or process, may appear to be, it is subject to the law of random marketplace variation, always ready to morph into something else or spawn an ancillary competency that obsoletes the original as the competition or the customer changes the rules of the game. The desire for a better mousetrap will always encourage entrepreneurs to gaze beyond what constitutes their comparative advantage in the pursuit of innovation.

2.1.4.4 The Commoditization of the Marketplace

The impact of globalization, hypercompetition, and accelerating innovation in products and services has resulted in a growing commoditization of goods and pricing that has begun to threaten established paradigms of marketing and the basis of exchange value. In the not too distant past, companies sought to gain market share by locking in customers based on their loyalty to their brands. In an exchange economy, companies motivate buyers by offering proprietary functional features and benefits at prices designed to discourage competitors from challenging their leadership. Customers, in turn, act as fundamentally rational buyers who carefully weigh value received for the value tendered, with the goal of choosing the highest value for the lowest price. In a market economy marked by scarcity in product/service availability and absence of choice, the seller determines the conditions of exchange value. What the customer really wants and the psychological needs and feelings arising out of the transaction are of minimal consequence.

In today's global world, where any product at just about any price, is just a mouse-click away, the traditional concepts of exchange value have been rendered obsolete. The key is found in the shift from an economy of scarcity and controlled exchange interaction, to one of abundance, inexhaustible choice, and rapid innovation. This fundamental shift in the relative power of the customer to decide what constitutes marketplace value and how companies will be rewarded with loyalty has ushered in a new era. Instead of the product/service content, what customers are really interested in is how the exchange process provides them with a source of special meaning, an emotion, an experience tailored just to their individual requirements. Acquiring products at the lowest price is no longer the customer's objective—the goal is find buying experiences that provide solutions to today's purchasing dilemmas caused by a bewildering range of choice, the constancy of change, and feelings of stress and anxiety that lead to alienation and decay in trust and loyalty.

Companies who seek to thrive and profit in today's *customer experiential economy* must understand that they need to transform strategies based on competing through brand and price to one centered on competing through *customer intimacy*, by cultivating engaging relationships that position their competencies and those of their supply chains as valued resources customers simply cannot do without. In a progressively commoditized marketplace where customers grow increasingly apathetic to the pull of brand and company loyalty, "the path to sustainable profits and growth for most companies," states John Todor in his book *Addicted Customers* (2007), "is through differentiation on the customer experience." Most companies have not as yet understood this new concept of *value* based on customer intimacy. The results for the ones that have—the Starbucks, Toyotas, and Zaras of the world—"is rapid growth, high profits, and a core customer base that indicates that their business model is sustainable."[10]

2.2 Activating Customer Value in a Global Economy

When economic historians look back at the business environment of the opening years of the twenty-first century, it is sure that they will identify the convergence of billions of people empowered by the Internet and capable of competing and collaborating in a global economy as perhaps the period's most salient feature. But, concomitant with this feature, historians will also point to the dramatic changes globalization is having on the very foundations of twentieth-century economics—concepts of competitive advantage, the nature of product/service value, and the role of labor and innovation. Globalization is increasingly requiring companies large and small to search for ways to synchronize the flow of goods, information, investment, and innovation to uncover new avenues of customer value that span national boundaries and time zones. It has become obvious that competitive leadership will go to those companies that can continuously transform their value networks by remaining agile and scalable, collaborative, and customer aligned.

The critical first step in this process is understanding the capabilities and objectives driving nations and individual enterprises. For example, emerging nations like China and India are clearly trying to develop positions in manufacturing and technology that leverage their enormous labor cost advantage to build a long-term, sustainable dominance in high-volume commodity/technology markets. First World nations have always been characterized by high selling price thresholds, which in turn act like a centrifugal force drawing in developing nations that can provide the necessary productive capacities or knowledge skills at a much lower cost to feed the demand. In the past, developed nations were able to stay one step ahead of the cost/value curve without losing competitive advantage by focusing on continuous product/service innovation, followed by another round of outsourcing of low-value work.

But as developing economies such as China and India continue to expand, and skills, experience, and funding grow, the pressure on innovation and need for customer intimacy for all nations has correspondingly increased. It is not dissimilar to what happens to local boutiques, department stores, and food-marts when Wal-Mart not only sets up a location nearby and plays its overwhelming low-cost leadership card in the volume-versus-value game, but then also begins to develop innovative ways to present radically new product and service formats to local customers. Boutiques can no longer take refuge by just depending on complex operations/services (value) to combat a volume-based competitor who, in turn, is intent on exploring new methods designed to erode the value advantage of seemingly more agile and entrenched local merchants.

Driving profitability and constantly renewable sources of competitive advantage in the twenty-first century's global economy requires companies to pursue the following strategies:

- Learning how to compete in an age of temporary advantage
- Generating new avenues of customer intimacy
- Creating new opportunities by reaching new markets
- Activating the power of collaboration

When companies interweave each of these strategies into a comprehensive fabric, they will collectively provide distinct value-centric directions that will enable businesses to succeed in today's global economic environment.

2.2.1 Competing in the Age of Temporary Advantage

Perhaps one of the most difficult adjustments for companies today is the requirement that they transform their business strategies from being product/service/technology driven to those that are focused on their ability to rapidly deconstruct and then reassemble people and process capabilities from inside their companies or externally from supply chain partners to meet new marketplace opportunities. In the past, businesses felt that competitive advantage could be sustained by developing a market-winning portfolio of products and services that optimized their productive assets and cost-versus-service tradeoffs while providing for the standardization and channeling of the customer experience. Such a strategy worked fine in the pre-globalization era. In many industries, executives and employees alike could count on relatively unchanging products, company structures, and customer approaches. Brands and marketing strategies often lasted beyond the careers of individual executives; workers could count on an immutable work environment with paternalistic programs that shaped and took care of employees from training and advancement to retirement.

Caught in the ever-increasing velocity of change characterizing today's global business environment, companies are finding that strategies that seek to lock in current advantages by encasing capabilities in rigid organizational and operational structures can be deleterious, if not fatal to corporate heath. Petrified organizations, like Ford and GM, are finding they cannot sustain their advantage forever, regardless of how securely they may have once thought they locked out the competition.

In contrast, today's best companies are not afraid to restructure both the organization as well as their business strategies in the search for competitive advantage. For example, Intel's decision in September 2006 to reexamine the direction of the business and eliminate 10,500 jobs (about 10 percent of its workforce) was a direct effort to abandon a strategy that had once made it one of Wall Street's top performers. The decision was driven by a combination of sinking profits and a bloated and inefficient organization as it sought to regain market share stolen by smaller rival, Advanced Micro Devices, Inc. (AMD). "These actions, while difficult, are essential to Intel becoming a more agile and efficient company, not just for this year or the next, but for years to come," said Chief Executive Paul Otellini in defense of the moves.[11] Intel had also been under intense pressure to unload money-losing divisions and halt the encroachment of AMD on its lucrative core business: making the microprocessors that act as the brains of computers.

While traumatic, Intel had been in a similar situation in the mid-1980s when it exited a business it helped create (making dynamic random access memory chips widely used to store information in computers) to focus on microprocessors. That shift prompted one of Intel's largest rounds of layoffs ever, with the company eliminating more than 7,000 jobs, about 30 percent of its workforce at the time. The critical point is that Intel had seen at both junctures in time that its existing competencies, its products, and the value they provided to its customers no longer drove competitive advantage. It was time to evolve or die. "They're going to lose a lot of share, the PC environment is tough, and they're bloated," said an industry analyst. "But if they can cut costs enough, we're going to see a different company."[11]

The bottom line is that whatever a company's current core strengths, be they innovation, product design, unique processes, or technology savvy, *all competitive advantage is temporary*. Companies today, regardless of the industry, are finding it increasingly difficult to build any kind of *sustainable* competitive advantage. Instead of building products and organizations capable of locking in competitive advantage, they are finding that even their best strategies are often countered by disruptive innovations in technology, breakthrough products and services from some competitor on the other side of the globe, radically new business models like Dell, Wal-Mart, or Amazon.com, or gigantic risks produced by global environmental disasters, the price of oil, or terrorism. The problem is that these often jarring shocks to the business environment are occurring more rapidly as changes from anywhere at any time on the globe can obsolete even the most rock-solid product or service.

In this age of temporary advantage, perhaps the *ultimate* strategic capability is not to be found in any product or service and their seemingly uncopyable internal core competencies. Rather as Fine has stated, perhaps the most important competency of a company is its "ability to determine which of those capabilities are going to be the high-value-added capabilities and which will be the commodity abilities—and for how long."[12] Successful companies will be those that can continuously anticipate which capabilities to invest in, which to outsource, and which should be discarded as they prepare for the moment current competencies no longer provide competitive advantage.

2.2.2 Creating New Avenues of Customer Intimacy

As stated in the first chapter, driving the enterprise toward greater customer intimacy is now *the* foremost frontier for competitive advantage. Much of the components traditionally ascribed to creating competitive advantage detailed above (low cost, brand dominance, product innovation, process uniqueness, technology enablers, and rapid and agile logistics response) while important, have become of secondary importance today in comparison to the capability of a company to deliver a consistent, enriching *customer experience*. In a market environment dominated by increasing product commoditization, exploding product line portfolios, global low-cost challengers, and revolutionary business models, the only path to successful competitive differentiation resides in the richness of a company's intimacy with its customers. The new competitive imperative is simple: *companies and their supply chains must migrate from strategies that collectively center on operational efficiencies to those that optimize the customer experience.*

While much more will be said about this principle during the course of this book, suffice it to say that engineering customer intimacy strategies to counter direct challenges from China, Inc. or Wal-Mart is the only way to stay competitive in today's global business landscape. And the fundamental objective is to continually deliver value to the customer that exceeds the competition. The more value customers can expect from a business, the more that business will be worth. The most effective strategies, therefore, will be those that can unearth the latent, unmet needs of the customer and capitalize on opportunities to sell new products and services that solve customer problems from a unique perspective.

For example, value-centric strategies could consist of the following:

■ *Process Capabilities.* It this strategy a company focuses on complex engineering and technology-driven design, manufacturing, and delivery processes that permit it to offer products/services to match the unique solutions customers want. The primary value-add in this strategy would be a company's ability to leverage unique in-house expertise, development processes, and technology tools that cannot be easily replicated. The competitive advantage would reside in the delivery of cutting-edge product/service envelopes, the ability to materialize and harness revolutionary processes, and the capability to mobilize resources to realize very narrow time-to-market or time-to-customer horizons. Succeeding with this strategy will require that companies be market masters providing a unique set of customer value enhancers (short delivery time, product configurability, technology enablers, etc.) that the competition simply cannot match.

■ *Mass Customization.* Another strategy would be to move to the opposite end of the spectrum and focus on internal strengths in manufacturing, service, and distribution to develop unique customer value. In this strategy businesses would focus on internal differentiating capabilities in areas such as mass customization and make-to-order manufacturing that, accompanied by supporting services, enable them to carve out a unique competitive position. The key drivers would be a combination of customer intimacy (which would alert the business to abrupt shifts in market value propositions) and operations excellence (which would utilize lean, flexible processes). The value of the strategy is that it enables companies to build marketplace advantage around late-stage product configuration, thereby insulating them from offshore, high-volume commodity competition.[13]

■ *Supply Chain Stewardship.* A third possible strategy to enrich customer intimacy is to utilize the competencies of supply chain partners. For example, rather than developing new capacities and technologies on their own, companies can adapt and channel the strengths of channel partners to rapidly construct and deploy solutions to meet tough competitive challenges. Termed *channel stewardship*, the goal of the strategy is not only to leverage specific partner competencies, but to transform the entire supply network into an integrated value ecosystem focused on pursuing the total customer experience. A channel steward can be a producer, an intermediary, or any other channel network participant. The result is the development of value propositions that are both as attractive as possible to the customer as well as profitable to channel members.[14]

Regardless of the strategy, the goal is to turn customer intimacy into a competitive edge. Converting strategies into actual programs to deepen the customer experience, however, is easier said than done. According to a 2005 survey by global research firm Strativity Group, while 76% of the executives surveyed placed customer strategies higher on the corporate agenda than they had three years previously, only 31% said they had the tools and authority to construct new avenues of customer intimacy.[15] To survive and thrive in today's global economy, companies will need to take a harder look at customer intimacy strategies that deliver an exceptional customer experience, cut costs, and increase profitability, while keeping one step ahead of the competition.

2.2.3 Reaching New Markets

In the popular view, the concept of globalization has often been equated with *offshoring* (the movement of manufacturing, IT, service, and other jobs overseas) and *outsourcing* (the movement of any process that is not a core competency to a channel partner that can do it better). While they are different strategies, offshoring and outsourcing primarily focus on providing companies with a variety of advantages, such as cost reduction, increased quality, access to alternative sources of supply, proximity to customer facilities, and increased agility, attained by shedding redundant jobs and unprofitable processes. *Globalization*, on the other hand, is about the growth and exploration of new markets, individual countries partnering with each other to produce and export goods and services, the networking of human knowledge and skills, and the exploitation of local comparative advantage centered on the diffusion of wealth. As Jeffrey R. Immelt, chairman of GE said, "Globalization has a bad name. But the world is inextricably global. We win by exporting and we win by sourcing."[16]

Globalization strategies are thus not simply about endlessly searching the globe for low-cost resources: they are also about *growth*. While low-cost sourcing is often seen as the driver, many companies are also noticing that developing economies, such as China and India, continue to expand and mature and are rapidly evolving from low-cost commodity producers to powerhouse consumers. According to Tom Dadmun, vice president for supply chain operations for Alabama-based telecommunications equipment firm ADTRAN, Inc., his company is growing operations offshore because that is where the customers are. "When you look," he thinks, "at the growth areas and emerging markets, they are not in the U.S. The growth in my business domestically will be in the single digits whereby the countries in Asia, South America, South Africa, and India are growing much faster; therefore you must set up global supply chains to reach these customers."[17]

And many companies are going global to capture this new market. For example, South Carolina-based Polymer Group, Inc., a producer of nonwoven fabrics used to make products such as diapers, baby wipes, and injection molders, has twenty-one sites in ten countries because its customers, who include Proctor & Gamble, Hanes Industries, and Johnson and Johnson, are located there. According to CEO James L. Shaeffer, "We're not in China, shipping back to Wal-Mart. We're there because there is a developing middle class, and there is a developing consumer base."[18]

Furthermore, it is simply a myth that U.S. manufacturers are making globalization decisions based solely on the cost of labor. While it is true that industries, such as textiles and toys, are being outsourced to countries with a comparative advantage in those products, the manufacturing of highly complex systems, such as automotive, aviation, and semiconductor, are actually being *insourced* to the United States. For example, Honda increased its U.S. workforce by 15 percent in 2005; Novartis recently relocated its R&D facility from Switzerland to Massachusetts; and Samsung is investing $500 million in its Texas semiconductor plant, where it employs some 1,200 Americans.[19] Looking for new markets does not mean that manufacturing in the United States needs to be abandoned. Successful enterprises will need to follow the role of companies like Ohio-based Nordson Corp., which leverages a U.S. workforce dedicated to the latest lean philosophies and supply chains concepts to gain global competitive advantage. While two-thirds of its sales are outside the United States, 70 percent of its manufacturing remains in the country.

An effective globalization program designed to explore new opportunities to engage and deepen customer intimacy should have the following key performance targets in mind:

1. *Reducing lead times to the customer.* Locating plants and supply chains in foreign countries will enable companies to decrease the lead time it takes to delivery customer-satisfying products and services at the lowest cost to global customers.

2. *Improving global performance visibility.* A local presence combined with robust supply chains should provide quicker and timelier intelligence regarding the direction and intensity of local customer demand. Such market information will enable companies to more effectively focus productive capabilities and channel inventories to service shifting patterns of demand on a global basis.

3. *Exceeding customer expectations.* When companies manage the entire customer relationship, they can gain an important edge. By engaging directly with the customer, businesses can develop innovative ways to enrich the customer experience, localize support to meet unique demand requirements, offer value-added services, and outperform competitors on key metrics such as delivery, responsiveness, and configuration of products and services that correspond to local needs.

4. *Managing value-focused global operations.* For many enterprises today, the goal is to drive customer-enhancing value across all points in the supply chain simultaneously regardless of geographical location. Effectively tapping into this vast reservoir of demand requires systems and operations capable of dealing with diverse economic, cultural, and national conditions, regulations, and business processes, as well as of providing the framework for collaboration with partners that span the globe.

2.2.4 Activating the Power of Collaboration

Without a doubt, today's networking technologies have truly enabled companies to deepen the relationships they have historically formed with their customers, suppliers, and business partners while opening up hitherto blocked or untraveled avenues of global partnership. More than ever before, the ability of companies to collaborate with their customers and suppliers has become the key to competitive success. But as customers' choices in products, services, and channels have dramatically expanded, so have their expectations of continuous value delivery and performance. The bottom line is that companies cannot solely focus on a strategy of reengineering processes and promoting infrastructure optimization to maintain marketplace leadership; such benefits are short-lived as competitors adapt and copy the method. Succeeding today requires companies to leverage and coordinate the competencies and innovative capabilities of their partners if they are to provide unique customer value innovation and rapid deployment.

Defining the content of *collaboration* can be a tricky affair. While the term describes an activity pursued jointly by two or more channel entities to achieve a common objective, its content and objectives can span a wide spectrum of functions. It can be interpreted in very basic terms as the process of periodically transmitting business data and intelligence between customer and supplier or between supplier and supplier, to the structuring of real-time technology architectures that enable partners to share and leverage highly interdependent infrastructures that permit the tight integration and synchronization of marketplace and product intelligence focused on enhancing customer value performance everywhere along the supply chain continuum.

As globalization expands in intensity, companies have become keenly aware that to enter the world marketplace without a strategy to collaborate effectively with the customers and suppliers constituting the value chain is a recipe for disaster. It can, in fact, be argued that perhaps there is no product, no process, no competency more pivotal than the collective capability of a superior partner network. The following points have surfaced as the main drivers:

- The relentless acceleration in the forces changing today's marketplace—the growing requirement for customer intimacy, globalization, outsourcing and offshoring, information technology enablers, emerging markets, the decreasing span of competitive advantage, and others—is requiring companies to deploy strategies focused on lean philosophies, nimble and quick-to-market development processes, and synchronized and mutually supporting channel collaboration. Simply, the faster the growth, the more dependent firms have become on utilizing the resources and core competencies of channel network partners to stay ahead of, if not drive the power curve.
- Market leaders have always known that the more integrated and efficient the passage of information and the performance of transactions the lower the cost. As the sophistication and deployment of collaboration technologies increases among networked partners, the more the cost of business declines and the intelligence necessary to effectively respond to customer needs increases.
- The challenges of the global marketplace have rendered obsolete the old strategies for creating renewable customer value. Companies simply cannot remain inward focused and dependent on historically successful product and service offerings and development processes. Rather, business strategists must look to merge existing core competencies with the innovative capabilities of business partners to enlarge the scope and scale of competitive reach or generate new competitive opportunities. Succeeding in this agenda means quickly gaining new efficiencies and capabilities made possible only by collaborating with channel network partners.
- The increasing customer centricity of the marketplace has dramatically changed previous marketing strategies. In the past, companies focused on offering product/service portfolios to the customer, who was then expected to choose motivated by price and brand awareness. Today's customers want suppliers, from wherever on the globe, to understand their individual needs and motivations,

and to offer solutions that meet those needs as completely as possible. Every decision made anywhere in the supply chain should center on the value it provides to the customer. And as channel partners network closer together, they will be able to understand more of what customers value from them and how they will be able to unearth latent demands and opportunities requiring the creation of new value propositions. An intimate supply chain is not concerned with just selling more products and services: it is focused on increasingly providing value-generating solutions that meet its customers' total needs.

■ Finally, the assets and material, financial resources, and intellectual capital required of each node in the supply chain today to meet the needs of an increasingly global and volatile marketplace are gradually outstripping the capabilities of even the largest of companies. World-class human capital as well as productive assets may be far cheaper to locate out in the supply chain through collaboration than to develop internally.

As whole supply chains ascend the collaboration-intensity continuum from casual to highly interdependent customer value–focused ecosystems, the level of cooperation and joint deployment of capabilities will also become more complex. The end result is the continuous sharing and re-creating of competitive value, which reveals the hidden paths to delivering the total customer experience.

2.3 Summary and Conclusion

There can be no doubt that the convergence of exploding economies and new forms of competition, the enormous enabling power of computer networking, the erosion of impediments to free trade, and the rising economic power of developing nations founded on comparative advantages in low labor and operating costs have had a tremendous impact on the competitive positioning of today's enterprise. In the past, companies could count on a relatively slow-moving business environment. Firms could painstakingly build core competencies and sustainable competitive strategies that often lasted the lifetime of both management and labor. Competition existed mainly among the highly developed Western nations who were separated by an iron curtain from almost 50 percent of the earth's populations who, in turn, were locked away behind the doors of centralized economies. The prevailing marketing objective was to win and lock in customers to a buying experience determined by the business's strengths in branding and service expectation. Performance measurements centered on increasing the value the customer provided to the firm.

Within a short decade or so this economic paradigm has been shattered by the emergence of a global economy. As the self-sufficiency of the industrialized nations began to evaporate dramatically, and once-backward nations began to exert an almost unstoppable comparative advantage in low-cost labor and operations, even the strongest Western corporation found itself searching for strategies to integrate itself with new supply partners, new markets, and pools of talent exploding everywhere across the globe. Instead of focusing on core competencies and long-established brands, globalization has forced, often painfully, all companies to realize that current core strengths, be they innovation, product design, unique processes, or technology savvy, are *temporary*. And as globalization increases in intensity through the first decade of the twenty-first century, the clock speed of temporary advantage will be quickening.

Globalization is not simply a fad: it is not going to go away by government legislation or erecting barriers to protect wasteful practices and obsolete strategies. In fact, globalization has more than ever forced companies to view the customer from an entirely new perspective. As customers gain greater control of the transaction process and increasingly find themselves able to source products and services from anywhere on the globe, companies are no longer able to compete simply by the strength of brand loyalty and processing advantages. They must be able to provide a level of intimacy and a completeness of experience that their customers simply cannot find with any other supplier. In the end, success will go to those companies that are able to constantly reinvent themselves, that are willing to seek out new marketplaces and form radically new alliances that are able to continuously migrate themselves and their supply chains from strategies that collectively center on operational efficiency to those that optimize their value to the customer. Regardless of what has happened in the past, the only viable competitive edge today belongs to those businesses fixated on customer intimacy.

Growing the capabilities to continuously treat customers as unique, very special individuals, while providing them with increasingly complex solutions to their product and services needs, requires a transvaluation of the traditional objectives of supply chain management. In the next chapter we will explore a new view of the supply chain and how its constituent parts must be reshaped to support continuous customer intimacy.

Endnotes

1. Thomas L. Friedman, *The World Is Flat: A Brief History of the Twenty-First Century* (New York: Farrar, Straus and Giroux, 2005).
2. Paul S. Bender, "Global Supply Chains," in James A. Tompkins and Dale Harmelink, *The Supply Chain Handbook* (Raleigh, NC: Tompkins Press, 2004), 33.
3. These figures quoted from David J. Lynch, "Enthusiasm for Globalization Ebbs," *USA Today,* January 15, 2007, 1B–2B.
4. These figures are quoted in Friedman, 182–183.
5. Bernard J. La Londe, "Education: The 'Seed Corn' of Competitiveness," *Supply Chain Management Review* 10, no. 5 (July/August, 2006), 7–8.
6. Charles M. Savage, *Fifth Generation Management: Integrating Enterprises through Human Networking* (Bedford, MA: Digital Press, 1990), 69.
7. Adam Smith, *The Wealth of Nations* (Book IV, Section ii, 12).

8. Deloitte & Touche, *The China Factor: Navigating Risk in a Land of Opportunity*, (New York, N.Y: Deloitte & Touche, June 2006). More data can be found on Deloitte's website, www.iwchinafactor.com.

9. These figures have been obtained from the U.S. Census Bureau, *Foreign Trade Statistics* (Washington, DC: Government Printing Office, www.census.gov/foreign trade 1997).

10. John I. Todor, *Addicted Customers: How to Get Them Hooked on Your Company* (Martinez, CA: Silverado Press, 2007), 16.

11. http://news.moneycentral.msn.com/provider/providerarticle.asp?Feed=P&Date=060905&ID =5994946&GT1=8506. Accessed Sept. 2006 Editor, *Intel revamps its business.*

12. Charles H. Fine, *Clock Speed: Winning Industry Control in the Age of Temporary Advantage* (Reading, MA: Perseus Books, 1998), 12.

13. Many of the points in this paragraph were found in Geoffrey Moore, "Taking on China Inc.," *Manufacturing Business Technologies,* February 2004, 21–23.

14. See the excellent discussion on channel stewardship as a strategy in V. Kasturi Rangan, "The Promise and Rewards of Channel Stewardship," *Supply Chain Management Review* 10, no. 5, (July/August, 2006): 42–49.

15. The results of the Strativity Group 2005 survey are quoted in Peppers & Rogers Group, *Turning Customer Experiences into a Competitive Edge: Nikon's Journey to Leadership,* Carlson Marketing White Paper (Norwalk, CT: Carlson Marketing, 2006), 1.

16. "Immelt's Big Cheer for Globalization," *Business Week Online,* February 27, 2004. http://www.businessweek.com/bwdaily/dnflash/feb2004/nf20040227_2342_db 039.htm. Accessed Sept. 2006

17. Jeff Moad, "Winning the Globalization Game," *Managing Automation,* July 2005, 25–32.

18. John S. McClenahen, "HOT!HOT!," *Industry Week,* January 2006, 23–26.

19. Marty Weil, "In Line with Insourcing," *APICS Magazine* 16, no. 6 (June 2006): 30–33.

Chapter 3

The Enabling Power of Supply Chains

Leveraging the Process Value Chain to Support Customer Intimacy

The dramatic growth in the power of the voice of the customer and the explosion of marketplaces across the globe have transformed the nature and purpose of the supply chain. As little as a dozen years ago, the concept of supply chain management (SCM) was just emerging from its roots in the logistics function. Historically, the practice of logistics had been about the synchronization of product and service availability with the time and place demands of the customer. Instead of seeing customers and suppliers as components in a strategic chain of product transactional and marketplace information flows, companies considered logistics as purely a tactical function concerned with the daily activities of warehousing, transportation, and cost management. Often companies segmented logistics activities, assigning responsibility to departments such as sales, production, and accounting.

Today, the concept and practice of SCM has evolved to embrace a radically different tactical and strategic place within the enterprise. *Tactically,* SCM seeks to integrate and optimize the capabilities of all company functions—finance, marketing/sales, manufacturing, procurement, and distribution—in the pursuit of lean principles and processes that will continuously uncover and activate opportunities for cost reduction and increased channel throughput by synchronizing customer demand with supply channel capabilities. *Strategically*, SCM has emerged as the prime mechanism for the creation of integrated networks of channel partners focused on the generation of total value for the customer. On this level, SCM is concerned with the establishment of collaborative partnerships characterized by the interplay of cross-channel correlative processes, tightly linked by the networking capabilities of today's technologies, and capable of creating unique sources of customer value by unifying the resources, capabilities, and competencies found anyplace along the supply chain continuum.

In this chapter the concept and components of SCM are reexamined in light of the tremendous changes brought about by an increasingly networked, customer-centered supply chain environment. The discussion begins with a new definition of the supply chain. The supply chain is seen as consisting of three major components. The first is the *demand channel*. This component provides the sales and marketing information arising from the marketplace and is the prime driver for SCM. The second component is termed the *process value chain* and is composed of the channel integrators that produce the products and services requested by the *demand channel*. The final component is termed the *value delivery network* and is composed of those channel intermediaries responsible for the distributive mechanisms involved in presenting the product/service to the end-customer.

Once the components of today's supply chain have been outlined, the chapter focuses on the first of the two SCM components—the *process value chain*. The role of the *process value chain* is to effectively leverage channel productive assets to ensure the cost-effective and timely flow of goods and services to the delivery network to meet channel intermediary and end-customer demand. Included in the discussion is a process matrix that can be employed in considering alternative delivery network designs. Analysis of the *value delivery network* is the topic of chapter 4.

3.1 SCM Foundations

While the concept of supply chain management can be traced to new thinking about channel management that is little more than a decade old, its emergence has its roots in the ages-old struggle of producers and distributors to overcome the barriers of space and time in their effort to match products and services as closely as possible with the needs and desires of the customer. Most texts attribute the foundations of SCM to the historical evolution of the logistics function.[1] Logistics had always been about synchronizing product and service availability with the time and place requirements of the customer. Over the past fifty years, the science of logistics management has advanced from a purely operational function concerned with the transportation and warehousing of products to become one of today's most critical business management strategies, designed not only to enable fast, flexible supply systems, but also to create value for the company, its supply channel partners, and its customers.

3.1.1 Supply Chain Basics

In today's global business environment it is virtually impossible to think of a company and its value offerings without considering the supply chains to which it is linked. While prior competitive strategies focused squarely on products and their market value generation potential, company productive processes, or the core competencies to be found *within* the organization, such a viewpoint was never really accurate. No company is an island. It is purely an illusion that businesses can develop and sustain market leadership sui generis. In reality, companies have always belonged to linked communities of customers and suppliers that reciprocally coevolve, using each others' competencies and capabilities to enable them to reach for new levels of productivity, profitability, and value to their customers.

Supply chains exist to solve a simple problem: *how can companies effectively satisfy the wants and needs of each individual customer by offering unique solutions that provide them not only with exceptional value, but also with an unequaled buying experience.* While it is true that brand recognition and innovation provide the mechanisms that drive the machinery of the marketplace, even the most ingenious and desirable products and services will fall fallow if producers do not build organizations and supply chains capable of enhancing the customer experience and deepening value exchange relationships. As the gap between customer engagement and producer ability to deliver widens, companies correspondingly risk the distancing of intimacy as to the evolving needs and desires of their customers.

3.1.1.1 Defining the Supply Chain Environment

Since its inception, the concept of SCM has been portrayed (Figure 3.1) as a pipeline-like mechanism for the movement of products and information up and down the channel of supply. As detailed, the supply chain pipeline can be composed of a variety of players, each occupying a critical position and each providing a range of specialized functions. Although Figure 3.1 portrays the full range of business entities, the actual design of a supply chain depends on a number of factors, the primary ones being the extent of vertical integration the product integrator pursues, the impact of the distribution network on costs and margins, the depth of customer experience and intimacy desired, and choice of selective versus intensive penetration of the marketplace.

As a pipeline, the supply chain provides the playing field for the merging of two opposing yet supportive flows. In the first flow, information in the form of intelligence about marketplace wants and needs, actual orders for products and services, and surrounding ancillary support components is communicated up the pipeline, passing through a possible variety of intermediaries, and eventually ending with the producer. Based on this information, supply and delivery functions derive forecasts and other drivers of demand management. Product/service wraps are then developed, built, and pushed down the supply pipeline in the expectation of matching

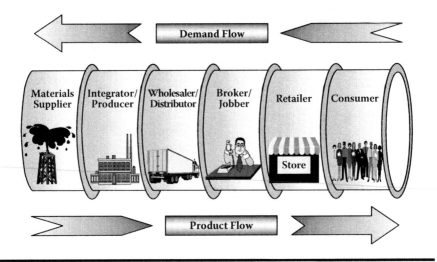

Figure 3.1 SCM flow.

anticipated market demand. The actual nature of demand is often independent of the available supply sources and is the product of customer search and conscious selection from an array of alternatives. This demand-side function can be termed the *demand channel.*

For the most part, channel demand has been seen as occupying a position at the conclusion of the supply chain process. In reality, customer demand is actually at the beginning of the supply chain and acts, not as a passive reciver of supply chain outputs, but rather as the driver of supply events. Such an understanding reverses the traditional performance goals of supply chain management, which focuses on such logistics attributes as delivery efficiency, quality, and cost containment. The demand chain is not only about communicating wants and needs to the supply chain; it is also about realizing components of the customer buying experience, such as supplier search, value acquisition, convenience, peace of mind, brand loyalty, and depth of relationships.

The second flow constituting the supply chain centers on the management of the downstream flow of goods and services from producer to customer. In this flow, the supply chain can be described as a collection of primary suppliers, producers, intermediaries, and retailers concerned with the acquisition, processing, and distribution of products and services down the supply chain. These functions encompass such activities as the timely and least costly production and delivery of products, services, support information, and other relevant deliverables, as well as the efficient execution of all sell-side transactions. This supply-side function can be termed *supply chain management* (SCM) and is represented in Figure 3.2 as a continuum of linked networked nodes of primary suppliers, producers, and distributors involved in the process of making a product or service available for use or consumption.

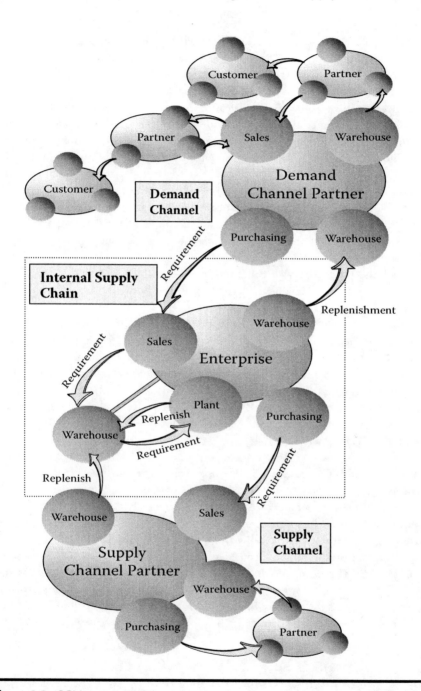

Figure 3.2   SCM components.

While the supply chain provides the conduit for the processing and distribution of products, it would provide no value if it did not assist all players in the supply channel to better understand, capture, create, deliver, and sustain value to the customer. In fact, the supply chain has often been termed a *value chain* because its real objective is to ensure that the goods and services it is creating and distributing continuously provide customer value. In its role as a value creator, the supply chain is best understood when divided into two separate yet contiguous flows. The first, termed the *process value chain*, is composed of those supply chain constituents that produce the goods and services as requested by the *demand channel*. This portion of the supply chain creates value by producing the portfolio of products and services that provide the greatest value to the customer. Often the *process value chain* consists of a network of materials, component, and resource suppliers that are used by channel integrators to manufacture or assemble the final product.

Once the product/service composite has been created, it is then up to the demand-satisfying portion of the supply chain to fulfill the wants, needs, and expectations specified by the *demand channel*. The goal of this side of the supply chain is the creation of a delivery network that enables final product differentiation and the effective distribution of the array of goods and services that reflects as closely as possible the values demanded by the customer. The actual design of the structure of the demand-satisfying portion of the supply chain is the responsibility of the integrators and intermediaries that constitute the channel and will be dictated by the nature of demand and the respective capabilities of the channel network constituents. The demand-satisfying portion of the supply chain is called the *value delivery network.*

The actual point in the supply chain where the productive versus the distributive function takes place depends on supply chain design. The key is to clearly identify the transition point where demand channel requirements meet supply chain capabilities. A manufacturer, for example, who sells direct to the customer, would be responsible for *process value chain* functions surrounding the sourcing and manufacturing of products as well as for *value delivery network* functions. On the other hand, a distributor would consider the chain of supply network constituents as beginning with feeding distributors who in turn would be delivering goods and services from upstream *process value chain* integrators. The *value delivery network*, in turn, would consist, perhaps, of other downstream distributors, broker/jobbers, and retailers who would be delivering the product to the end-customer.

3.1.1.2 Managing the Demand Channel

It is critical at this juncture not to confuse the *demand channel* with the *value delivery network*. The role of the demand channel is to serve as a conduit for the transmission of both actual orders as well as information about the products, services, and intensity of experience the customer desires from the array of available buying choices. In contrast, the role of the value delivery network is to translate the statement of demand, received either directly or indirectly, into a fulfillment channel system capable of providing the products and services that provide to the customer the most value and the optimum solution.

The effective management of the customer in today's environment is termed *demand management*. Traditionally, businesses have leveraged the science of marketing to uncover as well as influence patterns of customer demand. For the most part, when discussing customer demand, managers are focused on the following elements: database modeling for identifying and measuring demand, forecasting modeling for predicting demand, product/service profiling to determine the buy portfolio offered to the marketplace, and marketing strategies for increasing demand.

While it is true that deploying marketing techniques, such as promotions, advertising, and the annual sales campaign, to influence the customer is often identified with demand management, the actual process must be considered from a much wider perspective. To be effective it must embrace strategies that seek to integrate and optimize the totality of company and supply chain functions. Instead of purely a marketing and sales activity, demand management is also the responsibility of several operational departments, including production, logistics, distribution, planning, and finance. Outside the organization, demand management requires channel network partners to coevolve closely synchronized, collaborative strategies and processes that collectively enhance customer value by increasing the velocity of inventory, services, information, order management, and fulfillment at the critical "moment of truth" when the customer encounters a supply node in the *value delivery network*.

Supply chain participants normally embark on demand management strategies from two directions. To begin with, each channel node creates a strategy that directly serves performance and profitability goals. This strategy normally encapsulates the reasons why a firm chooses to participate in a specific supply chain in the first place. Encompassing and integrating individual company demand strategies into a collective supply chain demand strategy is the single greatest challenge before any supply network community. Normally this level of strategy is driven by the *channel master* or *supply chain steward*, who holds sufficient power to enforce the compliance of channel participants to a common demand management strategy. This role could be fulfilled by any of the participants in the channel—the product integrator, an intermediary, or a retailer.

Drafting a channel-level demand management strategy usually begins with a value proposition surrounded by strategic decisions associated with such factors as the type of market to be pursued, its geographic scope, the mix of products and services offered, and the capabilities of resources to be deployed. Once goals have been identified, the resultant demand management strategy could encompass one or multiples of the following approaches.[2]

- *Growth strategies* determine how companies can develop market leadership by acquiring competencies and synergies through merger or acquisition. By mapping the demand management terrain, corporate strategists can build value proposition models that enable them to leverage new resources to drive as well as capitalize on identified marketplace requirements for product/service mixes, pricing and promotions, delivery chain capabilities, and technology enablers.

- *Portfolio strategies* are concerned with the type, scope, nature, and life cycles of the range of product/services offerings constituting the customer value proposition. Based on demand feedback, portfolio management focuses on four critical criteria. The first, *design*, assesses the capability of product offerings to meet customer expectations of quality, usability, life cycle positioning, and opportunity to deploy intelligent services and activate logistics functions to speed *value delivery network* fulfillment. The second criterion, *cost*, requires companies to not only pursue opportunities for process improvement and cost reduction, but also to continuously squeeze the time it takes from product idea conception to sales. The third criterion, *services*, provides new tools to deliver product-enhancing values such as self-service, real-time pricing, credit management, documentation, even classroom and e-learning opportunities. Finally, *quality* enables supply chains to be more responsive not just to base expectations of performance, reliability, conformance, etc., but also to the ability to assist customers in selecting the right combination of product/service wrap, and then configuring the solution to meet individual requirements. Effectively managing these dimensions will ensure strategic diversification of the product portfolio to match demand expectations.

- *Positioning strategies* seek to continuously rearrange supply chain structures to optimize product/service placement within the various supply channel networks based on demand and operating economics. Among the most important activities is determining where the highest value-producing products should be located in the *value delivery network*, defining channel postponement strategies, utilization of geographic deployment, and enhancement of logistics capabilities.

- *Investment strategies* are concerned with assembling flexible clusters of assets that provide strategic planners with the capability to align capital, research, and development budgets, marketing expenditures, and human and physical plant resources with anticipated product/service demand and delivery capabilities. This approach would be critical in determining not only the content of product portfolios, but also what types of channel structures, network partnerships, and assets should be invested in to support overall supply chain objectives.

While most of the discussion regarding demand management lies outside the scope this work, it is the fundamental kickoff point for the construction of a competitive, customer-focused *value delivery network*. The next section will explore in depth the elements by which integrators and intermediaries design approaches to meet customers' demand chain needs.

3.1.2 Fundamentals of Process Value Chains

In the above discussion the supply chain was divided into two separate groups of participants: product/service producers (*process value chain*) and demand channel distributors (*value delivery network*). The role of the *process value chain* is to receive demand information in the form of marketing intelligence and actual orders, and then translate that demand into the products and services demanded by the customer. Once the anticipated portfolio of goods has been produced, it then enters the *value delivery network* where various intermediaries, from wholesalers to retailers, augment and complete the transfer to the end-customer.

The ability of supply chains to provide the level of value desired by the customer begins, therefore, with the capacity of channel integrators to optimize their productive resources and effectively leverage their materials suppliers to make and have available their products and services when the customer wants them at the least cost and with a minimum of effort. Effectively managing the *process value chain* starts with planning for and controlling internal productive resources, such as product design, fixed assets, labor, materials, and overheads, expended during the process of materials and component conversion or integration. Being able, however, to construct agile, flexible, and lean organizations and processes requires producers to engineer relationships with their suppliers marked by close cooperation, partnership, and communication.

The ability to optimize productive functions, however, is a dynamic process, and as the variables associated with product and process life cycles, quality, outsourcing, depth of supplier relationships, and other factors increase, so does the complexity of managing them. Without the effective management of the *supply value chain,* productive assets will be poorly utilized, and without the necessary outputs, the flow of goods and services to the demand chain pipeline will be erratic, and the profitability, even the very existence, of the entire supply chain network could be threatened.

3.1.2.1 Anatomy of Supply Chain Demand

As detailed in the previous section, the key to an effective *value delivery network* is the management of demand as it cascades from the end-customer through the various channel intermediaries and producers, concluding with the raw materials and component parts suppliers at the very beginning of the supply pipeline. The task of supplying goods and services to the demand presented to the supply chain requires the various channel nodes to recognize the type of demand to which they are expected to respond. Typically, supply chains experience not one, but three types of demand.[3] These types can be described as *independent demand, derived*

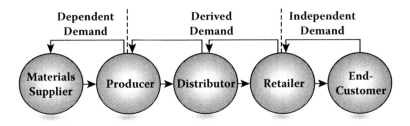

Figure 3.3 Demand in the supply chain.

demand, and *dependent demand,* and they are illustrated in a classical supply chain in Figure 3.3.

3.1.2.1.1 Independent Demand

This type of demand occurs only once in the supply chain and that is at the point when the end-customer purchases a product or service. The purchase point could be a retailer, a distributor, catalog sales, an Internet sale (B2C [business to consumer] or B2B [business to business]), or other transaction occurrence between a supplier and the end-customer. This type of demand is considered to be *independent* because it is not subject to any form of higher demand, and is therefore the prime mover that initiates activity in the supply chain.

3.1.2.1.2 Derived Demand

This type of demand is characteristic of all intermediaries that supply the network entity subject to independent demand. Depending on the number of intermediaries, derived demand could occur at several points in the delivery network, but will always culminate with the product/service producer. While it can indeed be stated that, in a transaction where a distributor receives demand from a retailer, the retailer is truly the distributor's customer, in reality that demand is strictly *dependent* on the demand the retailer experiences from the customer—hence it is *derived demand.* When it is considered that the sole reason for the existence of any supply chain is to bring value to the end-customer, it is absolutely critical that intermediaries carefully develop product, marketing, and logistics strategies that reflect the primacy of the end-customer as they are serviced through the channel entity that directly experiences independent demand.

3.1.2.1.2 Dependent Demand

This type of demand originates in the inventory requirements placed on the producer. Although the producer can be said to receive derived demand from downstream network entities, such as jobbers, distributors, and retailers, the demand it in turn passes on to materials and component parts suppliers at the origin of the *process value chain* can be described as *dependent* demand. In fact, the producer must actually manage two types of inventories. The first, finished goods, is subject to the same tools employed to manage independent and derived demand, such as forecasting, product life cycle management, customer portfolio management, and others.

The second type of inventory—production inventory—is, on the other hand, strictly managed as *dependent demand*. The process of identifying dependent demand on this class of items occurs at the conclusion of the MRP (material requirements planning) bill of material explosion. After finished goods demand has been determined, quantities and due dates are then calculated by the MRP gross-to-net explosion. Once completed, the next step is to communicate the requirements to materials and component parts suppliers for replenishment. In this way, these end-of-channel suppliers are subject to *dependent demand*.

Companies positioned along the *process value chain* continuum must be careful to develop the optimal *supply* and *value delivery network* management functions commensurable with the type of demand they receive. This can be difficult if they service multiple types of demand. For example, a business that sells movie CDs to retail customers, but then also sells directly to end-customers through the Internet, must be careful to develop inventory stocking, order fulfillment, and purchasing policies that reflect independent demand coming from the direct Internet sales and derived demand stemming from sales to retailers.

3.1.2.2 Role and Function of Channel Producers

Producers can best be represented as residing at the center of the supply chain process. As represented in Figure 3.4, channel integrators own, interface with, or drive almost every business within the supply chain. Because of their integral position, any changes in the productive segment of the supply chain are bound, therefore, to impact networked-in suppliers at the beginning of the supply chain as well as delivery network intermediaries that feed goods and services to the customer.

In today's global business environment, the pressure of competition, demand for perfect service by the customer, requirements for continuous cost reduction, outsourcing, need for agile, lean manufacturing processes, utilization of technology, and other factors have collectively negated previous forms of producer strategies. In the past, perfecting existing products and processes, and strategically acquiring new productive resources that expanded critical capacity and lowered costs, differentiated producers, and defined industry leadership. Today, producers have come under intense pressure to reduce investment in plant and equipment and reengineer the core processes that do exist to be as lean and agile as possible. Part of this shift in the fundamentals of manufacturing strategy is the result of ensuring that companies meet ROA (return on assets) expectations by removing

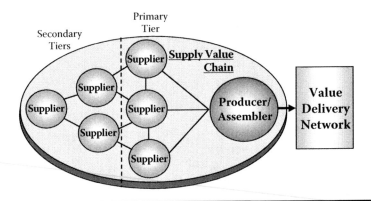

Figure 3.4 The supply value chain.

waste associated with inflexible equipment and inventories that are peripheral to the business or have poor utilization. Another factor is the declining shelf life of products. Obsolete products, and the processes that make them, simply add to the asset and not the income side of ROA. In any case, the strategies devised by the producer segment of the supply chain will have a direct impact on how the delivery network will function.

Gauging the impact of producers on supply chains requires at least a high-level understanding of their strategic role. Essentially, producers leverage the following activities in their role as *supply value chain* integrators.

3.1.2.2.1 Marketing Strategy

The products and processes producers provide are based squarely on the demand channel intelligence they receive from various sources in the supply chain. Whether it comes directly from the customer or through a complex network of *value delivery network* intermediaries, producers need accurate information to be able to make a variety of sound decisions. The starting point is the accurate identification of the wants and needs of the customers who buy from the supply chain. The essential objective is to determine what product/service choice sets provide the greatest utility, value, and satisfaction to the customer.

Once the nature of the marketplace has been detailed, producers can then correctly assemble the portfolio of products and services that will provide the best match to the widest manifold of values desired by the customer. Among the key determinants are the robustness of current and future volumes, the spectrum of buying behavior, industry practices and trends, and the relative power of key competitors. At the end of the process, producers should be aware of what competitive attributes, such as price, cost reduction, delivery speed and reliability, quality, etc., will enable them to win orders in the marketplace.

3.1.2.2.2 Process Choice

Producers can choose from a variety of productive processes in their effort to provide the optimal portfolio of products and services to be offered by the *value delivery network*. Depending on the nature of product and competitive attributes, producers could choose project, jobbing, batch, line, or continuous processing (or a combination) as methods by which goods are produced and presented to the marketplace. A short definition of these process choices is as follows:[4]

1. *Project.* Products produced in a project environment are normally unique and one of a kind, matched to an individual customer's requirements. This process produces a wide product range that is normally never repeated and is very high in cost and price.
2. *Jobbing.* Jobbers are normally focused on the processing of a wide variety of fairly unique products characterized by extensive features and options. Jobbers provide capacities and capabilities that enable them to repetitively build specialized products characterized by complex configuration, low volume, and high cost and price.
3. *Batch.* Between jobbing and line comes batch processing. Batch production consists in processing products in large lot sizes. While a range of products is offered, economies of scale in processing usually lead producers to offer several basic models with a limited variety of features. Batch production enables producers to migrate from a job shop to a flow pattern where batches of a desired model proceed irregularly through a series of processing points, or even possibly a low-volume assembly line.
4. *Line.* The next type of method is line processing. Producers in this region offer a limited number of models with no or an extremely limited number of features. Line production is characterized by connected, mechanized processes, such as a moving assembly line. Key attributes of this model are volume manufacturing, delivery, and concern with cost. Product design and quality are determined before the sale occurs.
5. *Continuous.* At the far end of the processing spectrum can be found continuous production. Producers utilizing this method sell a very narrow range of highly standardized, commodity products produced in high volumes. Continuous processes normally utilize dedicated equipment geared toward continuous output. Price is the key determining factor for this type of production.

While it can be said that the process choice determines a host of functions that dictate how products will be manufactured or assembled, it also has a critical impact on the structural mechanics of the *value delivery network*. For example, the selection of a line or continuous process will mean that products are sold *direct by customer*. This means that the product requires an extensive distribution chain to enable the customer to directly choose the product from the retail shelf or distribution point. In contrast, a product that is assembled to order by a batch or line process will normally have a *demand channel* mechanism to first transmit the order from the customer, and then a *deliver-to-customer* distribution chain that can be simple (direct from producer) or complex (from producer through various intermediaries). Ordering an automobile is a good example of this type of processing model.

A jobbing process environment is similar to the batch/line method in that actual products are configured to customer specifications and then delivered to the customer. However, products built by this method are usually highly customized and require searching for components and materials from an extensive supply chain. In addition, the distribution channel for this method is normally very shallow or even direct *delivery by producer*. Finally, project-based processing requires an even more disconnected upstream supply chain, while the distribution channel is extremely short with *delivery by producer* being the norm.[5]

3.1.2.2.3 Channel Configuration

While the choice of a specific productive process will dictate the selection of a host of planning and control mechanisms, from sourcing, financial investment, and physical assets to operating costs and infrastructure, it will also impact the strategies and structures of how demand value will be communicated to the customer. As illustrated in the supply chain attribute matrix (Table 3.1), the depth and complexity of the entire supply chain will be dependent on the process choice. Basically, as the product moves downward in the matrix from project to continuous process, the

Table 3.1   Process Value Chain Attribute Matrix

| | Supply Chain | | | | |
| | Process Value Chain | | Value Delivery Network | | |
Process Method	Process Intensity	Supply Channel Complexity	Market Penetration Intensity	Integrative Intensity	Distribution Intensity
Project	High	High	Low	High	Low
Jobber	High	High	Low	High	Low
Batch	Medium	Medium	Medium	High/ Medium	Low/ Medium
Line	Medium/ Low	Low	High	Medium/ Low	Medium/ High
Continuous	Low	Very Low	Very High	Low	Very High

⇐ Customization/ Single Source   Standardization/ ⇒ Distribution Intensity strategies, characteristics, and players in the supply and delivery value chains will correspondingly change.

The components of the matrix bear further explanation. In the *process value chain*, the complexity of the supply chain is driven by the scope and depth of the *collaborative partnership* existing between supplier and producer. Whatever the formal arrangement, supply partnerships can be described as cooperative alliances formed to plan for and access supply channel capacities involved in value analysis, quality assurance, contracting, cost management, materials requisition, procurement, and performance and product information exchange. The actual intensity of collaboration between producer and supplier, however, varies by the type of process employed.

For example, producers who select project methods normally form relatively loose, often intermittent supply partnerships, depend on a wide variety of suppliers, negotiate contracts focused on short-term objectives such as price and delivery, and clearly demarcate boundaries of responsibility for quality and process/product improvement. At the other end of the spectrum, continuous producers develop deep collaborative relationships with their suppliers. Such partnerships normally are limited to a small core of suppliers, centered on contracts built on long-term quality, cost reduction, and mutual benefits sharing, and characterized by close and continuous linkages of information, real-time communication of designs and specifications, and joint responsibility for total quality management. Continuous producers want to deal with a supply chain that acts as a virtual organization, networked and synchronized to provide agile responses to rapid changes in production requirements.

The choice of process method will also impact the nature of the *value delivery network*. Three characteristics, as detailed in Table 3.1, can be identified. The first, *market penetration intensity*, describes how deeply into the delivery network producers and/or intermediaries are prepared to go in order to increase market share among existing and potential customers. Often the level of penetration intensity will require the development of supporting *market development strategies* (to identify potentially new customer segments) and *product development strategies* (to identify new products/services and/or processes that will appeal to newly targeted customer groups). As indicated in the matrix, producers using a project method create highly customized products where complex market penetration strategies are not applicable. On the other extreme, line and continuous producers are constantly searching to expand penetration of commodity-type products and services in an effort to gain an ever-increasing share of the market.

The second demand chain process driver can be described as *integrative intensity*. This characteristic determines the level of integration backward, forward, or horizontally a producer chooses to pursue in the demand chain. The choice of backward/forward integration identifies how much control over predecessor intermediaries (backward) or downstream demand channel nodes necessary to reach the end-customer (forward) the producer desires. Horizontal integration describes another level of marketplace control whereby a producer acquires a channel intermediary. According to the matrix, the more a product/service is customized, the more intense will be the producer's relationship with channel processes. For example, a producer of highly configurable plant heating and cooling equipment will most likely control the entire demand chain from marketing, to production, to actual delivery. On the other hand, producers of commodity products/services will depend on a complex delivery network that in turn assumes the responsibility for a wide range of activities from promotion and pricing, to delivery, merchandizing, and retail.

The final delivery network process driver, *distribution intensity,* is concerned with deciding on the number of intermediaries to use at each channel level. There are four strategies that can be deployed. In the first, *single source distribution*, a producer retains total control over all aspects of *value delivery network* activities. This strategy is chosen by producers who want to keep exclusive control over elements such as delivery, price, promotions, and service. In the second strategy, *intensive distribution*, companies seek to utilize as broad as possible a network of internal and distribution partner channels to reach as many customers as are possible. The third strategy, *exclusive distribution*, is pursued by companies who want to limit the number of intermediaries who deal with the customer. This strategy can take two forms: *exclusive distribution*, in which a producer authorizes exclusive distribution rights to a small, select number of intermediaries, and *exclusive dealing*, where a producer requires intermediaries not to carry competing products or services. In the final strategy, *selective distribution*, companies will permit multiple, but not all possible intermediaries to handle and sell the product/service. This strategy enables producers to maintain a strong control over products, pricing, and service levels while leveraging select intermediaries on several channel levels to gain a desired depth of marketplace penetration.

The process method utilized by a producer will have a determining factor on which distribution intensity strategy is to be deployed. For example, line and continuous process-based producers (such as foods, low-cost electronics, and basic services) normally produce commodity goods or raw materials and seek as many outlets to sell to as possible. On the other hand, batch and line producers, who produce, assemble, and make-to-order goods (such as major appliances, automobiles, and designer apparel) often seek exclusive or selective distribution in order to retain control over pricing, promotions, and market image as well as to prevent the inroads of competitors. Finally, capital goods producers will normally use the single-source distribution strategy. Makers of highly customized, project-oriented processing either purposefully (to eliminate any form of competition) or unintentionally (due to the unique nature of the product/service) will pursue this strategy.

3.1.2.3 Role of Primary Suppliers

As illustrated in Figure 3.1, positioned at the beginning of the *process value chain* can be found the raw materials and component parts suppliers. For the most part, the role of these channel constituents is to supply the production inventories that are required by the producers of finished goods. The effective communication of producer demand and the corresponding matrix of replenishment activities, such as quality and on-time delivery, are at the very core of a competitive *value delivery network.*

Several key drivers come to mind. First, the efficient management of *dependent demand* plays a critical role in actualizing overall supply network delivery, flexibility, quality, and cost objectives. Second, the sheer size of raw materials and component parts purchasing affects the financial stability and profitability of virtually every node in the demand chain. Thirdly, the efficiency and quality of dependent demand procurement has a direct influence on the capability of the entire supply chain, regardless of configuration, to respond to derived and eventually independent demand. Finally, effective dependent demand management requires close collaboration between producers and suppliers. With the expansion of the global marketplace and the availability of Internet tools, dramatically new avenues have been opened for sourcing, cost management, concurrent product development, quality, and delivery.

Perhaps the most common response to the question "What is the role of dependent demand suppliers in the supply chain?" is to deliver to downstream channel nodes the right products/services, at the right time, in the right quantities, delivered to the right place, at the right price with perfect quality. Organizing effective procurement strategies around such a comprehensive list of objectives can be a challenging one, indeed. Rarely will buyers be able to achieve simultaneously optimal quality, service, and price objectives from a single supplier. In any case, dependent demand suppliers are expected to pursue the following objectives if they are to contribute to a supply chain that contributes the most value to the customer.

■ *Provide an uninterrupted flow of materials, component parts, and services.* Perhaps the most fundamental responsibility of dependent demand suppliers is ensuring that downstream channel producers or aggregators do not encounter production inventory shortages. Shortages cause processing downtime, interrupt the timely flow of product and cash through the channel, and strain relations with customers on one end of the pipeline and suppliers on the other. Ensuring the flow of dependent demand items, however, is not enough. Suppliers, producers, and aggregators must continually search for methods of increasing the velocity of the flow of goods and services through the distribution channel without accompanying increases in carrying costs.

■ *Facilitating effective dependent inventory demand planning.* Perhaps the most important difference between dependent demand suppliers and other supply chain players is the fact that the channel product requirements they receive are the result of calculations performed (most by MRP-based systems) by producers in response to value delivery network–derived or independent demand. Since the inventory requirements are thus always known *before* they are actually passed to the supplier, technology tools that provide for visibility and near-instantaneous transmission of demand and delivery information is critical for the effective functioning of all nodes in the channel ecosystem.

■ *Provide products at a competitive price.* Purchasers are always searching for suppliers that will provide the highest quality and serviceability at the lowest cost. Pursuing this objective means that suppliers must be informed about the market forces regulating prices and product availability. In addition, this objective requires producers and suppliers to understand channel cost dynamics, and then to negotiate quality, price, and service arrangements that achieve optimum value for both parties.

■ One purchasing objective that is growing in importance is expanding the scope of supplier *value-added services.* The goal of these functions is to reduce wastes in ordering and delivery, and facilitating the flow of goods and information through the supply channel. Three critical flows can be identified:

  – *Product flow.* This involves accelerating the physical movement of goods from the supply source to the point of consumption. As globalization expands, the velocity of materials and component inventories through the *process value chain* could be inhibited as the number of transfer points and the length of the delivery channel elongates.

  – *Information flow.* This reduces redundancies in the transmission of critical information up and down the channel, such as demand schedules, market data, inventory supply levels, warranty and product information, product specifications and application information, and post-sales support.

  – *Service flow.* This involves increasing value-added services that improve productivity and eliminate costs such as Internet order placement, advanced shipping notices, order status tracking, electronic transfer of payables and receivables, bar coding, packaging, and delivery.

3.1.2.4 Supplier Relationship Management

The relentless growth of the power of the customer and the ever-present requirement to continuously reduce costs everywhere in the supply chain has recently accentuated the importance of close partnership between buyers and suppliers and spawned a whole new concept called *supplier relationship management* (SRM). As pressures driving cost-effective product and service procurement and supply channel velocities intensify, the need for collaborative buyer/supplier partnering has likewise increased. The mission of SRM is to respond to this challenge by providing trading partners with opportunities to achieve simultaneously dramatic breakthroughs in cost savings, integrative formats for collaborative product development, new forms of sourcing, and new mechanisms for the linkage of channels of demand with the supply chain. By expanding collaboration, integration, and alignment of all buyer/supplier points of contact, SRM seeks to transform the entire supply chain into a seamless value-driven supply engine.

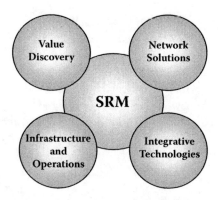

Figure 3.5 SRM dynamics.

The creation of truly value-driven SRM partnerships requires the synchronization of channel demand with the capabilities of supply chain partners. Reaching this objective requires the realization of several critical supply channel dynamics as illustrated in Figure 3.5. The first dynamic can be described as *SRM value discovery*. This dynamic is focused on determining the value propositions to be supported by the SRM partnership. The results of the process should reveal several critical value benefits. Among them can be found expected *cost savings* due to the removal of redundancies and the streamlining of demand and delivery, enhanced *process efficiencies* gained through increased collaboration on product and channel design, *inventory optimization* due to real-time planning and demand transfer, and increased *delivery performance* as a result of closely networked streams of information closely matching channel capacities and demand channel needs.

Once meaningful channel value propositions have been identified, *SRM-driven infrastructures and operations* can then be constructed. To be effective, SRM objectives will need to be executed by agile buyer/supplier functions capable of being rapidly deconstructed and reassembled based on customer needs as they cascade through the demand channel. Such flexible supply environments must be capable of quick integration with partners anywhere in the channel and the rapid deployment of new technologies and processes if channels are to fulfill, even anticipate the demands of the end-customer. Another opportunity can be found in the use of *outsourcing*. Companies have increasingly used channel partners to exploit core competencies in an effort to perform work more economically, locate needed technical expertise, free internal resources, and reduce overhead costs.

Supporting effective SRM partnerships are *integrative technologies*. Throughout history, the ability of buyer and supplier to communicate plans and requirements and accelerate the transaction process and delivery of goods has been driven by technology tools. For decades procurement activities have been facilitated by the use of

ERP (enterprise resource planning) systems, *collaborative planning, forecasting, and replenishment* (CPFR), and *electronic data interchange* (EDI), which have enabled trading partners to interface demand, order and shipment transmission, and electronic financial settlement. Today, Internet tools have dramatically enhanced SRM by providing for new forms of procurement, such as online catalogs, interactive auction sites, and radically new methods for sourcing and supplier management, and web-based toolsets that network channel partners with real-time, simultaneous synchronization of demand and supply.

Finally, SRM provides for the growth of *networked solutions*. The ultimate goal of SRM is to provide trading partners with the ability to continuously coevolve new processes that enable them to align, coordinate, and integrate pan-channel functions into a unified, seamless process. Overall, the goal is to migrate trading partners up what Poirier, Bauer, and Hauser term an SRM "maturity scale."[6] In the model, the focus of SRM is to advance the supply relationship from traditional negotiation and spot buying practices to a fully networked alliance. In the process, the relationship expands through stages characterized by progressively more integration between buyer and supplier. In the process, the relationship matures from a concern with volume, single-source alliances, through shared responsibility, mutual planning of supply planning, trust, and search for the application of lean techniques, and concludes with the full integration of the supplier with the customer's business in the joint search for increased supply chain value to themselves and their customers.

3.2 Summary and Transition

The demand for increased customer intimacy has required supply chains to reexamine the basic values and mechanics constituting their channel ecosystems. In the past, the supply chain was viewed as a simple pipeline. Demand and marketing intelligence was gathered from the points of customer contact along the supply chain continuum and transmitted upstream to channel producers and primary suppliers. In turn, products and services were produced and then pushed downstream to the various distributive intermediaries, who in turn passed them on to the end customer.

In today's increasingly customer-centered supply chains, such a definition of SCM has become increasingly insufficient. Customers are no longer passive recipients of standardized products and services: instead, they want to do business with value chains that treat them as unique, very special individuals, and they are demanding that their suppliers provide them with complete, configurable solutions with a minimum of effort and cost on their part. To be competitive, supply chains are now expected to provide not only the highest quality products and services, but also an outstanding experience that provides superior value at each touchpoint where customers interact with a company and its brands. Simply put, the customer experience has now become *the* battleground for competitive advantage.

Fundamental to pursuing more intense levels of customer intimacy is the need to deconstruct the former concept of the supply chain into three interactive components. The first is the *demand channel*, which provides intelligence regarding sales and marketing information arising from the customer channel. The second component is termed the *process value chain* and is composed of the channel integrators that produce the products and services requested by the *demand channel*. The final component is termed the *value delivery network* and is composed of those channel intermediaries responsible for the distributive mechanisms involved in presenting the product/service to the end-customer.

After introducing the components of today's supply chain, the primary focus of the chapter centered on detailing the various functions of the *process value chain*. This component was described as consisting of four critical functions. To begin with, the *process value chain* is responsible for the timely and accurate receipt of channel demand in the form of marketing intelligence and actual orders, and then the translation of that demand into the products and services demanded by channel customers. At the end of the process, producers should be constructing the product and service portfolios that enable them to leverage their unique competitive attributes to win orders in their marketplace.

The second main function of *process value chains* is the selection of the best process choice. Depending on the nature of the product and type of desired competitive attributes, producers could choose project, jobbing, batch, line, or continuous processing methods. Such a decision will drive the third main function, the actual structure of the *value delivery network*. As illustrated in the *process value chain* attribute matrix (Table 3.1), the depth and complexity of the delivery network will be determined by the process choice. Basically, as the process method moves from project at one end of the spectrum to continuous processing at the other end, the strategies, characteristics, and channel players will move from simple to complex distribution.

The final critical function of *process value chains* is the creation of ever-closer relationships with channel primary suppliers. Termed *supplier relationship management* (SRM), the objective is to provide producers and primary suppliers with opportunities to expand collaboration, integration, and synchronization of *dependent* demand with productive capabilities. For primary suppliers, the goal is to engineer highly networked replenishment engines capable of quickly responding to producers' requirements for the uninterrupted flow of materials, components, and services calculated by their MRP systems. For producers, the object is to construct supplier relationships that enable them to reduce costs, enhance process and design efficiencies, optimize inventories, and increase delivery performance. Such objectives can be executed only by agile supplier/buyer functions capable of being rapidly deconstructed and reassembled based on demands as they are identified at customer touchpoints in the *delivery value network*.

A fully networked *process value chain* facilitates the flow of goods and services through the distribution network. The quicker producers can respond to derived and independent demand signals, the more intimate channel delivery intermediaries can become with their suppliers. In the next chapter we will be turning to a full analysis of the delivery value network, and how it can be constructed to generate new opportunities to build outstanding customer relationships far beyond the capabilities of the competition.

Endnotes

1. For a more detailed history of the evolution of SCM see David F. Ross, *Introduction to e-Supply Chain Management: Engaging Technology to Build Market-Winning Business Partnerships* (Boca Raton, FL: St. Lucie Press, 2003), 4–18, and *Distribution Planning and Control: Managing in the Era of Supply Chain Management*, 2nd ed. (Norwell, MA: Kluwer Academic, 2004), 10–22.
2. These points can be found in James R. Langabeer, "Aligning Demand Management with Business Strategy," *Supply Chain Management Review* 4, no. 2 (2000): 68, and Ross, *Distribution Planning and Control*, 429–432.
3. The three-part division of demand was first detailed by John T. Mentzer and Mark A. Moon, "Understand Demand," *Supply Chain Management Review* 8, no. 4 (May/June 2004): 38–45.
4. For a complete overview of production strategy, see Terry Hill, *Manufacturing Strategy: Text and Cases*, 2nd ed. (Boston MA: Irwin McGraw-Hill, 1994), 93–124.
5. For further discussion on these points, see James W. Reeve and Mandyam Srinivasan, "Which Supply Chain Design Is Right for You?" *Supply Chain Management Review* 9, no. 4 (May/June 2005): 50–57.
6. Charles C. Poirier, Michael J. Bauer, and William F. Houser, *The Wall Street Diet: Making Your Business Lean and Healthy* (San Francisco, CA: Berrett-Koehler Publishers, Inc., 2006), 116–120.

Chapter 4

Designing and Maintaining a Delivery Channel

Creating Value Delivery Networks to Drive Customer Intimacy

In the previous chapter the supply chain was described by using the concept of a pipeline-like mechanism that enabled the smooth flow of products and services down the delivery channel to the end-customer, while serving as a conduit for the return flow of vital marketing and transaction intelligence up the channel of supply, ending with the raw material and component suppliers found at the source of the supply network. The first flow was termed *supply chain management* (SCM) and was defined as the network of materials suppliers, producers, and intermediaries concerned with the acquisition, processing, and distribution of products and services to the customer. The second flow was termed the *demand channel* and was defined as the mechanism for the transmission of demand for the products, services, and the intensity of experience customers expect to find available in the array of available buying choices presented by the supply chain.

Instead of a single process, SCM was divided into two separate yet intercon-nected parts. The first was termed the *process value chain* and was the focus of chapter 3. The role of this component of SCM is the production of the goods and services necessary to meet channel intermediary and end-customer demand. The second part of SCM was termed the *value delivery network*. This component is composed of those channel intermediaries responsible for the distribution mecha-nisms involved in the delivery of goods and services as they make their way to the end-customer. Exploring the nature of the *value delivery network* is the subject of chapter 4.

The chapter begins with an overview of the functions and goals of the *value delivery network.* In contrast to the *process value chain*, the nature, function, and structure of delivery networks are seen as varying dramatically. Often these net-works consist of very complex combinations of partnerships and alliances, some temporary and driven purely by selfish advantage, some contractual and governed by cooperation and long-standing patterns of behavior. The actual delivery format is determined by the number of intermediaries, depth of desired market penetra-tion, span of partner capabilities, relative power of the competition, and level of acceptable dependence and risk sharing among the various channel players.

The second part of the chapter undertakes a detailed description of the vari-ous types of delivery network intermediaries. A whole section is then devoted to a review of the various functions that must be performed by delivery intermediary specialists. The chapter concludes with an analysis of the different types of delivery network systems available and how successful channels manage conflict among members. In the end, delivery networks must provide the channel with the right blend of specialists capable of smoothly conveying the right products and informa-tion to the end-customer.

4.1 Value Delivery Networks—An Overview

Perhaps the most perplexing and least understood area of business management is the complex, interwoven fabric of relationships and enterprises constituting the *value delivery network.* Unlike the *process value chain*, which consists of fairly con-ventional relationships of primary material and component suppliers and product producers, the nature, functions, and structure of *value delivery networks* can vary dramatically, making it difficult for companies to easily identify and generalize about building any meaningful channel strategy. Each delivery network can be a labyrinth of partnerships and alliances among a variety of different types of busi-nesses, each participating for parochial interests and each calculating the return on investment and effort for the level of services and commitment tendered as the reward for channel membership.

An effective approach is to begin the discussion with a broad definition. The *value delivery network* can be defined as *an organized network of interdependent businesses voluntarily or contractually confederated together through which products and services are marketed and sold.* Such a definition is functional enough to cover the wide spectrum of possible delivery networks. Some networks, such as producer direct to the end customer, will often have complex intracompany channel structures and minimal extracompany participation. Others will contain intricate combinations of wholesale merchants and retailers who buy, warehouse, and resell merchandise; brokers and agents who do not take title to goods but rather act as middlemen bringing buyers and sellers together, or are contracted to represent the producer, or act in the role of a buyer; and export/import intermediaries who purchase and sell goods, arrange for logistics services, and provide consulting advice and financial assistance when dealing with foreign markets. Finally, there is a host of delivery network *facilitators*, such as third-party logistics services, financial institutions, and marketing and advertising agencies that expedite the distribution process.

The actual dynamics of such critical issues as delivery network structure, number of intermediaries, depth of desired market penetration, channel partner capabilities and costs, distribution of network power, and strength of the competition will have a dramatic impact on supply chain strategies. As delivery channels become more complex, they become more difficult to influence, as control of branding, pricing, promotion, and quality erodes. In addition, managing such hybrid supply chains requires channel masters who possess the coercive or persuasive power to ensure that each network entity remains focused on providing the end-customer with the desired level of value, intimacy, and buying experience.

4.1.1   Why Delivery Network Intermediaries Exist

Delivery channels exist to facilitate the marketing, buying, and selling of products and services beginning with the producer and culminating with the end-customer. In performing this singular objective, *value delivery networks* can be said to solve three critical distribution problems: *functional performance, reduced complexity,* and *specialization.*[1] Regardless of delivery network complexity, three critical functions— exchange, delivery, and facilitating—must be executed. These functions enable networks to span the time, place, and possession gaps separating producers from end-customers. As illustrated in Figure 4.1, the first function, *exchange*, enables the activities of purchase, title transfer, and settlement. The second function, *delivery*, enables the activities of transportation and storage. Finally, the third function, *facilitating*, enables the performance of optional support activities such as information transfer, promotion, risk bearing, and financial management. These functions could be performed solely by a producer who uses a direct-to-end-customer format or they might be performed separately by different network intermediaries who in turn must be carefully integrated together if necessary functions are to be successfully completed.

Another critical operation performed by *value delivery networks* is the removal of complexity from channel arrangements by participating in the *routinization* of

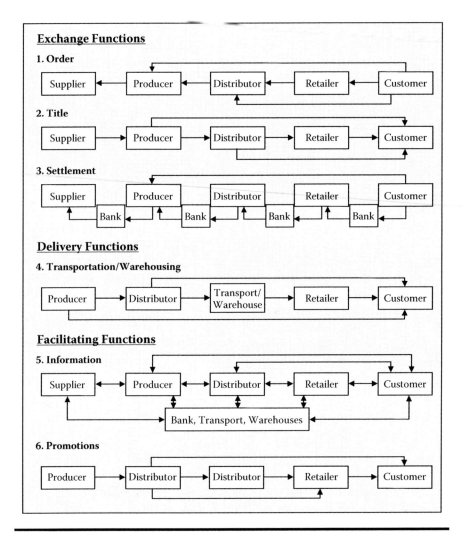

Figure 4.1 The value delivery network functional flows.

distribution functions and product *sorting*. Routinization refers to the commonly accepted policies and procedures drafted by each channel entity that collectively provide the network as a whole with common goals, governance, expectations, and mutually accepted channel information and exchange mechanisms driving intelligence collection and transactional efficiencies. Sorting refers to a group of activities used to transform products into the assortments and lot sizes demanded by network entities. Sorting processes consist of *sorting* heterogeneous groups of items into homogeneous subgroups (i.e., grading), *accumulating* groups of homogeneous products into larger groupings, *allocating* or breaking down large lots of products into smaller lots, and *assorting* or mixing related products into assortments.

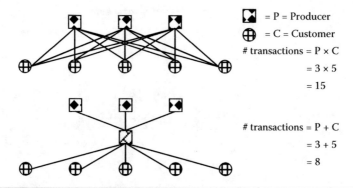

Figure 4.2 Impact of delivery network specialization.

The final reason why delivery networks are formed is to solve the problem of *specialization*. The goal of this function is to increase efficiency in the supply channel by assigning the performance of specific delivery network tasks to specialized business partners. The net effect is to increase the velocity of products and information through the delivery pipeline by reducing costs associated with selling, transportation, warehousing, value-added processing, order processing, and credit. As seen in Figure 4.2, by inserting just one intermediary into a channel composed of three producers and three customers, specialization can significantly reduce channel complexity. Even if a channel specialist is disintermediated from the network, the *function* that facilitator performed cannot be eliminated, but must then be assumed by one of the remaining channel nodes.

4.1.2 Designing Delivery Network Structures

While it can be said that the functions of the delivery network *must* be performed, the exact number of actual channel entities involved is found in the delivery network structure. When designing the delivery network, strategists can pick from four possible channel models (Figure 4.3). In the first, or a direct-marketing strategy, the producer sells directly to the end-customer. Companies who deploy this type of structure essentially sell two types of product. The first type consists of capital equipment, configured products, or unique, difficult-to-find items characterized by long lead times, tight brand control, complex delivery, and high price. The other consists of a range of commodity-type products and services sold door to door (Avon) or by mail order (LL Bean), telemarketing (Pella), producer-owned stores (Sony), or the Internet (CDs/publishing).

In the second delivery network strategy a producer will sell to a retailer, who in turn sells to the end-customer. This strategy is used by producers who want to maintain strong brand and pricing controls, but who are also looking for a much wider level of market penetration than a factory-direct format will permit. Such producers normally exercise a significant influence on retailers regarding product

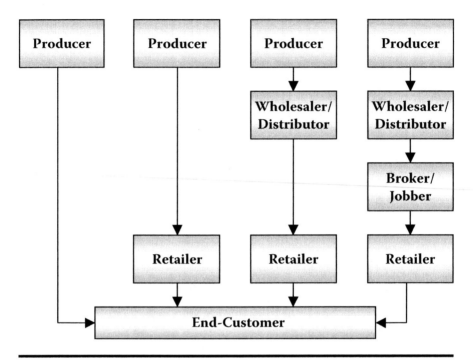

Figure 4.3   Types of delivery network structures.

display, competitive positioning, and promotion. The third delivery network strategy consists of a wholesale/distribution intermediary separating the producer from the retailer. Such an arrangement supports several strategies. A producer may utilize a wholesaler to assist in achieving levels of market penetration and distribution intensity unachievable when acting alone. On the other hand, a powerful wholesaler can leverage its strengths as an aggregator or sorter by acquiring products from many producers and selling them to a diverse group of retailers or perhaps even end-customers (i.e., W. W. Granger and McMaster-Carr).

The final delivery network strategy utilizes all available types of channel intermediaries. Such a complex delivery network is often characteristic of commodities, foodstuffs, and bulk goods. For example, produce distribution often moves from the grower to wholesalers, who in turn sell to local jobbers, who finally sell to local food markets. The goal of such complex networks is to ensure quick movement of product through the channel, the availability of a wide assortment for retailers, and as wide a market penetration as is possible. While the above delivery networks are descriptive of consumer channels, they will also apply to the distribution of goods to industrial customers. The only difference is that in industrial channels, producers will use internal *sales branches and offices*, *industrial distributors* (merchants selling exclusively to manufacturers), and *manufacturing representatives* (third-party sales reps selling only to manufacturers) to distribute their products.

4.2 Types of Value Delivery Network Intermediaries

The value delivery network can be said to contain several types of distribution businesses collectively focused on facilitating the flow of products and services either to other intermediaries or to the end-customer. As detailed above, the exact composition of any given delivery network is determined by a variety of channel strategy factors and can change over time. Channel intermediaries can be divided into four general types: manufacturers, brokers and agents, wholesalers and distributors, and retailers.[2]

4.2.1 Manufacturers' Sales Offices and Distribution Warehouses

The first type of delivery network entity is manufacturers who perform the functions of sales and distribution to the end-customer without the assistance of other types of channel intermediaries. Manufacturer-driven channel formats can be divided into several subtypes. In the first, *factory direct*, goods are shipped and serviced directly from the manufacturer's production facility. A second subtype, *sales offices and channel warehouses*, consists of manufacturers who distribute their own products through networks of company-owned sales offices and geographically dispersed warehouses. Channel warehouses are often responsible for replenishment planning from upstream manufacturing warehouses, transaction management, and financial profit and loss performance.

A third type is a *manufacturer-owned full-service channel distributor*. This format describes an acquired channel intermediary serving the parent's markets. When demand warrants, these intermediaries will also distribute the products of other manufacturers. Examples can be found in the clothing and apparel industries. The final subtype is a *license*. In this format, a manufacturer contracts with a third-party channel intermediary who is granted exclusive rights to market and sell the manufacturer's products/services or processes for a specific period of time.

4.2.2 Brokers and Agents

This type of channel intermediary differs from all other delivery network entities in that they usually do not take ownership of inventory, assume risk, or provide financing. In addition, they will normally offer a very limited range of services. For the most part, their function is to act as facilitators assisting other intermediaries in the buying, selling, and matching of products, network suppliers, and customers. The primary role of *brokers* is to serve as middlemen, bringing seller and buyer together and assisting in price, product, and delivery negotiations. Brokers are usually paid for their services by the party who contracted them.

There are several types of independent agents who represent or are contracted to represent either the producer or act in the role of a buyer. One variation, *manufacturers' representatives*, usually represent two or more manufacturers that produce complimentary product lines. Normally, they enter into a formal written agreement with each manufacturer, which governs issues such as pricing policies, sales territories, order handling, delivery, service and warranties, and commission rates. Most manufacturers' agents are small firms composed of highly skilled salespeople who have an extensive knowledge of the products they represent and the best marketplaces in which to sell them. This type of agent is often used to sell capital and high-tech goods such as furniture, apparel, and computers.

Another type of agent is the *selling agent*. This type of agent is contracted by manufacturers who do not have direct sales and marketing staffs. Because of their unique position, they often exercise significant influence over pricing, buying terms, and conditions of sale. Selling agents are often found in such industries as textiles, industrial machinery and equipment, coal and coke, chemicals, and metals. In contrast to selling, manufacturers can contract *purchasing agents*. This type of agent is normally a product expert who provides buying expertise and consultative services to their clients. In addition, they often not only offer purchasing, but also warehousing and shipping services. The final type of agent is the *commission merchant*. Often termed *commission houses*, this type of agent takes possession of goods from the producer and then sells them in the marketplace for the best price. After deducting a fee covering the commission and miscellaneous expenses, the balance is then passed back to the producer. They are most often used in agricultural marketing by farmers who do not wish to sell their own produce or who do not belong to a producers' cooperative.

4.2.3 Wholesalers and Distributors

This type of intermediary consists of several diverse independent businesses that buy finished products from channel producers and other intermediaries and then pass them to delivery network resellers for eventual end customer consumption. The term *wholesaler/distributor* can cover a wide spectrum of businesses, ranging from powerful multi-billion-dollar companies to small bulk breakers and aggregators servicing narrow markets with limited ranges of products and services. While dominant retailers, such as Wal-Mart and Home Depot, and alternative channel marketers, such as warehouse clubs and Internet sales, have been challenging traditional wholesaler/distributor formats, this type of channel intermediary accounts for at least 50 percent of sales volume and number of businesses in the typical delivery network. Generally speaking, this type of intermediary can be divided into three groups: full-service distributors/wholesalers, limited-service distributors/wholesalers, and export/import distributors.

4.2.3.1 Full-Service Wholesalers/Distributors

This subtype of distributor provides a wide range of products and services to the delivery network. Besides stocking goods and offering a variety of value-added functions, such as sales order management, transportation, and financial settlement, full-service distributors often perform services such as credit, EDI (electronic data interchange) transmission, and Internet networking. This type of channel entity can be said to coalesce around three types of distributor: *consumer distributors, wholesaler merchants,* and *industrial distributors.*

Consumer distributors provide products and services directly to the end-customer. Their primary value proposition is to be found in their capacity to serve as aggregators and bulk breakers. This type of distributor often sells through a catalog or the Internet in order to reach a global audience. Examples of companies using this format are W. W. Granger and McMaster-Carr Supply Company. *Wholesale merchants* provide products and a full range of value-added services to the retail industry and can be segregated into *general merchandise wholesalers,* who carry a full range of products spanning several merchandise lines, *general-line wholesalers,* who carry an extensive assortment of products limited to one or several targeted product lines, and *specialty wholesalers,* who carry the products of a single line.

The final type of full-service distributor is the *industrial distributor.* This type of distributor is composed of aggregators or bulk beakers who sell exclusively to manufacturers. Similar to retail distributors, they may carry a multitude of product lines (often called a *mill supply house*), a general line, or a specialty line. In addition, they normally offer manufacturers a full range of services from offering credit, to order and delivery management, to financial settlement.

4.2.3.2   Limited-Service Wholesalers/Distributors

In contrast to the full-service distributor, this type of channel intermediary offers a limited range of goods and services to retailers and end-customers. There are several kinds of distributor in this subgroup. *Cash-and-carry wholesalers* stock a limited line of fast-moving products that are sold to small retailers. *Truck wholesalers* or *truck jobbers* perform primarily a selling and delivery function only. They carry a limited line of products (such as milk, bread, and soft drinks) that they sell for cash to supermarkets, small groceries, restaurants, business and institutional cafeterias, and hotels.

Another type, the *drop shipper,* operates in industries associated with commodities handled in bulk, such as building materials, coal, lumber, and heavy equipment. *Rack jobbers* provide highly advertised, brand name, nonfood products and accompanying services to grocery, convenience, and drug stores. Examples are toys, paperback books, greeting cards, hardware items, and health and beauty aids. Another type of limited distributor is *producers' cooperatives.* Cooperatives are formed by a group of agricultural producers who assemble food products from co-op members for sale in local markets. *Mail-order wholesalers* sell products from a catalog to retail, industrial, and institutional customers.

4.2.3.3 Exporting and Importing Distributor

The third major subtype of wholesaler/distributor consists of internal branches or third-party companies that specialize in international distribution. Often global corporations will provide their own international supply channels, complete with foreign sales offices and warehouses. Other companies seeking a global footprint, on the other hand, may choose to contract with a third-party trade distributor who, in turn, will provide the necessary international exposure.

There are various types of international distributors. An *international trading company* will provide global companies with a wide range of services ranging from the purchasing and selling of goods, to logistics, financing, and consulting. *Export merchants* act in the role of an international wholesaler. These global channel entities purchase goods from domestic companies and then pack and ship them to distribution points in foreign markets. Often global enterprises will engage *resident buyers*. In this format companies will position their own buyers directly in an exporting country for the purpose of sourcing, purchasing, and shipping goods to facilities located in the home country or in foreign markets. A variation on this practice is an *export commission house*, which performs the same functions as a *resident buyer,* but is a contracted third-party agent.

A further type is an *allied manufacturer.* In this arrangement a company seeks to contract with a foreign business partner who exports/imports similar or supporting goods. By piggybacking their products, both firms can improve market share by presenting foreign markets with extended product lines or achieving high logistics utilization. The final type is an *export management company.* This type of distributor acts as a product line or foreign market specialist, who represents one or a group of noncompeting manufacturers and/or distributors.

4.2.4 Retailers

This type of delivery network intermediary can be described as any business engaged in the sale of goods and services directly to the end-customer. In the public's eye, retailers are normally seen as stores or discount outlets where customers physically shop for goods for take-home use. In reality, whether it is a manufacturer, a wholesaler/distributor, or an end-of-channel enterprise, any network entity selling to the end-customer (either directly, by phone, by machine, or by the Internet) is performing retailing functions. For the most part, retailer types can be distinguished by the level of services and the range of product assortments offered to end-customers.

Retailers can be broken down into two separate groupings. In the first group we have brick-and-mortar stores. This format controls the vast majority of retail sales (about 97 percent) and consists of *specialty stores* carrying a broad assortment within a narrow range of products (i.e., The Limited, Footlocker, Barnes and Noble); *department stores* carrying a very broad line of products—typically apparel, home furnishings, electronics, jewelry—with each department managed separately by a specialist marketing and merchandizing group (i.e., Macy's, Bloomindales, Nordstrom); *supermarkets* carrying a wide variety of low-cost, low-margin food-stuffs (i.e., Jewel, Dominck's, Alberston's); and *superstores* that attempt to provide a complete one-stop shopping experience (i.e., IKEA, Wal-Mart, Home Depot). Other retail formats, such as *discount stores, off-price retailers* (i.e., *factory outlets,* and *warehouse clubs*) and *catalog showrooms* focus on offering customers manufacturers' surplus, discontinued, and irregular goods, bulk purchase discounting, or high-volume, high-markup brand name goods available at a cash-and-carry showroom.

The second type of retailer can be described as businesses engaged in *nonstore retailing.* The overriding characteristic of this group is that they all use communications mediums, such as telephone, door-to-door sales, mail, television, and radio, to engage in sales and marketing activity. In this group we have *direct selling, direct marketing,* and *automatic vending* retailing formats. Perhaps the fastest growing segment is Internet businesses. In fact, at the height of the dot-coms in the early 2000s, it was suggested that channel distributors and retailers would eventually be disintermediated from the supply chain altogether to be replaced by cybermediaries. Essentially, e-businesses leverage the Internet to perform matching of products and buyers or coordinate marketing and transaction functions among trading network partners. Today, besides pure cybermediaries like e-Bay and Amazon.com, many companies provide Internet ordering formats, which allow their customers to directly manage their own buying experience.

4.3 Role of the Value Delivery Network

The primary role of the *value delivery network* is to provide for the effective distribution of goods and services that reflect as closely as possible the value and the place and time requirements demanded by the customer. Whether carried out by the sales and distribution division of a manufacturer, a wholesaler, or a megaretailer, there are a number of critical functions performed by delivery network entities.

4.3.1 Delivery Network Functions

The performance of the functions below are absolutely critical for the smooth transfer of goods and services through the delivery network. It must be said, however, that not all of the channel intermediaries assume responsibility for each one of these functions. A megaretailer like Wal-Mart, for example, actively seeks to dominate channel functions to the point where it can enforce its strategy for delivery function deployment among its channel partners. Other delivery networks might be composed of entities that seek to use specialized partners to perform targeted functions, such as transportation, financing, and warehousing, which they choose not to or cannot perform. The most critical functions performed by delivery networks are described below.

- **Selling and Promoting**. While it can be said that selling and promotion are the twin drivers of the delivery network, the actual form these functions take will be dictated by the channel strategy. These functions are perhaps the most difficult for producers. Producers have a very limited number of distribution points and have increasing difficulty executing sales, promotions, and fulfillment as end-customers are located geographically further from the home factory. To counter these deficiencies, producers can expand their own direct sales staffs and number of finished goods warehouses. A second strategy involves the use of delivery network intermediaries to carry out the responsibilities of product deployment. Wholesalers/distributors and retailers have direct-selling organizations, are often marketing experts in their industry, and have a strong footing in their target markets. In addition, because of their intimate knowledge of local customer needs and expectations, they can more effectively expand market share than producers by deploying targeted promotion campaigns using special pricing, product offerings, and value-added services such as short delivery cycles, financing, and transportation economies.

- **Buying and Building Product Assortments**. The ability to present the end-customer with as wide a range of products assortments as is possible constitutes the central pillar of the delivery network. Wholesalers/distributors are particularly structured to serve this requirement. By aggregating and consolidating product families from multiple manufacturers, they have the ability to transform products and product quantities into the assortments and lot sizes demanded by the marketplace. The value to the retailer or end-customer is obvious: the more products that can be sourced from a single supplier, the less the cost involved in purchasing, transporting, and merchandizing.

- **Bulk Breaking**. Along with building product assortments, this function is one of the fundamental reasons for the existence of network intermediaries. Bulk breaking refers to the ability of distributors to purchase from manufacturers in large lot sizes and then break those quantities down into much smaller quantities desired by retailers and end-customers. When combined with the ability to build assortments from several manufacturers, this function provides network middlemen with a powerful competitive position.

- **Value-Added Processing**. Today's delivery network intermediaries are increasingly involved in converting goods derived from the *process value chain* into their final form through the processes of sorting, labeling, blending, kitting, packaging, and light final assembly. This *value-added processing* function rests on the *principle of postponement*. Postponement seeks to minimize the risk of carrying finished forms of inventory by delaying product assortment, lot sizing, or even final assembly to the latest possible moment before customer purchase. This practice enables delivery network intermediaries to carry a great deal less product in the pipeline, shrink warehousing, handling, and transportation costs, and significantly reduce end-product obsolescence.

■ **Transportation.** The movement of goods from the manufacturing source through the *value delivery network* and out to the end-customer is the role of transportation management. Whether product is delivered directly to the end-customer by the manufacturer or moves through a complex delivery network, effective transportation is fundamental in assisting companies achieve time and place utilities. Poorly executed transportation results in lost sales, faltering customer confidence, and possible increased costs resulting from order expediting and returns. Transportation solves these problems by ensuring that goods are positioned properly in the delivery network by moving them as quickly, cost-effectively, and consistently as possible from the point of origin to the point of consumption.

■ **Warehousing.** Delivery networks use warehouses to solve a variety of problems. The most obvious reason that warehouses exist is simply because demand for products is often geographically located far from the place where they are produced. Warehouses ensure that network entities possess sufficient stock to satisfy customer requirements and act as a buffer, guarding against uncertainties in supply and demand. Other than brokers and some types of agents and Internet middlemen, most intermediaries perform some form of warehousing in order to assure the even flow of goods through the delivery network.

■ **Merchandizing.** Often retailers require the assistance of their delivery network suppliers to perform special product and display functions to ensure the optimal marketing of goods to the end-customer. Among the activities can be found simple value-added processing functions such as labeling, packaging, assortment, bulk breaking, and assembly into a store display unit determined by a retailer's marketing and sales campaign. Another example is a promotional pack that is assembled by the network producer or intermediary in response to a special sale.

■ **Marketing Information.** While actually the function of the *demand channel*, the timely transfer and quality of information arising from the customer purchasing experience is a critical responsibility of the *value delivery network*. As producers at the origin of the delivery channel are separated by distance and time from the end-customer, so the value of information becomes less reliable. The goal is to ensure that as the delivery network becomes more complex, all channel entities, regardless of their distance from the end-customer, can receive information regarding product, marketplace issues, and competitors' activities as quickly as possible.

■ **Reverse Flow Channels.** Over the past decade the growth of governmental and industry requirements for the reclamation of packaging materials, obsolete or unused products, and other wastes and backhaul to a central collection point for recycling has grown dramatically to the point where it has become a critical function of the delivery network. *Reverse logistics*, however, is more than just waste recycling. The real objective is the coordination of both the forward and reverse processes necessary for the full utilization of products and materials throughout the entirety of their life cycles.

4.3.2 Delivery Network Facilitators

While all of the above channel functions must be performed for the smooth and seamless transfer of products and services through the delivery network, they are not always performed by a single network entity. Those channel types that do take direct ownership of inventories and assume financial risk can be called *primary delivery network intermediaries*. However, if network intermediaries choose not to assume direct responsibility for one or multiple functions, they can employ the services of a *delivery network specialist*. In short, the role of a channel specialist is to perform specific functions for primary intermediaries for a fee. The use of a specialist, therefore, can be considered as a form of *outsourcing*, where a third-party specialist, who possesses special competencies beyond the core competencies of the contracting firm, is employed to perform key logistics operations. The following businesses are delivery network specialists.

- **Financial Institutions**. This type of specialist provides a wide range of banking functions ranging from cash management and lending to taxes, currency exchange, and payment. Other specialists in this area will handle additional functions like insurance and stock buying and selling.
- **Marketing and Advertising Agencies**. Many small distributors, wholesalers, and retailers simply do not have the competency to drive major marketing, advertising, and promotional campaigns. By contracting a specialist, network intermediaries can gain access to sophisticated marketing analysis and media outlets without direct investment in such resources.
- **Technology Services**. With the advent of the Internet and company-to-company networking, delivery channel intermediaries are, more than ever, required to deploy increasingly sophisticated technology tools that support ease of information transmission through the availability of wide-band data, voice, video, and text information transfer. Rather than support these often expensive resources internally, network businesses can turn to on-demand technology companies who will provide these computer solutions for a fee.
- **Logistics Service Providers**.[3] In today's fast-paced distribution channel intermediaries simply cannot stay competitive by providing end-to-end delivery network management without the support of *logistics service providers* (LSPs), often termed *third-part logistics* (3PL) providers. LSP services can be divided into five service areas:
    - *Logistics*—global trade services, inbound/outbound delivery, supplier management, inventory management, and payment.
    - *Transportation*—small package delivery; intermodal transportation; ocean, rail, and bulk transport; track and trace; fleet management; and equipment and personnel leasing.
    - *Warehousing*—storage, pick/pack functions, assembly, cross-docking, customer order management, and delivery fulfillment.

Figure 4.4   APL Logistics website.

- *Special services*—direct delivery to customer (UPS), import/export/customs functions, reverse logistics, market and customer management, consulting, and financial services.
- *Technology*—EDI, satellite/wireless communications, web enablement, and software solutions hosting.

In the past, channel businesses sought to utilize LSPs to outsource noncore functions, which could realize quick cost savings. Today, many managers see their LSPs as constituting a critical cornerstone of their logistics strategies, providing additional sources of value found in leveraging of technology to attain channel information, reductions in fixed assets, and reductions in overall channel costs. A typical 3PL service offering can be seen by visiting APL's website (Figure 4.4).

4.4   Value Delivery Network Decisions

It can be said as an axiom that supply chains are never created from nothing. Even in today's most innovative business environments, such as high-tech, electronics, or biomedical, enterprises can normally tap into an already existent, if not very mature, *value delivery network*. Why a particular channel is chosen depends on a matrix of factors, such as the desired level of market penetration, how deeply forward and backward integration with channel partners is to extend, and the targeted level of intensity of product/service distribution.

Of all the factors, however, perhaps the most critical in choosing a particular delivery network is the degree of *functional dependence* involved. Is the delivery channel to be characterized as purely transactional, unencumbered by channel dependencies, or is it based on a relational dependence among channel constituents? What are the required capabilities and costs of each network entity and how are they to be woven together? What is the distribution of power among channel players: who wields the most and who the least power? What are the strengths and weaknesses of the competition and how are existing channels responding to the initiatives of these alternative formats?

4.4.1 Delivery Network Systems[4]

The answers to many of the above questions are to be found in the network system a company chooses. There are three types of channel systems that could be used. In the first, *transaction-based systems*, there is minimal to no dependency among channel trading partners. Such systems, in fact, are formed for the performance of an often nonrepeatable transaction. The products or services sold are normally confined to very expensive durable goods, such as machinery or other processing equipment, and the services rendered are usually customized around a unique event. Once the transaction is completed, the likelihood of the delivery network re-forming again is remote.

In many ways the second type of delivery network system, a *limited channel*, is similar to a single-transaction channel in that businesses engage with other firms only to capture an opportunity and they do not seek to form extensive dependencies. Limited channels can be defined as loose arrangements of businesses that intermittently and opportunistically coalesce with delivery channel specialists in the buying and selling of goods. The overriding objective of such channels is achieving the best selling price and delivery, and their longevity is directly dependent on the ongoing usefulness of the arrangement. There is little or no loyalty in a limited channel, no effort to build collaborative partnerships, and no desire to improve channel efficiencies. Often channel relations are characterized as adversarial and arrangements can be dissolved at a moment's notice. Finally, limited channels do not view their success at providing value or an exceptional customer experience as stemming in any sense from the capabilities of their network partners. Each firm stands alone and autonomous, free to choose or disengage from any trading partner as long as it augments the internal objectives of the business.

The operating goal of a limited channel system is to utilize business partners to exploit a business opportunity on a product and service basis. In contrast, a *federated network system* is formed by businesses that acknowledge mutual dependencies and actively seek to integrate individual core competencies, resources, and customer market opportunities on a long-term basis. By pooling together the specialties of each channel member, a federated network can realize levels of efficiency, profitability, and customer value that could not be achieved by any of the individual firms acting alone. Critical factors driving coalescence are that all participating members perceive the relationship as fair and equitable, and they will financially and competitively benefit in the short and long term from the arrangement. Unlike the first two types of delivery channels where firms compete on their own, federated networks permit channel partners to compete as a unified delivery system.

Federated delivery networks are not new. Collaborative relationships among channel members can be found in a variety of forms, from partnerships, joint ventures, and strategic alliances to consortia, franchising, and royalty and licensing agreements. Several dynamics will dictate how the federated channel will work. To begin with, the presence of a powerful channel player, who either owns or franchises parts of the delivery network or, like a Wal-Mart or Home Depot, possesses so much power that network partners have no alternative but to fully cooperate, will result in networks that are driven by strong contractual arrangements where the channel master seeks to control partner behavior and diminish opportunities for conflict. Members benefit by participating in the economies of scale resulting from volume transactions, enhanced bargaining power, and removal of system redundancies. This type of federated delivery network describes about 80 percent of today's consumer market.

Another type of federated delivery network can be found in the form of partnerships and alliances. *Partnerships* arise when two or more firms integrate core competencies and resources in the pursuit of an emerging market opportunity. Each participant in such an arrangement agrees to surrender some of its independence to achieve long-term benefits arising from cooperative marketing, operations, and information sharing. A serious drawback of a partnership is the inability of the relationship to withstand conflict stemming from differences in operations or go-to-market strategies. When businesses agree to move to the next level of cooperation by jointly undertaking to improve performance, cost effectiveness, and competitiveness, this type of federated network is called an *alliance*. While it can be voluntary, most alliances are centered on contractual agreements. Examples are franchises, dealerships, and warehousing and transportation service agreements. Contracts provide network partners with a sense of permanence where risks, profitability, and accountability are shared legally.

4.4.2 Managing Channel Conflict

By their very natures, *network delivery channels* are difficult to change and often subject to conflict. Because they are really aggregates of independent companies, each with its own set of performance metrics and competitive objectives, constantly finding common ground where parties can realize their own goals in an atmosphere of mutual trust will continue to be a delicate and often complex management skill. Regardless of prophesies foretelling the disappearance of delivery networks as "Wal-Mart World" deconstructs the traditional distribution channel, the rise of new forms of network alliances driven by the Internet and globalization are sure to provide channel strategists with ever-new possibilities for delivery chain management.

Despite the fact that today's communications technologies have enabled companies to integrate more closely with their channel partners and customers, resistance to rather than the espousal of change is the norm for most delivery networks. While individual players may want to embark on new initiatives designed to promote increased competitiveness or closer customer intimacy, getting other channel constituents to go along can be difficult. According to Ragan,[5] there are three critical impediments to channel change.

1. Unless there is an overwhelming channel power player, like a Wal-Mart or a Hewlett Packard, influencing the behavior and policies of a community of independent companies is a complex one indeed. Besides constantly changing and recalibrating the strategic and performance targets of each channel member, there are also legal restrictions, contractual commitments, potential relationships with other delivery intermediaries, competitive practices, and marketplace conventions that make change difficult.

2. When channel changes are initiated, they are often undertaken by a single player. While a channel master like Wal-Mart possesses the power to mandate and orchestrate an initiative such as RFID (radio frequency identification), most channels do not have centralized leadership driving and coordinating improvements. Changes are normally seen as local, with no one overseeing the impact on overall channel capabilities, competitive positioning, and customer relations.

3. Because channels are opportunistic and voluntary, the operating conventions that do arise over time tend to get petrified. Even a strong leader like a Wal-Mart or Home Depot often must resort to threats and admonishments targeted at altering often decades-old ingrained systems of behavior. As a result, the changes that are made are often realized on a local level and rarely impact channel design.

Because delivery networks are by nature difficult to change, conflict between channel players can easily erupt. Conflict could arise over a decision to drastically change the channel, such as Dell's decision in the mid-1990s to abandon altogether its retail stores in favor of a purely Internet-driven business format. Additionally, conflict can arise over channel goal compatibility, such as moving from a low-cost, high-volume commodity focus to a more upscale product focus, such as pursued by Target's apparel strategy. Since channels are often nonexclusive, a company could find its products being offered by a downstream player alongside those of a direct competitor. Then again, conflict can arise over lack of specific demarcation in channel roles and rights, such as the conflict between major computer companies and their VARs (value-added resellers), who sometimes find themselves competing for the same customer. What is worse, a network partner could assume control over the end-customer relationship, even usurping brand identity and product pricing and promotions.

Conflict can arise between players at the same level in a channel, at different levels in a channel, and between two or more channels that sell to the same market. For example, when Sony opened its own retail store format, the strategy was in conflict with both large and small retailers who sold Sony products along with other brands. In some mega-electronics stores, Sony has been able to set up its own store within the retailer's store. Another example is the desire of companies to open e-commerce sites. Selling directly to the customer has the effect of disintermediating downstream delivery partners; sometimes such a strategy would be in violation of long-held contracts, such as between auto makers and car dealerships. For the most part, it can be stated that as delivery networks elongate and become complex, the more difficult it is for producers to control brand and pricing issues. On the other hand, the more powerful a channel player, the less room network members have to create sources of channel conflict.

Since revenue growth and profitability are directly linked to a company's ability to manage its delivery network partners, identifying and quickly resolving conflict is essential to ongoing channel success. According to an Aberdeen study on sell-side channel management,[6] firms that can optimize the value of their delivery networks can maximize their benefits, while those that poorly manage their channels find their prices, margins, and marketing power squeezed to commodity status and their customer relationships seized by more powerful sell-side players. While some channel conflict can be constructive and supportive of responses to a dynamically changing marketplace, much of it is dysfunctional. There are several methods for ensuring effective conflict management.

1. *Leadership.* In lieu of a powerful channel member who can enforce behavior and conformance to policies and established metrics, much conflict among network members can be reduced by the emergence of a *channel master* or *steward.*[7] The steward can be a producer, an intermediary, or any other participant in the delivery chain. The role of the steward is to design a *go-to-market strategy* that simultaneously addresses customers' best interests and generates profitability for all participants. The steward then acts as an advocate for change, transforming discordant partners into a unified channel for customer value and profitability.

2. *Integration.* As customers demand more not fewer multichannel sources for products and services, the need to develop integrated, collaborative channel processes is imperative. This method of alleviating channel conflict will require network partners to share sell-side data and analytics, construct metrics to more effectively chart channel revenue contribution, search for ways to continuously reduce overall costs, construct new avenues to deepen customer intimacy at each level in the delivery network, and search for ways to rationalize new sources of channel conflict.

3. *Technologies.* An important source for the removal of channel conflict is the visibility of sell-side data from every source in the delivery network. Technologies such as marketing portals, *customer relationship management* (CRM), and contract, service and *partner relationship management* (PRM) computerized solutions provide integrative tools for lead management, proposal and order management, global pricing and contract management, and service management that link the regions together and provide the end-customer with a single delivery entity.

4. *Performance Intelligence.*[8] Realizing the opportunities found in the marketplace requires looking at the performance of not just one company, but of all the firms comprising the entire end-to-end delivery channel. The optimal delivery channel has a keen understanding of customer demand and how it impacts producer capacities and schedules, logistics capabilities, and inventory. This knowledge will reveal two critical sets of metrics necessary for the alignment of demand and supply: the cost to serve customer objectives and the performance management metrics used to measure best practices across the delivery channel. Such intelligence permits the establishment of a single version of the entire delivery network and enables modeling of the best combination of network partners, superbly integrated to provide the deepest forms of customer intimacy.

Removing delivery network conflict must be conceived as an *evolutionary* process. Whether driven by a megachannel power or an emergent channel steward, *federated delivery networks* need leadership focused on guiding and directing changes in channel design and management, while at the same time ensuring customer intimacy and profitability for all network participants.

4.5 Summary and Transition

While the role of the *process value chain* is to produce the products and services required by the *demand channel*, it is the responsibility of a supply chain's *value delivery network* to ensure their timely and cost-effective distribution to channel intermediaries and end-customers. The *value delivery network* can be defined as *an organized network of interdependent businesses voluntarily or contractually confederated together through which products and services are marketed and sold.* Delivery networks can be simple, such as producer direct to the end-customer, or they can be composed of complex combinations of partnerships and alliances where goods and related issues, such as pricing and promotions, can change dramatically as they make their way to the end-customer.

Delivery channel decisions are perhaps one of the most critical activities facing management. Decisions regarding the number of intermediaries, depth of desired market penetration, span of partner capabilities, and level of acceptable dependence and risk sharing between the various channel players will have a direct effect on the probability of overall delivery channel success. All delivery networks are designed to handle three critical functions: *functional performance, reduced complexity*, and *specialization*. Decisions as to who the various players are, from internal manufacturers' warehouses and sales offices, to brokers/agents, wholesalers, and retailers, and what their direct role is in selling and promoting, value-added processing, transportation, warehousing, and merchandizing, will determine the level of cooperation, distribution of power, and dependency among delivery channel members.

Dividing the SCM into a *process value chain* and a *value delivery network* provides a useful method to describe what the supply chain looks like and its basic functions. The goal of the next chapter is to describe *how* these two components of SCM work in tandem to create highly competitive supply networks. As we shall see, SCM as a philosophy and a management practice can exist on several different levels and utilize a variety of different tools as it moves from the performance of simple logistics functions to embracing the full capabilities of the intimate supply chain.

Endnotes

1. This section has been adapted from David F. Ross, *Distribution Planning and Control: Managing in the Era of Supply Chain Management*, 2nd ed. (Norwell, MA: Kluwer Academic, 2004), 80–82; Donald J. Bowersox and David J. Closs, *Logistical Management: The Integrated Supply Chain Process* (New York: McGraw-Hill, 1996), 94–100; and Donald J. Bowersox and M. Bixby Cooper, *Strategic Channel Management* (New York: McGraw-Hill, 1993), 4.
2. These classifications were obtained from the U.S. Census Bureau, *North American Industry Classification System—United States, 2002. www.census.gov/epcd/www/naics.html*
3. This section is summarized from Ross, 658–666.
4. I have been assisted in the preparation of this section by Bowersox and Closs, *Logistical Management*, 119–125; Philip Kotler, *Marketing Management*, 11th ed. (Upper Saddle River, NJ: Prentice Hall, 2002), 522–526; and Steven L. Goldman, Roger N. Nagel, and Kenneth Preiss, *Agile Competitors and Virtual Organizations* (New York: Van Nostrand Reinhold, 1995), 201–234.
5. V. Kasturi Ragan, *Transforming Your Go-to-Market Strategy* (Boston, MA: Harvard Business School Press, 2006), 9–12.
6. Chris Selland, *Sell-Side Channel Management*, Aberdeen Group White Paper (Boston, MA: Aberdeen Group, September 2004).
7. This is the thesis of Ragan's *Transforming Your Go-to-Market Strategy*.
8. For further reference, see Michael P. Haydock, "Supply Chain Intelligence," in *Achieving Supply Chain Excellence through Technology*, vol. 5 (San Francisco, CA: Montgomery Research, 2003), 15–21.

Chapter 5

The Evolving
Supply Chain
From Logistics to the
Lean Supply Chain

Over the past decade, the concept of *supply chain management* (SCM) has undergone dramatic transformation. Originally conceived as an approach to more effectively execute logistics functions and closely integrate customers and suppliers into a common supply and delivery stream, SCM today describes both a business philosophy and a practical operations toolkit focused on the efficient movement of goods and services from producer to end-customer. Despite the codification it has undergone in what has become an enormous body of literature, SCM is still in the process of evolving to meet the changing needs of the marketplace. As discussed in the two previous chapters, the foundations of SCM were redefined by dividing it up into three distinct yet integrated processes: the *demand channel*, the *process value chain*, and the *value delivery network*. In this and the following chapter, the work of SCM redefinition will continue by investigating it from the perspective of three new management approaches based on cost reduction, operations excellence, and the creation of customer value.

This chapter begins with a review of the fundamentals of the SCM concept. As a management function, SCM is about the timely and cost-effective delivery of goods and services to the customer. SCM is, however, more than just logistics in that it also seeks to utilize network supply and delivery partners to assist companies reach markets and reduce costs, goals they simply could not achieve acting in isolation. This enabling aspect of SCM is explored in depth by deconstructing it into six critical competencies. These competencies will be seen as driving supply chains to achieve three critical success factors: the creation of continuous competitive advantage, the development of unified channels capable of delivering superior customer value, and the identification of technology tools capable of providing supply networks with visibility to total channel profitability and performance.

Although providing a concise definition, today's marketplace challenges have driven SCM to morph into three possible approaches coalescing around cost leadership, operations performance, or customer-centered organizations. The first approach, known as *lean supply chain management*, is the focus of the second half of this chapter, with the remaining two approaches comprising the content of chapter 6. After exploring "lean" concepts and principles, the lean supply chain will be discussed by exploring its six key competencies. The chapter concludes by detailing the benefits of the lean supply chain and the steps that must be followed if the desired level of supply chain success is to be achieved.

5.1 Supply Chain Management—An Overview

From the very beginnings of modern production and distribution management, companies have been faced with the fundamental problem of how to optimize the dispersion of goods and services to the marketplace. When producers and customers are in close proximity to each other, demand signals can be quickly received by suppliers and products and services in turn promptly delivered to the customer. As the time and distance separating production and the point of consumption increase, the ability of companies to deliver to an expanding range of markets rapidly diminishes. Without the means to effectively move product rapidly from the supply source to the customer, producers find their ability to expand their businesses restricted and markets themselves limited to a narrow array of goods and services.

Bridging this gap between demand and supply has required companies to employ two critical functions. The first is the application of the concept and practice of *logistics*. The role of logistics is to provide efficient and cost-effective warehousing and transportation capabilities ultimately focused on satisfying the day-to-day requirements of goods receiving and customer order fulfillment. The second function that has emerged is the utilization of other companies located in geographically dispersed markets who are willing to assume responsibility for the distribution of goods and services as representatives of producers. This function is termed the *supply value chain*, and the relationships governing the rights, duties, and behavior of producers and partners is termed *supply chain management* (SCM).

5.1.1   Fundamentals of Logistics Management

Over the centuries, logistics has been associated with the planning and coordination of the physical storage and movement of raw materials, components, and finished goods from manufacturer to consumer. There are many definitions of logistics. The Council of Supply Chain Management Professionals (CSCMP) defines logistics as "encompassing the activities involved in the forward and reverse flow and storage of goods, services, and related information between the point of origin and the point of consumption."[1] A very simple yet comprehensive description defines logistics as consisting of the *Seven R's*: that is having the *right product*, in the *right quantity* and the *right condition*, at the *right place*, at the *right time*, for the *right customer*, at the *right price*. Logistics provides *place* utility by providing for the transfer of goods from the producer through the *delivery value network* to the origin of demand. Logistics provides *time* utility by ensuring that goods are at the proper place to meet the occasion of customer demand. Logistics provides *possession* utility by facilitating the exchange of goods. Finally, logistics provides *form* utility by performing postponement processing, which converts products into the final configurations desired by the customer.[2] Together, these utilities constitute the value-added role of logistics.

Another way of defining logistics is to separate it into two distinct yet closely integrated spheres of contiguous processes as illustrated in Figure 5.1. The *materials management* sphere is concerned with the *incoming flow* of materials, components, and finished products into the enterprise. The operations functions in this sphere support the flow of goods originating in purchasing, progressing through inbound transportation, receipt, and control of production inventories, and concluding with production and presentation of finished goods to the delivery channel system. In contrast, the *physical distribution* sphere is associated with the *outbound flow* of goods and services from the place of production to the customer. Operations functions encompass warehouse management, transportation, value-added processing, and customer order administration.

Finally, logistics can be defined not as a series of functions, but rather as a system of nodes and links.[3] *Nodes* are the physical locations where products are stored as finished goods or processed into assemblies for further conversion or for sale to the customer. The other component of the system consists of the *links* or the various modes of transportation (rail, motor, water, air, or pipelines) that connect the nodes. As illustrated in Figure 5.2, logistics nodes and links can be simple or complex depending on how deeply the logistics system penetrates into the marketplace. A simple system can consist of as little as a materials supplier linked to a producer who is in turn linked to the end-customer. On the other hand, a complex logistics system can consist of multiple plants linked to a series of warehouses, which are in turn linked to retailers who then sell to the end customer.

Regardless of how it is defined, logistics performs five critical functions. The first, *network design*, is concerned with the physical configuration of the production

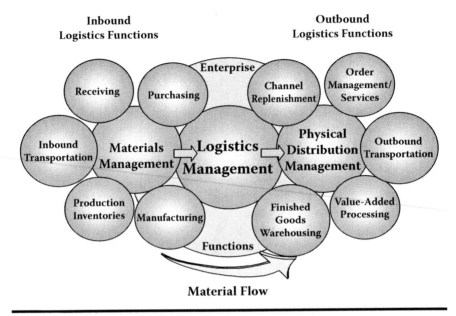

Figure 5.1 Logistics management functions.

plants and distribution warehouses a company uses to move products to the customer. Logistics planners must continually review network strategies to ensure they are providing optimal levels of customer service and competitiveness. The second element, *operations planning and execution*, is focused on the effective performance of a number of supply and delivery functions, including order management, production

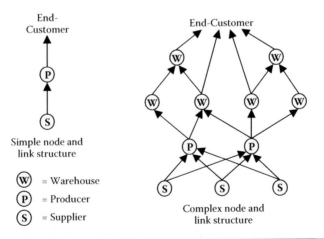

Figure 5.2 Logistics nodes and links.

and procurement, freight and service management, warehouse management, transportation routing and scheduling, fleet management, and reverse logistics.

The third logistics element, *logistics partnership management*, enables companies to utilize the capabilities offered by logistics partners to augment internal logistics services by providing special expertise in such areas as cartage, parcel delivery, warehousing, value-added processing, financial settlement, technology connectivity, and consulting. Increasingly, companies are turning to the fourth element, *information technologies*, to assist them in logistics management. Today's technologies provide tools to facilitate the flow of order management, shipment tracking, and alert messaging/notification. They also provide visibility tools that assist companies to monitor, simulate, control, and measure logistics functions in an effort to automate and increase the accuracy of logistics decisions. Finally, the last element, *performance measurement*, provides the logistics productivity, service performance, and measurement systems metrics necessary to ensure the achievement of targeted levels of customer service and financial performance.

5.1.2 Fundamentals of Supply Chain Management

In their effort to reach deeper into the marketplace and rationalize and accelerate the distribution process, companies have always known that using the capabilities and resources of specialist firms could dramatically enhance the footprint of their own core competencies. From the beginning, businesses sought to integrate internal logistics functions, such as transportation and warehousing, with those of channel partners in an effort to reach new markets, increase pipeline velocities, and cut costs. By the final decades of the twentieth century, however, it had become abundantly clear that the prevailing use of logistics partners needed to be dramatically expanded and elevated to a strategic level. In place of the opportunistic, tactical use of channel specialists that temporarily coalesced and collaborated to achieve a short-term objective, strategists began advocating the transformation of these transient relationships into integrated, mutually enriching partnerships. Logistics channels were to be replaced by *value networks*.

Although it can be said that logistics remains at the core of what supply chains actually do, the concept of SCM encompasses much more than simply the transfer of products and services through the supply pipeline. SCM is about a company integrating its process capabilities with those of its suppliers and customers on a strategic level. SCM recognizes that the real power of supply chains is to be found far beyond the narrow management of channel trading dyads (one-to-one businesses relationships). Effective supply chains, rather, consist of many trading partners participating simultaneously in an interactive network containing multiple levels of competencies and driven by various types of relationships. SCM enables companies to activate the synergy to be found when a community of firms utilizes the productive capacities of each member to build superlative supply and delivery processes that provide total customer value.

What exactly is SCM? While several definitions have been proposed, consensus on a definitive statement is still to be reached. For example, APICS (Association for Operations Management) defines SCM as:

> The design, planning, execution, control, and monitoring of supply chain activities with the objective of creating net value, building a competitive infrastructure, leveraging worldwide logistics, synchronizing supply with demand, and measuring performance globally.[4]

In their text, *Designing and Managing the Supply Chain* (2003), Simchi-Levi and Kaminsky define SCM as:

> a set of approaches utilized to efficiently integrate suppliers, manufacturers, warehouses, and stores, so that merchandise is produced and distributed at the right quantities, to the right locations, and at the right time, in order to minimize systemwide costs while satisfying service level requirements.[5]

Finally, the Council of Supply Chain Management Professionals (CSCMP) defines SCM very broadly as:

> encompassing the planning and management of all activities involved in sourcing and procurement, conversion, and all logistics management activities. Importantly, it also includes coordination and collaboration with channel partners, which can be suppliers, intermediaries, third-party service providers, and customers. In essence, supply chain management integrates supply and demand management within and across companies.[6]

SCM-driven organizations possess the capability to move beyond a narrow focus on optimizing internal logistics to a strategy that identifies and leverages the best core competencies and collaborative relationships among their supply chain partners to architect value networks capable of realizing continuous breakthroughs in product design, manufacturing, delivery, customer service, cost management, and value-added services before the competition. This strategic, channel-building attribute of SCM revolutionizes the role of the supply chain and provides all channel players with the capability to view themselves and their network partners as extended, virtual organizations possessed of radically new methods of responding in unique ways to provide total customer value.

5.1.3 Supply Chain Competencies

The supply and delivery network-building attributes of SCM revolutionize the role of every channel constituent and infuse them with radically new ways of providing

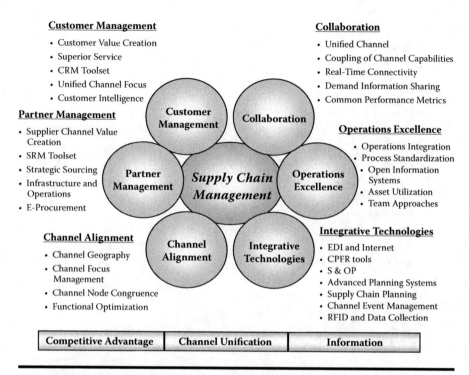

Customer Management

- Customer Value Creation
- Superior Service
- CRM Toolset
- Unified Channel Focus
- Customer Intelligence

Partner Management

- Supplier Channel Value Creation
- SRM Toolset
- Strategic Sourcing
- Infrastructure and Operations
- E-Procurement

Channel Alignment

- Channel Geography
- Channel Focus Management
- Channel Node Congruence
- Functional Optimization

Collaboration

- Unified Channel
- Coupling of Channel Capabilities
- Real-Time Connectivity
- Demand Information Sharing
- Common Performance Metrics

Operations Excellence

- Operations Integration
- Process Standardization
- Open Information Systems
- Asset Utilization
- Team Approaches

Integrative Technologies

- EDI and Internet
- CPFR tools
- S & OP
- Advanced Planning Systems
- Supply Chain Planning
- Channel Event Management
- RFID and Data Collection

Competitive Advantage	Channel Unification	Information

Figure 5.3   Supply chain management competencies.

total customer value. Establishing and sustaining SCM requires whole supply chains to pursue unflaggingly the following competencies (Figure 5.3).

5.1.3.1   Customer Management

In the past, companies sought to compete by optimizing economies of scale and scope, pushing standardized goods and services into the marketplace regardless of actual customer wants and needs. Today, instead of logistics systems focused solely on volume and throughput, companies have had to evolve into a supply chain perspective where the collective competencies and resources of their channel eco-systems can be leveraged in the pursuit of unique avenues of customer value and superior service. As customers migrate from being passive recipients to active partners in product/service design and development, pricing, and configuration of their own buying solutions, companies have come to understand that creating customer value rests on establishing enriching customer relationships—in short, customer management has become *customer relationship management* (CRM).

In today's era of the customer-centric marketplace, businesses cannot hope to survive without seamlessly working together with their supply chains. The goal is to create closely integrated end-to-end channel systems capable of providing complete visibility and information about customer requirements from any place along the supply chain continuum. CRM attempts to realize this merger of suppliers and intermediaries through the following points:

■ CRM is supportive of the strategic missions of all channel network players by providing the mechanisms necessary to align their resources and capabilities in the search to build profitable, sustainable relationships with customers.
■ CRM is focused on optimizing the customer experience wherever it occurs in the supply chain. Such an objective requires the use of metrics and analytical tools capable of providing a comprehensive, cohesive customer portrait, which in turn can drive acquisition and retention initiatives.
■ CRM assists in gathering intelligence as to which customers are profitable, what products and services will spawn differentiating customer value propositions, and how each channel member can architect sales and marketing processes that consistently deliver to each customer the values they desire the most.
■ CRM is about nurturing mutually beneficial, long-term relationships resilient enough to sustain continuous improvement opportunities and tailored solutions beyond immediate product and service delivery.
■ CRM is a major facilitator of supply chain collaboration. Customer value delivery must be considered as a single, unified event that ripples up and down the supply chain. Firms participating in integrated, synchronized supply networks capable of providing a seamless response to the customer will be those that will achieve sustainable competitive advantage.

Effective customer management requires the application of methods and technology tools that enable companies to span supply chain boundaries in their search to both identify new customers as well as to retain current ones. CRM provides the mechanisms necessary not only to quantify customers' behaviors and preferences, but also to invite customers to be value chain collaborators. Finally, CRM provides the operational mosaic of processes and toolsets necessary for the generation of fast flow, flexible, synchronized delivery systems that enable customer self-service, configuration of customized, individualized value solutions, and fulfillment functions providing the highest level of service and value.

5.1.3.2 Partner Management

Effective management of the acquisition of products and services to satisfy the demands of the customer resides at the very core of competitive supply chains. The need to more closely integrate the capabilities and resources of suppliers while reducing channel costs has rendered obsolete former sourcing practices and spawned a new concept—*supplier relationship management* (SRM). The mission of SRM is to activate the real-time synchronization of inventory and service offerings with the capabilities of channel partners in order to execute a customized, unique buying experience for customers while simultaneously pursuing procurement cost reduction and continuous improvement in supply network performance. SRM seeks to fuse supplier management functions—information systems, logistics, resources, skills, cost management, and improvement—found across the entire supply chain into an efficient, seamless process driven by relationships founded on trust, shared risk, and mutual benefit.

Reaching such objectives requires realization of several key components. To begin with, companies must establish the value propositions to be gained through supplier partnership. Among the benchmarks are expected cost savings, enhanced process efficiencies, reductions in cycle times, channel inventory minimization, and increased process optimization as a result of a closer matching of channel demand with network capabilities and resources. Once the value of SRM has been quantified, a strategic sourcing program can be launched. This component of SRM ensures that a company has engaged the right set of suppliers, that they provide the desired skills and competencies, that they can execute expected levels of product delivery and quality, and finally, that they can activate innovative thinking and a willingness to collaborate.

The third key component of SRM is the application of integrative technologies. Throughout history, the efficacy of supply activities has been driven by technology tools. Today, the Internet has enabled buyers and supplier to leverage new forms of procurement, such as online catalogs, buying exchanges, interactive auction sites, and other web-based toolsets, which both automate functions associated with purchase order management and synchronize, in real time, demand and supply signals from anywhere, anytime in the supply chain network. Finally, the last component, SRM-driven channel infrastructures, requires supply chains to possess agile procurement functions capable of being rapidly deconstructed and rebuilt to meet the changing needs of customers and shifts in performance and improvement metrics.

5.1.3.3 Channel Alignment

The geography of any supply chain is composed of its supply and delivery nodes and the links connecting them. Often, this network is portrayed as a series of trading dyads as exhibited in Figure 5.4. In this model, supply channels are seen as consisting of series of primary and secondary trading relationships where supply and delivery functions are performed one channel partner at a time. In reality, a channel intermediary, such as a large retailer like Wal-Mart, could literally be dealing with hundreds of suppliers and customers. For most channel constituents, the supply chain looks less like a pipeline (see Figure 3.1) and more like a grid representing an extensive network of customers and suppliers, many simultaneously interacting with each other (Figure 5.5).

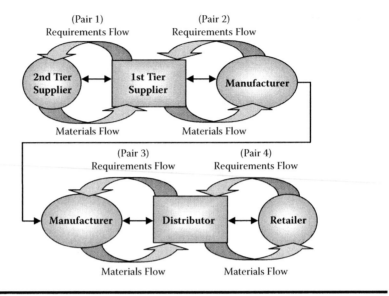

Figure 5.4 Channel dyads.

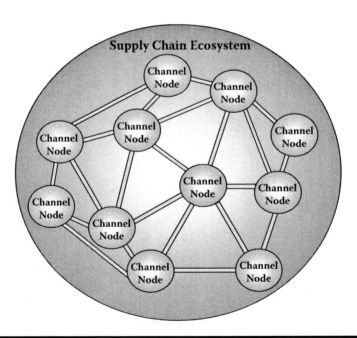

Figure 5.5 Supply chain as a network grid.

Since it is virtually impossible to manage such large supply ecosystems, each channel node must first clearly identify the supply and delivery channel it directly uses to acquire products and services and drive delivery to the end-customer. This extended network should be constructed around a common strategy and set of operational objectives that support the channel's collective best interests. This step should also reveal incongruities between the strategies and metrics of individual partners and regions of potential conflict. The goal is to tightly integrate the various links that constitute the reach of the supply chain. Without strategic and operational alignment, the chain will have weak links that will easily break as the pressure of demand variability and asset investment appears at critical points in product or marketing campaign life cycles.

Finally, as direct supply chain convergence matures, the number of nodes occupying peripheral positions, both upstream and downstream, can be more closely integrated into the direct channel (see Figure 5.6). The goal is to increase the length of the contiguous supply chain, thereby expanding opportunities for collaboration, focus on customer value, operations excellence, and supplier integration. However, supply chain strategists must be careful not to overexpand a unified channel system to the point where resources and benefits can be diluted by conflicts and compromises over costs, performance metrics, service value propositions, and delivery velocity targets. In fact, some companies may find themselves working with several separate supply chain and delivery networks as their business ecosystems evolve in new directions.

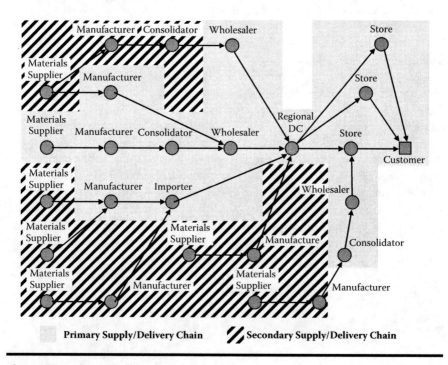

Figure 5.6 Channel alignment structures.

5.1.3.4 Supply Chain Collaboration

The keystone of SCM can, perhaps, be found in the willingness of supply network partners to engage in and constantly enhance collaborative relationships with each other. By way of definition, *collaboration* can be described as:

> an activity pursued jointly by two or more entities to achieve a common objective, and it can mean anything from exchanging raw data by the most basic means, to the periodic sharing of information through Web-based tools, the structuring of real-time technology architectures that enable partners, and leveraging highly interdependent infrastructures in the pursuit of complex, tightly integrated functions ensuring planning, execution, and information synchronization.[7]

The essence of collaboration is about bringing together often-diverse members of the supply chain in an effort to enrich capabilities and maximize value to the entire network and the customers they serve by sharing processes, technologies, skills, resources, and information. The *value* of collaboration is gauged by how effectively leveraging the competencies of the distributed knowledge of the channel base, reducing redundant functions and wastes, sharing a common vision of the supply chain, and constructing the technical and social architectures for making it happen enable whole channel networks to achieve superior levels of marketplace leadership.

The creation of viable collaborative relationships involves a variety of processes. According to Finley and Srikanth,[8] there are several critical imperatives that must be pursued if collaboration is to reach its potential. To begin with, it is essential that individual company strategies and goals be aligned across all network partners. Convergence of objectives ensures suppliers, intermediaries, and customers are pursuing linked strategies, planning and execution processes, and performance metrics that create benefits not only for themselves, but also for the entire supply chain. Next, it is crucial that companies segregate the various channels in which they participate. Because each channel (i.e., wholesale, export, retail, mass merchandize, etc.) possesses a range of different processes, delivery dynamics, and performance indicators, a tailored strategy for each channel, rather than a global approach, would produce an array of unified channels, each with its own level of shared perspective and operating commonality. Finally, unified channel collaboration makes it easier to ensure connectivity of all channel nodes, availability of the proper technology tools for information visibility and real-time transfer, acceptance of common performance metrics and benefits, and access to demand patterns and expectations as they stream across the supply chain to guide the collective activities of the channel network.

5.1.3.5 Operations Excellence

All organizations seek to optimize productive functions while removing costs and this objective becomes even more critical in SCM. If the role of each network partner is to exercise its distinctive competency in support of total channel optimization, then, as each competency is increasingly integrated in collaboration with other participants, the more individual firms will have access to a range of processes and benefits they would be incapable of achieving acting on their own. Thus, in addition to competing on the merits of its own organization, each channel member must also see itself as dependent on the collective success of the entire supply chain. Even those firms that are less dependent on the overall success of their supply chains must still seek to continuously explore new opportunities for fostering cooperation and shared benefits.

Interorganizational operations excellence provides the mechanism that runs the engine of supply chain collaboration. The goal is the establishment of mutually agreed upon business processes and performance metrics that will drive competitive advantage. Operations excellence can cover a wide range of performance areas and includes:

Information technologies integration	Asset utilization
Cost reduction	Quality performance
Process standardization	Reverse logistics
Cycle time reduction	Inventory reduction
Increased customer service	Increased logistics utilization
Increased market share	Joint project collaboration

Implicit in achieving operations excellence in these areas is the need for joint supply chain team approaches. Such teams are essential in creating common ground on organizational practices and providing insight into areas of agreement and potential conflict. SCM teams, whether informal or formal, broaden and mature supply chain relationships by building the following attributes:[9]

- *Trust*: This attribute is perhaps the foundation of SCM. While trust is hard to quantify, it means that channel partners can have faith in the intentions and actions of each other, that individual company strategies are formulated with the good of the entire network in mind, and that companies will not use positions of power to abuse more dependent members.
- *Reliability*: Being reliable means that a company can count on its partners to exhibit consistent, predictable, and honest behavior over the long run. Lack of congruence between commitments and behavior erode supply chain relationships. In addition, the use of coercion to force partners to act in a prescribed way often results in less than reliable behavior and is antithetical to the establishment of strong channel relationships.
- *Competence*: This attribute is concerned with the capability of a partner to support and perform the role in the supply chain as initially promised. Competence refers to the ability of the partner's organization to provide the people, processes, knowledge, experience, technology, and resources that will ensure the viability of the relationship.

■ *Risk Sharing*: Risk is part of every business endeavor. Risk in a supply chain relationship, however, often extends beyond normal uncertainties because there is an implied external vulnerability arising from dependence on partners to perform their agreed upon roles. On the other hand, without the presence of some form of risk, the intended partnership will never flourish.

■ *Loyalty*: Trust, reliability, and the willingness to risk all contribute to a sense of loyalty between channel partners. Loyalty is a two-way street; each partner not only performs predictably, but is also willing to assist other partners to resolve problems or ameliorate risk. Loyalty enables parties to engage in deeper commitment to the relationship and by extension enriches the entire supply chain ecosystem.

5.1.3.6 Integrative Technologies

Gaining visibility into orders, inventory, and shipments across the extended supply chain is a critical priority of SCM, and providing that intelligence is the role of technology. In today's highly competitive global marketplace, having the best product or service is simply not enough; now, having the best *information* has become the decisive differentiator among market leaders and followers. Supply channel transparency requires a single version of data encompassing demand, logistics, demand/capability alignment, production and processes, delivery, and supplier intelligence across the firms comprising the entire end-to-end supply chain. Generating a single view of the supply chain requires information technologies that enable collection, processing, access, and manipulation of complex views of data necessary for determining optimal supply chain design and execution configurations.

The technology tools capable of providing supply chain transparency can be separated into three spheres. The first sphere seeks to utilize technology to improve operational efficiency and channel visibility. Technologies ranging from strategic systems like ERP (enterprise resource planning) to tactical devices like EDI (electronic data interchange), web, and RFID (radio frequency identification) provide connectivity, information sharing, event tracking, exception management, and dynamic optimization to reduce lead times, wastes, and increase supply chain agility. Included in this area is advanced supply chain planning systems, such as *collaborative planning, forecasting, and replenishment* (CPFR) and *sales and operations planning* (S&OP), which seek to balance demand and supply by optimizing inventory. The second sphere contains technologies that assist in the execution of regulatory compliance, security, and oversight. This area includes shipment tracking, channel disruption management, supply chain improvement, and regulatory functions available in such toolsets as supplier collaboration portals, 3PL (third-party logistics), and transportation systems. The final sphere, customer experience enhancement, centers on customer order and service management solutions that improve everything from on-time delivery and self-service order configuration, to delivery synchronization and status visibility.

5.1.4 The Impact of SCM

The intense focus of today's academic and business communities on SCM is the result of the realization that companies cannot hope to gather, on their own without channel partners, the necessary resources and core competencies that permit them to efficiently and profitably design, manufacture, market, and distribute goods and services to what has become a global marketplace. The six SCM competencies, as portrayed in Figure 5.3, enable companies to realize the three essential success factors shown at the bottom of the figure. To begin with, by creating customer-centric business environments and closely synchronizing channel demand with suppliers' capabilities, SCM enables the building of integrated, relationship-driven supply chains focused on creating continuous *competitive advantage*. Second, by converging the collective resources and innovative capabilities found among network partners, SCM enables whole supply chains to act as if they were a single *unified channel* capable of delivering customer value seamlessly across intersecting supply chains. And finally, by leveraging the tremendous repositories of skills and innovative capacities found collectively within the people resources and technology tools found across the supply channel, SCM provides the necessary *information* to keep supply networks focused on providing total customer value as well as overall profitability.

Case Study 5.1

Customer Intimacy at NetApp

Network Appliance (NetApp), the Sunnyvale CA-based manufacturer of data storage solutions has worked hard at developing a distribution network that enables it to stay close to the needs of its customer base. The $2 billion a year company services a global market with 110 offices worldwide.

The key to its ability to deliver consistently a 99.5 percent global fill rate across its service organization stems from its unique distribution philosophy. The centerpiece of the strategy is NetApp's decision to establish regionally specific infrastructures to support customers in different geographies. NetApp's field service operation includes one global distribution center supplying five regions worldwide through four hubs (Louisville, Miami, Amsterdam, and Singapore) and 200 forward stocking locations. The flexibility of its infrastructure and its information technology has allowed NetApp to develop individual fulfillment strategies appropriate for different regions, right down to the local level.

Such a strategy is critical in remaining as close to the customer as possible. Due to the vital nature of its customers' data centers, NetApp's service chain offers two- and four-hour and next business day delivery commitments on more than 1,500 parts to keep its customers up and running.

Besides keeping as close to its customers as possible, NetApp's system has enabled it to shrink channel inventories by mapping out tight linkages between the stocking model and customer entitlements.

Source: Editorial Staff, "Managing a Global Supply Chain in a 'Flat' World," *Supply & Demand Chain Executive*, June/July, 2006, pp. 18–20.

5.2 SCM Process Approaches

Although SCM provides an organized, comprehensive methodology for managing logistics and integrating supply chain partners in the pursuit of total customer value at the lowest cost, it does not detail how to tackle the difficult task of creating the strategies, developing the cross-channel plans, and optimizing the supply network's collective capabilities that will enable supply chains to reach superior levels of performance. In fact, the need to leverage SCM concepts to both improve logistics functions as well as to increase the collaboration and synchronization of supply chain members has never been greater. Today's supply chains are besieged by immense challenges that range from strategic issues, such as effectively responding to the continuous changes occurring in the marketplace, increased need for asset agility, product proliferation, and globalization, to operational assaults on logistics capabilities brought about by constraints on transportation capacity, crumbling or nonexistent infrastructures, spiraling energy costs, and security.

What is needed are practical approaches to utilizing the basic tenets of SCM to fashion new strategies and best practices that will provide fresh insights into today's supply chain issues and enable a seaway into realizing tomorrow's opportunities. Such an understanding illuminates the very nature of SCM, which is always evolving to respond to the changes incessantly occurring in the marketplace. Today, SCM has the following six challenges before it:

1. Creating new avenues for supply chains to be more intimate with the customer by understanding what constitutes *individual* customer value and providing an unsurpassed buying experience.
2. Ensuring the long-term profitability of the supply chain and each network partner by removing barriers to higher levels of supply chain efficiency and effectiveness.
3. Increasing the level of collaboration and access to channel partner competencies by sharing data, intelligence, and more closely aligning organizations.
4. Architecting supply chains consisting of productive assets that are agile and flexible enough to respond to any marketplace challenge.
5. Increasing the velocity of inventory and delivery network processes while continually reducing costs.
6. Enabling greater levels of connectivity to more closely interweave the knowledge and skills of cross-channel teams.

While there are many variants, supply chain strategists have narrowed the response to these challenges to three distinct approaches. The first has coalesced around *cost leadership* and encompasses a set of principles and tools designed to increase supply chain productivity and profitability by ruthlessly reducing wastes found anywhere in the channel network. This method is known as *lean supply chain management*. The second approach, *operations performance*, is focused on ensuring supply chain execution functions are as agile as possible in the face of demand variability. This method can be concerned with supply flexibility and is known as *adaptive supply chain management*

Table 5.1   SCM Strategies

SCM Strategy	2006	2005	2004	2003
Cost Leadership	10.9%	12.6%	16.4%	22.9%
Customer-Centered	34.2%	39.9%	35.9%	29.9%
Operations	14.4%	13.6%	17.1%	16.6%
Performance Brended Approach	40.5%	39.9%	30.6%	30.6%

Source: Data from Peter D. Moore, Karl B. Manrodt, Mary C. Holcomb, and Mike Riegler, "Year 2006 Report on Trends and Issues in Logistics and Transportation," Capgemini White Paper, February 2007, 8–10.

or it can be concerned with delivery flexibility and is known as *demand-driven supply network management*. The final approach, *customer centered*, is concerned with the continuous development of supply chain capabilities and resources to provide total value to the customer. This method is known as *intimate supply chain management*. The remainder of this chapter will focus on lean SCM. Chapter 6 will then proceed to a discussion of the concepts and principles of adaptive supply chains and demand-driven supply networks. Finally, chapters 7 and 8 will complete the analysis with a review of today's most advanced form of SCM, the intimate supply chain.

It is important to note that companies will often pursue not just one, but a mixture of these strategies. No firm today can ignore the requirement to cut operating costs; however, just eliminating costs will be a hollow exercise if not linked to strategies that increase customer value. For example, in a survey of businesses conducted by Moore, Manrodt, Holcomb, and Riegler over the years 2003 to 2006, it was found that the most popular SCM strategy was actually a hybrid of the three approaches outlined above.[10] As detailed in Table 5.1, it was found that a single focus on cost reduction had fallen into last place behind other methods. What was more interesting is that a blended approach accounted for over 40 percent of the respondents. The analysis simply points to the fact that today's best supply chains are attempting to pursue cost management, operational flexibility, and superior customer service *simultaneously*.

5.3 Lean Supply Chain Management

Perhaps the most practical approach to SCM is to consider the supply chain as a source for both the continuous reduction of cost and for process improvement. What goes on in a supply chain must pass the simple litmus test applied to any process: *Do the functions being performed add value to the customers, the companies involved, and the supply chain in general?* In other words, do the inventories, policies and procedures, supply and delivery processes, and operating cultures of a supply channel provide rich sources of continuous value or do they produce too little value and too much cost? The concept of the *lean supply chain* centers on the principle that the continuous reduction of waste must not only be unflaggingly applied to the processes inside an organization, it must also be applied to all customers and suppliers found anywhere in the supply chain.

5.3.1 Primer on Lean

The story of the foundation of lean business process management is well known to all professionals in the field of production and distribution management. Springing out of the teachings on quality management of W. Edwards Deming and the assembly-line practices of the Ford Motor Company, the concept was adopted by Japanese manufacturers and nurtured to maturity in the 1980s in the Toyota Production System (TPS). Over the decades, lean has been enhanced by the addition of the concepts and techniques to be found in Total Quality Management (TQM), Six Sigma, and the Theory of Constraints (TOC). Today, lean has emerged as a *philosophy* preaching the total elimination of all wastes and the optimization of all resources, a *toolbox* of techniques for process improvement, and a *system* through which companies and their business partners can deliver continuous improvement and customer satisfaction.

Perhaps the best summary of lean can be found in the following five principles detailed in Womack and Jones's groundbreaking book, *Lean Thinking* (1996):[12]

1. *Produce value.* The value a company offers must be determined from the perspective of the customer—whether that value is lowest cost, best delivery performance, highest quality, an engaging buying experience, or a unique solution to a product/service requirement.
2. *Optimize the value stream.* Production and fulfillment processes must be closely mapped to expose any barriers to optimizing value to the customer from concept to product launch, from raw materials to finished product, from order to delivery.
3. *Convert the process to flow.* Once waste is eliminated, the goal is to replace "batch and queue" thinking and related performance measures with a mindset enabling the continuous flow of goods and services through the channel pipeline.
4. *Activate the demand pull.* Espousing the process flow mindset means producing and delivering exactly what the customer wants just when the customer wants it; this means migrating from demand driven by forecasts to demand driven by the customers "pulling" products to meet their individual wants and needs.
5. *Perfection of all products, processes, and services.* With the first four principles in place, supply chains can focus their attention on continuously improving efficiency, cost, cycle times, and quality.

These principles provide companies with a practical road map to apply lean concepts and tools to reduce inventory and cycle times, improve productivity and quality, and generate customer-focused organizations capable of delivering increased levels of customer value. Although such goals are critical for the survival of every company, it has become evident that true realization of lean lies in extending its principles and tools to the supply chains to which they belong.

5.3.2 Definition of Lean SCM

Although many companies can point to the impact on costs and profitability of a successful internal lean initiative, it can be argued that for lean thinking to drive the level of increased value and continuous improvement it promises, companies *must* look beyond the narrow boundaries of their own businesses and encompass the entire supply chain. In fact, regardless of the size of the initial benefits, they will rapidly diminish in value as they experience the entropy encountered when interacting with the wasteful processes of channel partners. According to research by the Aberdeen Group,[13] lean strategies are designed to respond to the following five supply chain pressures:

- Continuing requirement to improve operational performance
- Continuing requirement to reduce operating costs
- Responding to customer demand for the ongoing reduction in order cycles
- Achieving competitive advantage in pricing and service
- Meeting customer demands for reduced prices

Lean SCM speaks directly to all these issues by enabling entire supply chains to identify new ways to cut costs while improving productivity, quality, and customer satisfaction.

What makes a supply chain lean? To begin with, a lean supply chain seeks to reduce wastes found anywhere in the supply network, standardize processes across traditional, vertical organizations, and optimize core resources. Lean supply chains seek to create customer-winning value at the lowest cost through the real-time synchronization of product/service needs with the optimum supplier. Achieving such objectives requires supply chains to be both *responsive* (capable of meeting changes in customer needs for requirements such as alternative delivery quantities and transport modes) as well as *flexible* (adapting assets, pursuing outsourcing, and deploying dynamic pricing and promotions). Finally, lean supply chains are dedicated to the continuous improvement of people and processes throughout the extended supply chain.

All of these elements can be combined to construct a useful definition of the lean supply chain. Manrodt, Abott, and Vitasek define it as:

> A set of organizations directly linked by upstream and downstream flows of products, services, finances, and information that collaboratively work to reduce cost and waste by efficiently and effectively pulling what is needed to meet the needs of the individual customer.[14]

In a similar vein, Poirier, Bauer, and Houser consider the lean supply chain to be:

> A collaborating set of businesses linked by the end-to-end flows of products and service, information and knowledge, and finances, resulting in total enterprise optimization gained through total elimination of waste and increased revenues gained through greater customer satisfaction.[15]

This text offers a simple definition: A supply and delivery network of firms capable of supplying the right product at the right cost at the right time to the customer with as little waste as possible.

5.3.3 Six Competencies of Lean Supply Chains

While the above definitions provide a concise foundation, deeper investigation reveals that lean SCM can be better understood when it is deconstructed into six competencies as illustrated in Figure 5.7.

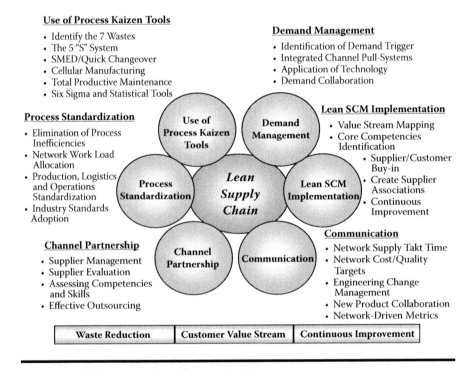

Use of Process Kaizen Tools
- Identify the 7 Wastes
- The 5 "S" System
- SMED/Quick Changeover
- Cellular Manufacturing
- Total Productive Maintenance
- Six Sigma and Statistical Tools

Demand Management
- Identification of Demand Trigger
- Integrated Channel Pull-Systems
- Application of Technology
- Demand Collaboration

Process Standardization
- Elimination of Process Inefficiencies
- Network Work Load Allocation
- Production, Logistics and Operations Standardization
- Industry Standards Adoption

Lean SCM Implementation
- Value Stream Mapping
- Core Competencies Identification
- Supplier/Customer Buy-in
- Create Supplier Associations
- Continuous Improvement

Channel Partnership
- Supplier Management
- Supplier Evaluation
- Assessing Competencies and Skills
- Effective Outsourcing

Communication
- Network Supply Takt Time
- Network Cost/Quality Targets
- Engineering Change Management
- New Product Collaboration
- Network-Driven Metrics

| Waste Reduction | Customer Value Stream | Continuous Improvement |

Figure 5.7 Lean supply chain competencies.

5.3.3.1 Application of Process Kaizen[16] Tools

"Lean" is about the reduction of waste found anywhere in the supply chain. Wastes can occur not only in inventory and processes, but also in time, motion, and even digital waste. According to the Toyota Production System, there are potentially "seven wastes" found in any process: *overproduction, transportation, unnecessary inventory, inappropriate processing, waiting, excess motion*, and *defects*. Lean advocates have argued that an eighth waste exists: *underutilization of employees' minds and ideas.*[17] An understanding of "waste" enables awakening of its antipode: that which adds *value*.

Lean advocates have identified a toolbox of methods designed to attack wastes anywhere in the company or the supply chain. Among the methods can be found the *"5S" system of improvement* (sort, set in order, shine, standardize, and sustain work management), *SMED* (single-minute exchange of dies)/*quick change over* (reduction of operational lead times inhibiting process performance anywhere in the supply chain),[18] *process flow analysis* (linking of processes and removal of barriers between channel nodes and delivery points enabling the acceleration of the flow of goods to the customer), *total productive maintenance* (TPM) (ensuring the availability of all equipment everywhere in the supply chain), and *Six Sigma and statistical methods* (providing mechanisms to ensure total quality across the supply chain).

5.3.3.2 Process Standardization

The purpose of lean SCM is to identify opportunities for the application of process kaizen to ensure the continuous elimination of waste found anywhere in the supply chain and the removal of all barriers to the smooth flow of goods and information. Process standardization should be applied to every repeatable process, whether manufacturing or logistics, including productive processes, product/service delivery, and inventory management. Standardization enables companies to effectively apply kaizen methods to any process and track, measure, and demonstrate the effects of the kaizen initiative. Standardization also enables identification of all inhibitors of flow, such as batch and queue processing, unnecessary transportation, and product storage.

The goal of SCM kaizen standardization is the removal of process, product, and service complexities across the supply chain. Inside the organization, kaizen standardization is achieved by value stream mapping; when applied to the supply chain, it is called *extended value stream mapping* and it is concerned with the application of kaizen tools to the value stream of products and information as they flow across suppliers, delivery intermediaries, and customers. As the supply chain becomes more complex and outsourcing expands, lean efficiencies are increasingly coming to depend on collaborative efforts aimed at cross-channel value enhancement and waste reduction. Reducing supply chain wastes by eliminating batch-and-queue thinking and activating *pull systems* enables the entire supply chain to reduce costs to the customer. By uncovering channel redundancies, supply chain partners can collaborate to standardize critical processes and shift work to the most efficient node in the supply network. By improving the extended value stream, all channel partners will be strengthened and their individual contribution to the supply network and the customer will be dramatically enhanced.

5.3.3.3 Channel Partnership

The effective utilization of channel partners stands at the core of lean SCM. If companies could cost effectively and efficiently produce all of the materials they needed and execute all the services they offered to their customers, they would have no need of supply partners. Channels exist because no enterprise can hope to sustain leadership across all business competencies simultaneously. Channels fill this gap by providing noncore strategic and operational competencies that reduce manufacturing, distribution, and service costs, improve flexibility, keep companies focused on core competencies, provide access to global networks and superior technology, improve quality and service, and reduce capital investment and increase cash flow.

The decision to outsource noncore functions to partners can take a strategic or operational form. *Strategically,* outsourcing has been pursued as a method to survive in today's increasingly global, complex marketplace driven by cost reduction, speed to market, and the need to provide consistent, satisfactory customer experiences. Strategic alliances can assist firms to overcome barriers to growth by enabling them to pool resources and expertise. Partners can also help companies add value to products by improving time to market, decreasing delivery time, expanding market access, or tapping into the success of complimentary products offered by suppliers. Finally, alliances can enable firms to develop core competencies while keeping them lean and agile to respond to new marketplace challenges.

Operationally, supply partners can assist companies realize performance targets they would otherwise be incapable of reaching using their own limited competencies. Partner alliances, such as third-party logistics (3PL), buyer/seller associations, collaborative product development, retailer–supplier partnerships, and distributor integration assist businesses to streamline transaction processing, lower system costs and cycle times, enhance technology systems, and enable resources to be used more efficiently and effectively.

The utility of an outsourcing program is based squarely on the strength of the business partner. Ensuring that a partner will be able to fill the necessary resource and competency gaps requires the creation of sourcing methods for effectively evaluating, auditing, and developing partners. A successful program requires planners to

- Validate the desired competencies of the partner by charting key operational metrics such as lead time, inventory turnover, and on-time delivery.
- Confirm the financial health and stability of partners through financial statements and outside analysts.

- Evaluate the level of technical functionality of the partners. This involves a review of the technology tools to be used to process information and to guide the flow of products and services to the customer.
- Determine the fit of the partner's culture and values with those of the company.
- Develop a contract that explicitly details expectations on both sides, identifies resources up front, specifies short- and long-term objectives, and outlines performance metrics, reporting content, calculation, and timing of delivery, states fee structures, and stipulates the nature of legal recourse for nonperformance.
- Agree on continuous improvement efforts in operations, managing change, sharing risk, and expanding the depth of the outsourcing relationship.[19]

5.3.3.4 Demand Management

In the past, satisfying customer demand was driven by the creation of mass-production and distribution infrastructures, which served as a conduit for the flow of standardized goods and services from the producer to the mass market. Today, this view of managing demand has been largely exploded. Twenty-first-century supply chains have found that *push* systems are incapable of operating in an era of rapid product proliferation, dramatic declines in product life cycle, and the high-velocity response necessary to meet high customer service targets, exceptional levels of quality, low cost, and the capability to configure products at any stage in the fulfillment process. Lean supply chains are responding to this challenge by designing *demand pull* systems, which trigger supply commencing at the point of sale, and then pull the requirement from upstream delivery nodes point by point all the way back to the producer.

In a *pull-driven* supply chain, production and delivery decisions are initiated by the entry of a customer order rather than a forecast. Enabling the demand pull requires information and management technologies capable of providing the fast flow of customer demand information, not to just the next immediate channel partner, but to the entire network simultaneously. According to Manrodt, Abott, and Vitasek,[20] there are four toolsets available to assist in breaking through the trading dyads of most supply chains and enabling the flow of the demand signal from the end-customer all the way back to the original product supplier.

The first, *point-of-sale systems* (POS), enables real-time communication of the customer demand signal from the retailer all the way back to the partner. POS enables products to be pulled through the downstream supply network by actual usage. While only a small fraction of today's supply chains have operating POS environments, many are looking to the second toolset, *demand collaboration*. This toolset is focused on utilizing forms of electronic communication, such as the Internet, to pass real-time sales data to supply chain partners. Besides sales data, supply chains can also share *sales and operations plans* (S&OP), which provide a window into expected demand and supply planning. Finally, companies can share *inventory management practices* driven by their supply chain management systems.

For example, communication of customer demand and product re-supply *takt* times will provide each channel member with a detailed knowledge of channel work (processing) times. Other information, such as costing, engineering change management, new product offerings, and individual company target inventories will reduce overproduction and excess channel stocks.

The goal of demand pull management is to provide advanced warning of demand and the channel's collective ability to respond effectively. This lean SCM competency directly attacks waste created by the *bullwhip* effect caused when inventory is added to the original demand signal as it moves upstream in the supply channel. Effective demand management removes wastes by reducing channel uncertainty, variability in fulfillment processes, supply lead time, and linking channel partners together in networks that enable them to respond as a team to the demands emerging in the marketplace.

5.3.3.5 Lean SCM Implementation

The decision to extend lean concepts and practices to the supply chain should take place only after a company has successfully implemented lean on the company level and there is clear evidence that there are significant benefits to be achieved by extending it to the value chain. According to Dolcemascolo,[21] a lean supply chain implementation effort consists of a series of planning and process steps (Figure 5.8).

In the *planning stage* implementers will need to execute three critical steps. In the first, *value stream mapping*, a company's supply chains are identified, a likely candidate is selected for improvement, metrics detailing current competitive values are developed, and finally, a future-state map is drafted that will show attainable value stream improvement. The second step, *core competency definition*, will assist in isolating those competencies the firm performs poorly and which should be outsourced to the supply chain. The final

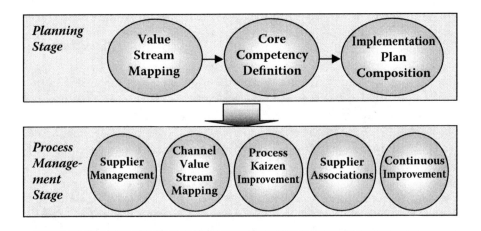

Figure 5.8 Lean value stream implementation stages and steps.

planning step, *plan composition*, requires drafting a workable implementation plan that will realize the goals of the value stream map and bridge gaps in internal competencies.

Once the planning steps are complete, the *process management stage* is executed. In step one, *supplier management*, new and existing suppliers capable of providing critically needed competencies are identified and contracted. In step two, *channel value stream mapping*, the actual supply and delivery streams to be activated with each customer and supplier are created and fused with the objectives found in the future-state map developed during the planning stage. In the third step, *process kaizen improvement,* the lean improvement toolkit is deployed to increase supply channel value. As improvement processes gain traction, implementers can formalize the lean initiative by founding, in step four, a *supplier association* focused on sustaining, improving, and expanding the lean value chain initiative. Finally, even after successes are scored, implementers should enable what will be a perpetual step—*continuous lean value chain improvement.*

5.3.3.6 Strong Communication

The lean supply chain requires all channel constituents to work together as a virtual enterprise to ensure the highest value to the customer. Unfortunately, while lean kaizen can be crisply focused and enforced *within* an organization, applying it to an entire supply chain, composed of multiple levels of independent companies, each pursuing individual and often-contradictory objectives, becomes a significant challenge. Although *extended value-stream mapping* can succeed in illuminating the actual process flows within the supply chain, and pinpointing and quantifying areas for improvement, communication and collaboration between channel members will actually determine the level of ongoing success.

Perhaps the most important driver of the lean supply chain is the ability of the channel's kaizen leaders to integrate into a single vision the different pictures each network partner perceives of what constitutes the value stream. Unification of purpose and lean mechanics rests on two elements: the creation of an effective lean SCM team and agreement on toolsets. A lean SCM project organization can germinate from several sources. Poirier, Bauer, and Hauser[22] discuss the establishment of a *partnering diagnostic laboratory* (PDL) to assist supply chain participants to effectively establish consensus on improvements to existing and potential cross-channel processes. A PDL consists of the channel parties involved and a knowledgeable facilitator who can lead a lean kaizen encompassing a single or mixture of product development, technical, transactional, procurement, or logistics lean efforts. In a similar fashion Dolcemascolo[23] advocates the formation of *supplier associations*. A supplier association is a network of supply chain partners organized to share the information and expertise necessary to sustain a lean system across the entire supply channel. The key functions of the association are the establishment of a top management team, utilization of committees targeted at specific supply chain kaizen objectives, performance of quality audits, and consulting and advisory assistance.

The second driver is agreement on a set of kaizen tools. A lean initiative should detail the mechanisms by which the entire supply chain can utilize training workshops that provide information and methods to effectively manage topics such as process mapping and other lean tools, conducting a kaizen event, application of new technologies, lean accounting techniques, problem-solving and statistical methods, and team building.

5.3.4 Impact of Lean Supply Chain Management

Today's best supply chains relentlessly pursue the six lean competencies as portrayed in Figure 5.5. Effective execution of these competencies enables companies to realize the three essential success factors shown at the bottom of the figure. To begin with, application of kaizen tools and process/industry standardization enable lean cross-channel project managers to effectively pursue *waste reduction* at all supply chain levels. Closely integrated supply chain partnerships and the development of technology tools providing real-time information regarding customer demand will keep all supply network nodes focused squarely on how to continuously build and sustain a *stream of value* to the customer. And finally, well-designed lean supply chain implementation projects and the capability to broaden and enrich cross-channel communications concerning quality, change management, collaboration opportunities, and joint metrics will enable supply chains to maintain a focus on *continuous improvement* as they drive toward network competitiveness and profitability.

In addition, those firms that embed lean techniques into core business processes and institutionalize them into their own organization and their supply chain cultures can expect significant benefits. According to an Aberdeen survey on lean supply chain practices (Table 5.2), all levels of lean practitioners undertaking a lean supply chain initiative exceeded expectations relating to reductions in inventory and assets and product development costs, and increases in channel flexibility, product quality, and customer services. Achieving such results requires companies to grow a culture of lean kaizen both inside and outside organizational boundaries, devise methods to quantify existing and new improvement projects, gain deeper commitment and collaboration of channel partners, and apply information tools that enable synchronization and visibility of channel network demand planning and demand pull mechanisms, optimization of channel inventory, and the most appropriate usage of outsourcing for warehousing, transportation, and logistics.

Achieving such results requires communication and resolve among all members of the supply network. According to Buxton and Jutras,[24] best-in-class lean supply chains follow and continuously seek to expand on the following steps to success.

1. *Champion a lean culture everywhere in the supply chain.* The goal is to continuously seek to eliminate barriers to lean by empowering customer-focused, cross-functional teams with the task of not only improving cross-channel processes, but also actively promoting the lean philosophy to supply and delivery networks.

Table 5.2 Lean SCM Benefits

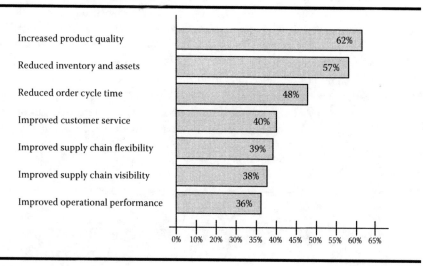

Increased product quality	62%
Reduced inventory and assets	57%
Reduced order cycle time	48%
Improved customer service	40%
Improved supply chain flexibility	39%
Improved supply chain visibility	38%
Improved operational performance	36%

0% 10% 20% 30% 35% 40% 45% 50% 55% 60% 65%

Source: Maura Buxton and Cindy Jutras, "The Lean Supply Chain Report," Aberdeen White Paper, September 2006, 12.

2. *Improve supply chain collaboration.* Closer collaboration ensures that suppliers, intermediaries, and customers are not only included in the lean supply chain effort, but that they are expected to be active participants. Collaboration is fundamental in mapping and evaluating the applicability of lean concepts and principles to channel processes.

3. *Implement effective technology solutions.* Technology tools enhance communication and visibility of information for all members of the supply chain. Networking and business system applications provide access to demand forecasts, customer shipments, production schedules, and disruptive events that assist channel partners to work collaboratively to ensure synchronization of the highest levels of customer value at the lowest cost with collective channel resources and competencies.

4. *Implement the lean tool kit.* Commitment to deploying lean tools to the supply chain environment ensures all channel partners are actively engaged in the continuous pursuit of workplace improvement and work standardization. Conducting cross-functional kaizen events centered on executing the demand pull and removing wastes concentrates supply chain efforts on illuminating weaknesses in the value stream and focuses attention on high-impact supply chain areas.

5. *Require performance to meet lean supply chain metrics.* The foundation of lean resides in the ability of organizations to pursue continuous improvement. Although gaining consensus and tracking cross-channel performance is

challenging, without common metrics the impact of lean is unknown. Customer service, postponement, lead times, warehouse efficiencies, transportation costs, and average channel inventory are all candidates for lean supply chain metrics.

6. *Engage in long-term lean strategies.* Although supply chains can gain easy and early benefits from a lean initiative, the true power of lean can be realized only in a long-term commitment where network partners can work together over time to utilize lean to effectively manage customer value. A lean supply chain is better positioned to redirect resources, undertake innovation, and respond rapidly to change to capitalize on marketplace opportunities, channel restructuring brought about by events like mergers and acquisitions, or the rise of new competitors.

Case Study 5.2

Lean SCM at Sun Microsystems

In 2004 Sun Microsystems redesigned its supply chain system to increase the velocity of moving products between its suppliers and customers. In the past computers were built by Sun's Asian partners who acquired the materials and built the system to Sun's specifications. The systems then were moved to Sun's operations where the software and final configuration was completed before going to a distributor and, finally, the customer.

Today, Sun has streamlined the process by moving information to the supplier, who's configuring the systems and shipping directly to the customer. According to Eugene McCabe, VP of worldwide operations, the new system has enabled the company to dramatically reduce logistics and inventory costs, while increasing delivery accuracy. "The big benefits," declared McCabe, "are speed and efficiency. More than 50 percent of Sun's machines are never touched by a Sun employee."

Achieving these metrics was a Herculean effort. "Nobody was doing this when we started," McCabe recalls. The project began by first process mapping the entire Sun supply chain, which extended from the Far East, through the United States, to Western Europe. The goal was to eliminate needless process, move, and storage wastes, and review costs, while meeting Sun's objectives.

During the process Sun developed its own software solution to match the targeted process design. Throughout the process, Sun relied on the Six Sigma framework for options management and decision-making.

The results of the Lean SCM initiative has resulted in a 20 percent reduction in logistics costs and a 40 percent reduction in finished goods inventory. Sun was also able to increase predictability, which rose from 85 percent to 95 percent.

See Editor, "One Touch Saves $89 Million," *World Trade*, January 2007, 32.

5.4 Summary and Transition

During the early 1990s, companies responded to marketplace challenges by expanding on the functions of logistics and tapping into the wide range of productive capabilities to be found in the matrix of business partners constituting their supply chains. The driving force of this new concept, SCM, sought to create integrated organizations that spanned company boundaries and linked critical competencies in the search for new avenues of competitive advantage. Today, the original concept and practice of SCM has, however, proven to be insufficient to counter the pressures of globalization, financial markets demanding more effective use of capital, accelerating innovation cycles, and customers demanding to be treated as unique individuals. Competitive SCM now requires companies to move beyond the standard definitions and embrace new ideas and technologies if it is to provide new sources of market leadership.

This chapter was concerned with the evolution of SCM from its foundations in logistics to the generation of new process models driven by the tremendous breakthroughs occurring in today's technology and management methods. After providing a redefinition of SCM based on a reexamination of its six critical competencies, the discussion moved to a consideration of the variations emerging in the science of SCM. Three distinct approaches were identified. The first, coalescing around *cost leadership,* is known as *lean supply chain management.* The second approach, *operations performance,* can be concerned with either supply flexibility and is known as *adaptive supply chain management* or with delivery flexibility and is known as *demand-driven supply network management.* The final approach, *customer centered,* is known as *intimate supply chain management.*

The second part of the chapter centered on detailing the lean supply chain. After outlining the origins and contents of lean concepts and practices, several definitions of the lean supply chain were advanced. The text offered a simple definition: *A supply and delivery network of firms capable of supplying the right product at the right cost at the right time to the customer with as little waste as possible.* Next, the lean supply chain was described as consisting of six competencies. The first two were concerned with the application of kaizen tools and process standardization. These components enable the pursuit of *waste reduction* at all supply chain levels. The second set of competencies, supplier relationship and customer relationship management, enable supply chains to be closely integrated and synchronized to provide a continuous stream of value to the customer. Finally, the last two competencies, effective lean implementation and cross-channel communications, enable supply chains to maintain a focus on *continuous improvement* as they drive toward network competitiveness and profitability.

Although the lean supply chain provides companies with the tools to pursue the elimination of waste and the pursuit of continuous improvement, it has become apparent that in today's hypercompetitive environment an exclusive focus on lean principles and techniques provides companies with the bare minimum for survival. As we shall see in chapter 6, only adaptive, demand-driven, intimate supply chains together with lean can produce the level of flexibility and customer centeredness so necessary to grow and prosper in today's business climate where constant, disruptive change is the norm and expectation for a superior customer experience dominates all decisions.

Endnotes

1. The Council of Supply Chain Management Professionals.
2. This definition can be found in David F. Ross, *Distribution Planning and Control: Managing in the Era of Supply Chain Management,* 2nd ed. (Norwell, MA: Kluwer Academic, 2004), 37.
3. This concept of supply chains can be found in John J. Coyle, Edward J. Bardi, and C. John Langley, *The Management of Business Logistics,* 7th ed. (Mason, OH: South-Western, 2003), 55.
4. John H. Blackstone and James F. Cox, eds., *APICS Dictionary,* 11th ed. (Alexandria, VA: APICS, 2005), 113.
5. David Simchi-Levi, Philip Kaminsky, and Edith Simchi-Levi, *Designing and Managing the Supply Chain: Concepts, Strategies, and Case Studies,* 2nd ed. (Boston, MA: McGraw-Hill Irwin, 2003), 1.
6. The Council of Supply Chain Management Professionals. http://cscmp.org/aboutcscmp/Definitions/Definitions.asp
7. David F. Ross, *Introduction to e-Supply Chain Management: Engaging Technology to Build Market-Winning Business Partnerships* (Boca Raton, FL: St. Lucie Press, 2003), 53.
8. Foster Finley and Sanjay Srikanth, "7 Imperatives for Successful Collaboration," *Supply Chain Management Review* 9, no. 1 (January/February 2005): 30–37.
9. These points have been summarized from Robert B. Handfield and Ernest L. Nichols, *Introduction to Supply Chain Management* (Upper Saddle River, NJ: Prentice Hall, 1999), 83–89.
10. See the discussion in Peter D. Moore, Karl B. Manrodt, Mary C. Holcomb, and Mike Riegler, *Year 2006 Report on Trends and Issues in Logistics and Transportation,* Capgemini White Paper, (City, State: Capgemini, February 2007), 8–10.
11. Figures in table 5.1 can be found in Moore et al., 2007, 8–10.
12. James P. Womack and Daniel T. Jones, *Lean Thinking: Banish Waste and Create Wealth in Your Corporation* (New York: Simon & Schuster, 1996), 15–26.
13. Jane Biddle, *Best Practices in Lean,* Aberdeen Group White Paper (City, State: Aberdeen Group, June 2005).
14. Karl B. Manrodt, Jeff Abott, and Kate Vitasek, "What Makes a Lean Supply Chain," *Supply Chain Management Review* 9, no. 7 (October 2005), 18–24.
15. Charles C. Poirier, Michael J. Bauer, and William F. Houser, *The Wall Street Diet: Making Your Business Lean and Healthy* (San Francisco, CA: Berrett-Koehler Publishers, Inc., 2006), 63.
16. *Kaizen* is the Japanese word for "continuous improvement."
17. Darren Dolcemascolo, *Improving the Extended Value Stream: Lean for the Entire Supply Chain* (New York: Productivity Press, 2006), 134.

18. The concept of SMED or *single-minute exchange of dies* was introduced by Shigeo Shingo in his book *A Revolution in Manufacturing: The SMED System* (New York: Productivity Press, 1985).

19. This list of outsourcing benefits has been abstracted from James A. Tompkins, Steven W. Simonson, Bruce W. Tompkins, and Brian E. Upchurch, *Logistics and Manufacturing Outsourcing: Harness Your Core Competencies* (Raleigh, NC: Tompkins Press, 2005), 28–36.

20. Karl B. Manrodt, Jeff Abott, and Kate Vitasek, *Understanding the Lean Supply Chain: Beginning the Journey*, APICS White Paper, (Falls Church, VA: APICS, November, 2005), 10–12.

21. Dolcemascolo, 8–10.

22. Poirer et al., 179–184.

23. Dolcemascolo, 169–180.

24. Maura Buxton and Cindy Jutras, *The Lean Supply Chain Report*, Aberdeen White Paper, (Boston, MA: Aberdeen Group, September, 2006), 12.

Chapter 6

The Adaptive, Demand-Driven Supply Chain

Using the Supply Chain to Manage Risk

The shock waves sent reverberating through the U.S. economy caused by Hurricane Katrina dramatically highlighted how dependent the nation was on the timely and efficient delivery of goods and services. For a vital few weeks, all sectors of the economy held their breath to see how devastating the impact was going to be. Although supply chain professionals everywhere were quick to respond to the challenge by exploring new ways to bypass the potential bottlenecks the devastation seemed to portend for water, rail, and truck traffic in the very center of the nation, the disaster acutely illustrated the need to build supply chains agile enough to meet the next major disruption, whether it be a terrorist attack, a catastrophe at a key port, or another devastating natural event. Simply, how adaptive are today's supply chains in effectively responding to the threat of disruptive events in an era of lean and super efficiency?

Suddenly, companies that had formerly sought to make their supply chains as lean and as streamlined as possible were having second thoughts. Although it was true that implementing lean principles had dramatically drained away much of the waste in production, inventories, and transportation, and dramatically increased throughput velocities, strategists were now beginning to worry that while the fat had gone, the supply chain pipelines that were left were perhaps too thin, that they had actually become too brittle to withstand even small ripples, not to mention a major disruption, in the supply network. To counter this lurking threat, supply chains began to focus on two new supply chain management models. *Operationally*, they began to see that while lean was critical, it could become destructive if supply network players were not also capable of rapidly adapting processes and competencies in response to a changing marketplace. Simultaneously, they saw that a purely operations focus was insufficient: they also needed to be *demand driven*, to be organized around receiving and responding to the demand signals arising from the customer.

This chapter seeks to detail these two emerging approaches known as the *adaptive supply chain* and the *demand-driven supply network* (DDSN). While building on SCM and lean supply chain principles, these two concepts provide companies with the opportunity to move beyond managing supply chains focused solely on throughput and low cost, to strategies that consider operational agility and customer centeredness as the central operating attributes of an effective channel network. The use of the word *network* is critical. In a supply network all channel participants are integrated together. This integration permits them to sense, analyze, transmit, and react to changes in real time, whether it is a shift in customer tastes or major supply disruptions, as a unified supply and delivery community. As we shall see, interactive networking enables companies to merge their competencies and resources into a virtual, seamless supply and delivery engine capable of adapting to absorb risk and to profit from any marketplace opportunity.

6.1 Managing Risk in the Lean Supply Chain

The objective of the lean supply chain can be summarized as consisting of two fundamental drivers: the *elimination of waste* found anywhere in the channel network, and the *pursuit of continuous improvement* targeted at optimizing the value stream. The implementation of lean solutions requires companies to move beyond basic *supply chain management* (SCM) by applying the concepts of lean manufacturing, reengineering, TQM (Total Quality Management), Theory of Constraints, and Six Sigma not only to internal operations, but also to their supply chains. Lean is such a powerful tool because it enables individual companies and their supply chains to continuously expunge the root causes of process error, purge all wastes, and efficiently manage global supply chains while retaining speed and flexibility, high levels of quality, reduced product roll-out time to cash, and access to customer intelligence, which generates revenues and creates differentiating customer value propositions in an era of shrinking margins.

Even as companies strive for greater efficiency, today's marketplace turbulence is also requiring them to strive for greater *speed* in responding to the threat of increasing variability in demand and supply. Effectively meeting this challenge is driving businesses to move beyond lean to the next stage of SCM: they need to embrace the concept of *adaptive, demand-driven supply chain management*. This stage involves replacing less-responsive linear supply chains with highly agile networks capable of rapidly adapting to marketplace changes. Adaptive networks seek to be *responsive* (i.e., able to meet changes in customer needs for alternate delivery quantities, transport modes, returns, etc.) and *flexible* (i.e., able to manipulate productive assets, outsource, deploy dynamic pricing, promotions, etc.). In addition, they need to be able to proactively reconfigure themselves in response to market events, such as introduction of a disruptive product or service, regulatory and environmental policies, financial uncertainty, and massive market restructuring, without compromising on operational efficiencies.

6.1.1 Understanding Supply Chain Risk

Supply chains have always been subject to risk. Since the dawn of the age of exploration and commerce in the fifteenth century, when caravans crossed the Steps of Central Asia and Venetian merchant ships hazarded the crossing around the Cape of Africa in search of trade with the Orient, risk has always haunted the supply chain. Although the mystery of exotic lands, novel products, and curious cultures has long passed, the problem of risk in the production, purchase, conveyance, and marketing of goods has lost none of its complexity, nor has the threat of uncertainty disappeared from the execution of commerce. As this decade has shown, the trauma of war in the Middle East, the threat of terrorist attacks, the devastation caused by tsunamis and hurricanes battering whole continents, and the lurking specter of a global pandemic has demonstrated that a short-term focus on supply chain cost reduction can result in catastrophic disruption in the flow of materials and products and bring disaster to whole economies.

In today's closely integrated, global business environment, the requirement to effectively manage risk has risen to become one of the critical components of building not only a successful but also a *resilient* supply chain. Recently, the need for supply chain contingency planning has moved from an optional to a required strategy. As inventories shrink across global supply sources, companies become increasingly dependent on outsourcing, and the disruptions caused by political, social, and natural events become much broader and pervasive, the shadow of risk has expanded to threaten the integrity of both demand and supply chains. According to John Cummings, i2 Technologies chief marketing officer, "Risk isn't a side issue of supply chain management; it's the entire issue. You can really boil the whole equation down to risk."[1]

6.1.1.1 Components of Supply Chain Risk

The threat of supply chain disruption can be described as belonging to two main types of risk. According to Kiser and Cantrell,[2] risk can be broken down into *external risks*, or those outside of the control of individual companies, and *internal risks*, or those within the control of a company. External risks can arise anywhere in the supply and demand channel and can be characterized as originating from:

- The presence of unpredictable customer or delivery network demand.
- Disruptions in the availability of materials and inventories caused by variances in supply delivery.

- Shocks to supply/delivery caused by climatic, political, economic, or social factors.
- Risks arising from economic issues such as outsourcing, rising interest rates, recession, bankruptcy, mergers, and divestitures.
- Disruptions caused by problems in channel partner plants such as environmental violations, regulatory compliance failures, shut down, fire, unfavorable community reaction, and labor unrest.

In contrast to risks arising from the marketplace, internal risks are much narrower in scope and are within the control of individual companies. Internal risks can arise from:

- Changes to operations, policies and procedures, personnel, financial shortages or redirection, and information and communication systems.
- Disruptions to manufacturing stemming from materials shortages, process variability, design discrepancies, labor shortages, and equipment failure.
- Inaccurate data, poor practices, communication failures, poor demand/forecast management, and inadequate systems for the management of production.
- Incomplete planning for disaster and recovery, inadequate performance metrics, and failure to build in redundancies for key processes in case of catastrophic failure.

In practice, external and internal risks can and do overlap. For example, a dramatic jump in product demand may find a producer without adequate supplier sourcing along with insufficient internal staffing and equipment to respond to the increased volumes.

Case Study 6.1

 **Impact of Supply Chain Risk**

As global markets shrink in distance, outsourcing becomes critical to corporate survival, and lean supply chain objectives reduce excess wastes and redundancies in the supply network. The impact of a channel disruption, even a comparatively small one, can be significant.

According to Dirk de Waart, in a study conducted by consulting firm PRTM, supply chain disruptions over the past decade have been growing in number and have made risk management a critical business strategy. In its study of more than 800 companies, it was found that supply chain disruptions resulted in 33 to 40 percent lower stock returns relative to the disrupted company's industry peers. Share price volatility in the year after the disruption was more than 13 percent higher when compared with volatility in the year before the disruption.

Source: De Waart, Dirk, "Getting Smart About Risk Management," *Supply Chain Management Review*, Vol. 10, No. 8., November 2006, p. 27.

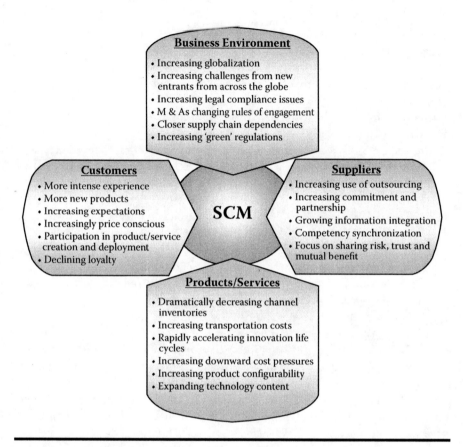

Business Environment
- Increasing globalization
- Increasing challenges from new entrants from across the globe
- Increasing legal compliance issues
- M & As changing rules of engagement
- Closer supply chain dependencies
- Increasing 'green' regulations

Customers
- More intense experience
- More new products
- Increasing expectations
- Increasingly price conscious
- Participation in product/service creation and deployment
- Declining loyalty

SCM

Suppliers
- Increasing use of outsourcing
- Increasing commitment and partnership
- Growing information integration
- Competency synchronization
- Focus on sharing risk, trust and mutual benefit

Products/Services
- Dramatically decreasing channel inventories
- Increasing transportation costs
- Rapidly accelerating innovation life cycles
- Increasing downward cost pressures
- Increasing product configurability
- Expanding technology content

Figure 6.1   Challenges to SCM.

The fact that companies are today coming under extreme pressures to be able to adapt to an increasingly volatile marketplace is hardly a secret. In the past businesses could count on brand recognition, superior delivery systems, and relatively slow-moving product life cycles to retain competitive advantage. In contrast, companies today are finding their products, their customer relationships, and their profits being squeezed from a variety of different sources. As illustrated in Figure 6.1, these forces can be described as follows.

6.1.1.1.1   Business Environment

There can be little doubt that the fastest growing dimension of today's business environment is *globalization*. As discussed in chapter 2, globalization has presented SCM with an array of radically new challenges. Globalization has forever altered the basis of competition by giving birth to new forms of digital business, virtual enterprises, and innovative management methods. It can even be said that the explosion in mergers and acquisitions, as well as the rise of new entrants from emerging markets, has altered the rules of engagement by consolidating players into larger, more powerful entities equipped with powerful capabilities to leverage a global marketplace. In turn, companies have responded to the downward pressure on margins and the increased need to reduce cost by outsourcing production and distribution, forming collaborative partnerships, and constructing value streams that span the globe.

But while globalization presents a host of new opportunities, it has also left supply chain professionals with as many new anxieties. For example, according to an Aberdeen Group survey on the global supply chain,[3] although regulatory pressures and the immaturity of logistics infrastructures in low-cost countries have been given the lion's share of the press, a lack of visibility, control, and integration across supply chain processes was identified as the most serious issue confronting supply chain managers. This concern was followed by the uncoordinated nature of multitiered supply chain processes, which cause an imbalance of demand and supply across tiers. Lesser concerns focused around loss of operational control and difficulty managing third-party providers, inability to manage growing global operations and distribution networks, rising logistics costs, inflated lead times, and lead time variability.

The inability to peer into the global supply chain renders a full commitment to lean SCM a risky business. Poor visibility and uncoordinated multitier processes negate efforts designed to eliminate wastes and continuously improve processes by forcing supply nodes to carry "just-in-case" inventories, absorb premium freight costs, and extend cycle times. As supply networks are increasingly expanded from a domestic to an international perspective with their dependence on multiparty players, a dependence on lean SCM alone is fraught with risks of greater unpredictability in product delivery, quality, costs, and compliance, which could result in catastrophic supply chain disruption.

6.1.1.1.2   Customers

While constraints on the supply side threaten to degrade the effects of lean SCM, the growing power of the customer poses as significant a challenge to the demand side of the equation. In fact, it can be argued that lean SCM is not really focused on the demand side of the supply chain at all, and that lean's preoccupation with the removal of wastes and streamlining of processes is actually antithetical to managing the inherent variability constituting marketplace demand. The requirement that supply chains have more flexibility and a little more fat seems logical in an era where customers are demanding more individualized service, more products uniquely configured to answer specific solutions, and a greater say in how products and services are built, priced, and delivered.

Several factors coalescing around the management of demand have made a dependence on lean SCM problematical. To begin with, the hypercompetitiveness of today's global markets have increased the volatility of demand, escalated requirements for product customization and variety, shortened product life cycles, and intensified expectations of a personalized buying experience. All of these factors have made it increasingly challenging to match demand with supply. In addition, as demand volatility expands, supply chain planners are having a harder time closing the gap between demand and supply. Most supply chain plans are constructed only on an aggregate basis, formulated on inaccurate data regarding inventory and capacities, and are poorly communicated to and synchronized with those of channel network partners.

6.1.1.1.3   Suppliers

There can be little doubt that supplier quality, reliability, and performance are the foundations of an effective supply chain. It is also true that supplier management has been one of the prime targets of lean SCM. Under extreme pressure to simultaneously be more innovative while continuously reducing costs, improving quality, and shrinking cycle times, supplier management has undergone a virtual revolution over the past decade. As companies expand their use of outsourcing strategies, intensify their search for supply partners willing to broaden and deepen commitment and partnership, and more closely synchronize special competencies enabling whole network ecosystems to better manage risk while sharing benefits, today's supply chain has placed a premium on lean strategies designed to promote growth and performance.

However, while effective supplier management can result in a savings of an average of 10 percent over traditional strategies, in addition to benefits resulting from contract compliance, performance measurements, and joint process improvement, companies' growing dependence on lean supplier management practices pose severe risks to supply chain effectiveness. To begin with, one of the key mantras of lean—*single sourcing*—while enabling reductions in price and administrative costs, can also increase the vulnerability of supply chains if the supplier cannot perform or even goes out of business. Beyond supply continuity disruption and price volatility, supplier consolidation can inadvertently create bottlenecks in the supply chain that can stress resources and suppliers to the breaking point. Even corporate moves, such as an acquisition, can introduce risk with the addition of relatively unknown suppliers and new assets that can traverse the entire supply chain.

Then again, while outsourcing can reduce costs and activate new sources of productive competencies, it also can dramatically expand the possibility of supply chain disruption. For channel interdependencies and synchronization to function effectively, partners must be willing to collaborate, tightly integrate information, and provide visibility into each other's operations. Persuading even close partners to engage in investments to change information systems and performance metrics, as well as to cooperate in sharing risks, building trust, and positing mutual benefits, are difficult initiatives to achieve. The result can be an escalation in supply chain complexity and decline in process visibility resulting in possible disruptions due to inefficiencies stemming from elongated transportation distances, governmental restrictions, and other factors driven by the vagaries at the heart of time and space.

6.1.1.1.4   Products and Services

As the impact of such sources of supply chain risks as natural disasters, strikes and bankruptcies, the price and supply of oil, and port congestion and infrastructure inadequacy dominate the headlines, the heightened exposure of supply networks brought about by a decade-long mandate to decrease inventories everywhere in the supply chain has become painfully visible. Competitiveness today requires companies to rapidly accelerate the rate of product life cycle development, increase product configurability, and apply advanced technology as an integral component of the product itself. But, simultaneously, they must decrease inventory everywhere in the supply network while increasing speed to market.

Of all the risks before a supply chain, the occurrence of inventory shortage is perhaps the most damaging. Production lines can be halted, transportation schedules disrupted, and customers left unsatisfied. One group of researchers found that inventory shortages had a deleterious effect on company profitability and financial well-being. It was discovered that stock prices for companies with disruptive parts shortages underperformed their benchmarks by an average of 25 percent. In addition, they experienced a median decrease in operating income of 31 percent, a decrease in sales of 1.2 percent, and an increase in costs of 1.7 percent.[4]

There can be little doubt that the application of lean to the supply chain has reduced overall costs and diminished the sting of the bullwhip effect. Still, while initiatives reducing inventory and excess capacity and promoting economies of scale and volume pricing have resulted in highly integrated supply network nodes, it has also left companies with little margin for error and susceptible to serious disruption arising from even minor sources of trouble. Furthermore, a focus on sole sourcing and outsourcing has increased dependencies on a single supplier. Such dependency reduces the ability of supply chains to respond effectively to change and makes them insensitive and immobile in the face of a global business environment increasingly dominated by volatility in tastes and fashion.

In many ways the application of lean SCM can be said to actually diminish risk in supply chains. By continuously seeking to reduce aggregate channel inventories, promoting standardization and routinization of processes, and shrinking product development life cycles, lean SCM can assist companies to become more adaptable to marketplace changes and more focused on creating customer value. Despite such advantages, however, lean's single-minded focus on the removal of wastes and search for continuous improvement can leave supply chains perilously thin in the wake of even minor disruptions. Simply put, supply chain efficiencies introduce risk. In the long run, it is safe to say that lean concepts and principles are a necessary, but not the only, component in the SCM strategic toolkit. Succeeding today requires supply chains to move beyond lean to other strategies that will make them more adaptive, demand driven, and intimate with the customer in order to survive and prosper in a global economy.

6.1.1.2   Solutions to Supply Chain Risk

As supply chains expand across continents, dependency on outsourcing increases, and buffers of everything from inventory to lead times shrink, the potential for disruption in supply chains has been greatly amplified. Responding to the rising crescendo of risk requires supply chain strategists to search for alternative methods of countering threats that range far beyond traditional SCM. It is important to remember that risks to supply chain security can arise from the business environment (supplier failures, new competitive entrants, quality failures, financial irregularities, technology change, and marketplace redirection) as well as from natural disasters, regulation, and geopolitical instability. The goal is to find solutions that ensure uninterrupted product and service availability for supply chains operating in an increasingly lean and volatile business environment.

Managing supply chain risks requires adapting policies and strategies capable of mitigating all levels of possible disruption. A pragmatic approach would be to apply what has been dubbed the SMART model to risk management. The five sequential stages constituting the approach require companies to be *specific* about all possible threats, *measure* the type of risk they pose to the supply chain and how damaging they would be, identify the *actionable* risks and determine the initiatives necessary to solve them, be *realistic* as to the resources required to effectively respond to the specific risks, and then *time-phase* in plans with detailed roles and responsibilities to tackle the threat. The purpose of the methodology is to be able to utilize resolution actions that are measurable and analytical rather than subjective.[5]

Once such an analysis has been performed, the next step is to devise solutions to counterbalance the impact of each risk. According to A. T. Kearney,[6] potential approaches to managing risk are: *avoidance* through proactive action, *transference* by shifting risk to a third party, *mitigation* by reducing possible financial impact, *minimization* of the probability of occurrence, *responding* through predetermined actions once an event has occurred, *monitoring* the disrupted environment and applying proper alternative solutions, and *acceptance* of the risk exposure. Plans should also include methods to track events and metrics that measure performance.

Detail solutions to risk management can be divided into three areas: *strategic, operational,* and *event driven.* Strategic solutions focus on the ability of the entire supply chain to establish viable alternatives to risk that ensure enterprise resiliency in the face of a catastrophic threat. Among the actions available can be found building redundancies into channel processes so that adequate information-processing capabilities, channel capacities, and inventories can be quickly redirected to network points of need. Another technique is to simply disperse risk among multiple sources of supply so that a range of viable options in time of need can be speedily identified. Such a strategy will require increasing collaboration and cooperation with network partners whereby joint problem solving and decision making can provide effective alternatives. Finally, strategists can strive to build increased flexibility into the supply chain by requiring that network partners pursue product designs that utilize standardization and modularity to counter sudden shifts in design content, sourcing strategies capable of executing various forms of purchasing from contracts to e-market exchanges, and agile manufacturing and distribution functions capable of quickly switching capacities and resources to capitalize on abrupt marketplace changes.

In contrast to strategic solutions, operational solutions involve the implementation of medium-range actions that assist in providing visibility and supplying functional alternatives to supply chain risk. Without a doubt, a critical initiative is to deploy technologies that reveal the status of internal operations, marketplace demand, supplier capabilities, inventory, capacity availability, and critical assets. Technology tools can assist in activating key problem indicators, collecting and analyzing data, and communicating data by deploying Web-based systems capable of linking databases across supply chain partners. Supply chain event management systems can also provide a window into supply channel events as they occur. If abnormalities begin to appear, the system can send out alerts and messages to the proper supply chain nodes.

Case Study 6.2

 **Benefits of a Secure Supply Chain**

A secure, agile supply chain provides an enormous number of benefits. According to a 2006 study by Stanford University, the Manufacturing Institute, and IBM, benefits include:

- Improved inventory safety (28% reduction in the ft/loss/pilferage and a 37% reduction in tampering)
- Improved inventory management (14% reduction in inventory and a 12% increase in on-time delivery)
- Improved supply chain visibility (50% increase in access to supply chain data and a 30% increase in shipping information)
- Improved product handling (43% increase in automated handling of products)

- Process improvements (30% reduction in process variances)
- Better customs clearance (49% reduction in customs clearance and inspections)
- Velocity improvements (29% reduction in transit times)
- Response (30% increase in problem identification and resolution)
- Customer satisfaction (26% reduction in customer attrition and 20% increase in new customers)

Source: Quoted in Blanchard, David, "Protecting the Global Supply Chain," *Industry Week*, December 2006, p. 43.

Other operational solutions could include better integration and synchronization of planning and execution across the supply chain. Today's advanced planning suites can assist planners gather real-time supply chain demand and supply intelligence, use advanced processing simulations to develop effective sense-and-response solutions to counter material-flow disruptions, and then communicate decisions and alternatives in real time to network partners. Furthermore, the impact of risks can be reduced by implementing decision-support tools, which assist supply chain planners to rapidly reconfigure the supply chain in real time. These systems provide network flow models that can illuminate the ramifications of the cost versus the benefits of alternative supply chain recovery options. Examples of alternatives to head off a major supply chain disruption include activating prequalified suppliers, switching transportation modes, redirecting transportation routes, outsourcing production, and moving to alternative delivery channels.

And finally, event-driven solutions provide short-term responses designed to ameliorate the impact of possible day-to-day threats to supply chain functions. For example, supply chains should strive to make productive processes, people, and materials as interchangeable as possible. Flexible resources will enable supply chains to seamlessly transfer operations to alternative networks. Companies should also design products and delivery processes to capitalize on channel postponement. By deferring final differentiation to the farthest node in the supply network, inventories can be kept flexible by delaying final product configuration to the actual point of sale. Then again, other functions, such as improving forecast accuracy, reducing the mean and variance of lead times, reducing the length of transportation lines, reducing compliance and regulation risks, and better leveraging third-party logistics partners, can assist in draining risk out of the supply chain.[7]

Case Study 6.3

 **Creating Flexible Transportation**

In its efforts to reduce supply chain risk, Limited Brands has started a program to reduce transportation content while increasing speed of delivery. Rather than use a "one-size-fits-all" approach to transportation, the strategy seeks to "switch on" alternative choices depending on shipping volumes. Designed in conjunction with the opening of regional DCs, the strategy will allow product to move in full truckloads as far as possible into a market before bulk break. This will minimize excess movement by keeping product produced in the region to satisfy local demand while reducing the overall cost of product delivery.

Similarly, Garden Ridge, a chain of home décor stores, in the southeast U.S., has looked to reducing transportation content by implementing a direct-to-store shipping program during peak seasons. The initiative calls for consolidating loads in Asia and shipping directly to stores versus sending products into the Houston DC where it is then transported to stores.

Source: Crone, Mark, "Are Global Supply Chains Too Risky." *Supply Chain Management Review*, Vol. 10, No. 4 May/June 2006, p. 34.

6.2 Advent of the Adaptive, Demand-Driven Supply Network

Effectively responding to risk requires companies to move beyond managing supply chains based solely on the criteria of throughput and low cost to a strategy that places agility and nimbleness as the central operating attributes. Lean supply chains are primarily focused on parochial efforts to balance their ability to increase throughput of goods and services to meet marketplace demand with the need to continuously reduce costs. Because of this inward focus, corporate continuous improvement objectives can leave companies fairly isolated, despite efforts to extend the enterprise out to network partners. As a result, while focused on pursuing enterprise-centric optimization objectives, companies often lack an understanding of the full impact their initiatives have on other channel constituents and customers found along the supply chain continuum. Such a lack of visibility undermines the collaboration necessary to coordinate the competencies and resources to respond effectively to unplanned supply chain risks.

The tendency of lean initiatives to direct corporate vision inward also has a deleterious effect on the robustness and timeliness of supply chain information. Despite their espousal of supply chain management principles, companies are often unable to sense or respond to changes happening in some other sector of the supply chain until it is too late to respond effectively to specific processes, events, and metrics. In order to be far more responsive than is possible with traditional supply chains, companies must be closely connected to other channel network partners in order to leverage the highest visibility to demand and supply events, the greatest velocity to generate value creation, and the strongest capability to redirect resources and inventories.

While it is of course critical that companies continue to extend the principles of lean SCM outward into their supply chains, it has become increasingly evident that they must simultaneously pursue the transformation of their supply channels into adaptive, demand-driven networks. The use of the word *network* is critical. As described in chapter 3, the concept of a *supply chain* denotes a linear, sequential process where goods and information are passed serially through a supply and delivery pipeline. In contrast, in a supply network all channel participants can sense and transmit, in real time, knowledge of local shifts in demand and supply concurrently to all channel points as they occur so that the entire ecosystem can respond intelligently to potential risks.

Interactive networking enables companies to merge their competencies and resources into a virtual, seamless supply and delivery engine capable of adapting to absorb risk and to profit from unexpected opportunities. Supply and delivery networks consist of a complex array of partner relationships interconnected by physical distribution, information, and customer and internal value flows. The system is driven by intelligence regarding channel demand and is controlled by feedback arising from planning and execution processes, sense-and-respond technologies, and performance measures. Supply networks by definition enable cross-channel demand identification and the adaptability to be designed in and leveraged across the supply chain, they are founded on actual capabilities of channel partners, and they are capable of interpreting event intelligence as it occurs so that inventories and capabilities available anywhere in the supply and delivery network can be quickly accessed and adapted to respond to both challenges and opportunities.

Adaptive, demand-driven SCM is an *operations performance* approach to SCM and is focused on ensuring supply chain execution functions are not only lean, but as agile and responsive as possible to marketplace variability. When viewed from a wider perspective, this approach can be said to consist of two separate but integrated concepts: one is concerned with *supply flexibility* and is known as *adaptive supply chain management,* and the other is concerned with *delivery flexibility* and is known as *demand-driven supply network management.* Providing an understanding of these two approaches is the focus of the next sections.

6.2.1 Fundamentals of Adaptive Supply Chain Management

As detailed above, the problem with lean supply chains is that they can be too brittle to withstand the unpredictable shocks caused by a host of potentially damaging events. In fact, even as companies strive for greater efficiency, today's marketplace turbulence is also requiring them to strive for greater velocity in responding to the threat of increasing variability in demand and supply. Simply put, lean without adaptability leaves an organization without room to refocus competencies and resources to respond to new marketplace conditions, and adaptability without lean can result in inflated costs structures.

Effectively meeting the challenge to deploy both efficient and adaptable organizations is driving businesses to move beyond lean to a new perspective where success is measured by a supply chain's ability to be strategically and operationally nimble while pursuing efficiency and total process improvement. This mandate involves replacing less responsive linear supply chains with lean, highly agile networks capable of rapidly adapting operations and resources to be more *responsive* and *flexible* as well as *resilient* to withstand the threats posed by marketplace changes.[8]

6.2.1.1 Defining the Adaptive Supply Chain

The *adaptive supply chain* can be defined as:

> A virtual networked supply chain community possessing the capacity to sense marketplace changes as they occur anywhere in the channel and then to communicate, through interactive information sharing and synchronized functions, the critical intelligence necessary to enable rapid decision making and optimal execution to not only survive but leverage risk to secure competitive advantage.

Agile supply chains are inherently dynamic, aggressively change focused, and growth oriented. While they embrace lean as a fundamental operating principle, they are distinctly about seizing leadership in today's fast-changing global marketplace by being able to rapidly adapt regardless of the level of possible supply chain risk. Adaptive supply chains cannot be implemented by just one company: they succeed by networking channel partners through real-time information and collaborative processes to drive collective value to the customer.

Supply chains that seek to be adaptive must possess the following attributes.

- *Customer Demand Driven.* Agile supply chains are capable of sensing and responding to demand as it actually occurs. Conventional supply chains attempt to predict demand by developing sophisticated forecasting techniques based on past sales histories. In contrast, agile supply chains utilize demand-gathering, planning, and execution technologies to capture real-time information that enables them to sense both planned and unplanned demand events as they occur. Such intelligence in turn enables them to rapidly adapt and synchronize distribution, transportation, and logistics capabilities to meet new demand patterns, and activate and apply visibility, collaborative, and analytical toolsets to every company in the network to keep the right products flowing to the right customers. Finally, demand driven means having the ability to adapt the entire supply network to increase delivery velocity by intimately understanding customers and their needs, and the solutions and delivery values each customer wants.

- *Supply Flexibility.* Adaptive supply chains require companies to link themselves together into networked federations focused on intense collaborative integration between buyers and suppliers. The goal is to erect mechanisms by which partners can focus their special competencies on accelerating joint product development, sourcing, order management, and delivery that enables rapid deployment of inventories and transportation capabilities to respond to demand as it actually happens at every point in the network. Suppliers that are seamlessly integrated into the channel system can continuously work on reducing lead times, possess the knowledge to and are capable of quickly responding to product changes, and are committed to transparency and openness.

- *Delivery Flexibility.* The supply chain delivery process has often been described as a pipeline through which product flows. As a pipeline expands to serve an ever-widening market, the volume of goods flowing through it correspondingly grows. As pipeline inventories increase, however, so do the costs of ordering, storing, and moving them. What is worse, the longer the pipeline the greater the chance that weak points will emerge as the membrane of the delivery network continuum is stretched to the breaking point. Countering delivery risk requires companies to continuously search for technologies to accelerate the velocity of pipeline flows. Critical to this objective is gaining *visibility* of total channel demand. Visibility enables trading networks to share in real-time transactional, operational, and performance data by leveraging event-monitoring technologies, which render transparent virtually pooled inventories and capacities. A closely networked delivery channel enables coordinated understanding of demand, assessment of fulfillment alternatives, and selection of optimal solutions that ensure joint execution of strategies sensitive and responsive enough to capitalize on unplanned demand events.

■ *Organizational Flexibility.* At the core of the adaptive supply chain stand organizations agile enough to rapidly alter resources and competencies in response to real-time demand events while concurrently devising alternative, intelligent plans to be implemented by the entire supply network. Organizational adaptability requires organizations that both understand the content of their core competencies and have the flexibility to select and blend in outsourced capabilities. Then again, adaptive organizations invest in technologies enabling them to easily access intelligence occurring anywhere in the supply network. Such tools provide transparency of potential problems early enough to consider multiple resolution options in response to the changing dynamics driven by a marketplace event or trend. Finally, the adaptive organization actively promotes and embraces standardized performance measurements both internally and across the expanse of the supply network pipeline. Operating standards enable supply chains to unearth unnecessary costs and wastes that cloud visibility of channel events and hamper organizational flexibility to rapidly adapt to changing conditions.

6.2.1.2 Adaptive Supply Chain Management

All supply and delivery chains exist to facilitate the marketing, buying, and selling of products and services beginning with the producer and culminating with the end-customer. Regardless of whether they are purely transaction based with minimal dependency on other channel players or organized into federated networks characterized by close collaboration and partnership, all supply channels must begin by establishing strategic plans and operations execution tactics that are targeted at delivering value to the customer. These planning and execution processes are founded on demonstrated levels of service and consider patterns of demand to be both recurring and stable.

Risk to the demand–supply equilibrium is marginalized through a variety of techniques. First, each level in the supply and delivery chain can strive to better predict the occurrence of possible marketplace variation by developing more sophisticated forecasting techniques that smooth and trend expected demand. Practical actions can result in the addition of inventory buffers staged strategically at various network points to dampen the impact of demand variability. Other approaches may go in the opposite direction with the activation of lean and process improvement toolsets that seek to diminish variability by shrinking assets and channel levels to speed pipeline flows, or leveraging outsourcing partners to quickly enable virtual capabilities in the wake of out-of-bounds demand.

Case Study 6.4

Adidas's Flexible Supply Chain

When Greece's soccer team scored a surprise victory in the European Championship, Adidas was able to capitalize on its adaptive supply chain to deliver more than 145,000 Greece team jerseys to stores across Europe just days after the winning match. Adidas's victory to capture market share was the result of the nimbleness of its global procurement and logistics network to respond with "just-in-time" products.

By synchronizing orders through a maze of contract manufacturers, subcontractors, and suppliers in more than a dozen countries, Adidas was able to repeat the Greece jersey delivery feat for each country as they progressed through the Championship. In addition, Adidas's supply chain was able to drive sales without significant pre-investment in materials or finished goods.

Adidas's success can be directly attributed to its ability to blend a very flexible supply chain strategy with the capability to effectively manage a global outsourcing network. By tapping into the competencies of internal and partner resources, Adidas succeeded by using the skills of each segment of the supply and delivery network by moving work to the best channel location. Such capabilities enabled Adidas to exploit its supply chain to attain strategic goals and not just focus on reducing costs.

Source: Puryear, Rudy; Singh, Banu; and Phillips, Stephen, "How to Be Everywhere at Once," Vol. 11, No. 4 May, June 2007, p. 10.

In contrast to these traditional methods of managing supply and delivery channels, adaptive networks seek to counter demand variability by abandoning static plans in favor of mechanisms that provide immediate feedback regarding the marketplace and the flexibility to quickly devise alternative plans that can be rapidly communicated to channel partners. As illustrated in Figure 6.2, adaptive networks possess information tools that permit them to *sense* changing conditions in the supply and demand channel when they occur. Illuminating potential or actual problems anywhere in the network requires *technologies* that quickly provide visibility to threats concurrently to all channel partners. Data is crunched to reveal potential troubles, and then aggregated to disclose systemic patterns of variation and contributing factors. Awareness of variation and understanding of the level of potential risk is then driven by system *alerts* that provide detailed action messages to all network planners. Exception

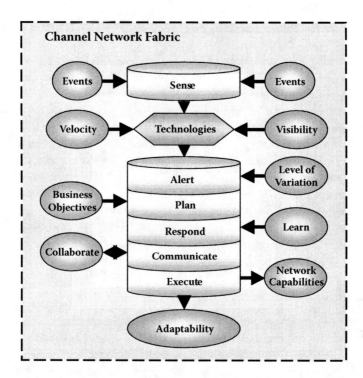

Figure 6.2   Components of adaptive SCM.

messaging supplies warnings on both tactical and strategic levels. Strategically, alerts may reveal emerging challenges that endanger the fundamental assumptions of the supply chain. Tactically, alerts may indicate that market conditions have altered the supply chain's ability to execute originally planned courses of action.

Exception messages enable channel planners to assess the degree of required *plan* revision. For example, action to correct a tactical problem, such as an inventory shortage at a network supply node, would result in an emergency effort to relocate stocks from other channel warehouses to the affected location. On the other hand, a major disruption at a critical supplier might require a fundamental revision of the entire supply chain strategy. The goal is to ensure that events occurring anywhere in the supply network are visible to all participants so that effective analysis, ending in changes to the plan, can begin. Actually, the intensity of the resulting *response* is dependent on the information supplied by the live event. The simplest response may be correcting an out-of-balance process. A more complex response would involve replanning a local supply/delivery point in order to put the plan back on track. Finally, a significant disruptive event may require complete reformulation of the entire channel strategy. In all cases, event data should be complete enough so that standard operating procedures and planning optimization tools can rapidly and accurately assess the resulting impact on performance of a fundamental change in plans.

Before a determined response can be executed, it is critical that possible solutions be *communicated* to affected supply network participants. The speed of response by channel partners to plan revision is driven by two factors: the level of existing network *collaboration* and the availability of communications tools. The more integrated and collaborative channel relations the quicker alternative plans can be communicated and consensus reached. The actual message must be delivered via communications enablers that present data and analysis in a format and style that can be easily transposed into local planning and diagnostic dialects. Once solutions have been agreed upon, plan *execution* can follow. Disruptions can be handled by adjusting the standard channel process by applying an alternate solution to the problem area and directing it back on track to the original plan. Incremental, focused event adaptation permits event obstacle resolution without adversely disturbing and destabilizing standard processes occurring at other network points. If the volume or magnitude of adaptive planning becomes too great over time, fundamental change to the overall supply network is probably warranted.

6.2.1.3 Advantages of an Adaptive Supply Chain

Adaptive supply chains enable companies to directly address demand and supply risk by providing the mechanism to continuously optimize operations anywhere in the supply network. The ability to leverage demand/supply event management, provide visibility to variations, and enable collaborative decision making empowers whole supply chains to focus on sources of disruption, resolve exceptions, and respond rapidly with solutions that minimize fracturing of supply network process continuity. Among the critical advantages are:

- *Customer focus*—being able to rapidly respond to changing marketplace conditions keeps the supply network agile and capable of rapidly refocusing resources regardless of possible disruptions occurring in the marketplace.
- *Event visibility*—high visibility of evolving demand and supply changes enables supply chains to quickly adapt processes without significant channel disruptions.
- *Lean strategies*—supply chain nimbleness enables supply networks to continuously reduce channel wastes, increase efficiencies, and inaugurate continuous improvement initiatives while pursuing supply and delivery optimization.
- *Increased channel collaboration*—closer cooperation and information sharing between network partners promotes rapid decision making and problem event resolution, which reduces overall channel costs, accelerates product design, shrinks time to market, and leverages increased channel service as a competitive differentiator.
- *Exploit new revenue opportunities*—flexible supply and delivery networks can pursue emerging marketplace opportunities much more effectively than companies that follow a more rigid channel strategy.[9]

6.2.2 Fundamentals of Demand-Driven Supply Networks

Although the application of lean, adaptive methodologies to the supply chain represents a dramatic enhancement to SCM principles and practices, succeeding in today's global marketplace also requires companies to be *demand flexible* as well as *supply flexible*. Supply-oriented networks are focused on gaining visibility and receiving event notifications regarding the management and allocation of productive resources and inventories in the channel pipeline. In the product-centered supply chain, the goal is to continuously reduce channel costs and wastes, optimize asset utilization, and construct internal and external processes agile enough to rapidly respond to unexpected trends and disruptions, thereby minimizing threats from the bullwhip effect and cycle-time variability. Operationally, companies first formulate production and new product launch objectives by unearthing past demand and translating it into forecasts, which in turn can be used to plan and execute production and distribution strategies. Finally, the resulting products are then pushed through the supply pipeline to the customer.

Accelerating the speed of pipeline inventories and enhancing the flexibility of productive resources, however, can no longer be considered as constituting a long-term competitive differentiator in today's marketplace. The traditional focus on the order-to-delivery cycle (order receipt, purchasing, manufacturing, warehousing, and transportation) is shifting to a concern with meeting the exact needs of the customer. Simply, supply chains are now being expected not only to lower costs and become more efficient, but also to become more responsive to customer demand. This means that companies must move beyond lean, adaptive optimization and restructure their supply chains to be able to sense and proactively respond to actual demand signals rather than just forecasts or jockeying to counter emerging disruptions in the supply network.

Being *demand flexible* requires a transformation of supply chain processes, infrastructure, and information flows that center on the *demand channel* as it moves upstream through the supply chain versus concentrating on the constraints or performance of *value delivery networks* and *process value chains* as product is moved downstream through the value network. Transitioning from networks oriented around supply to networks oriented around customer demand optimization is a significant leap and involves enhancing collaboration between sales and operations everywhere in the channel, closer logistics and transportation coordination to increase customer delivery speed and efficiency, and new forms of technology capable of sensing and communicating demand as it occurs anywhere, anytime in the supply network. Demand-driven networks are the prerequisite for the next stage of SCM—*intimate supply chain management*.

6.2.2.1 Defining Demand-Driven Supply Networks

The term *demand-driven supply network* (DDSN) was introduced in 2003 by AMR Research. A DDSN is defined as "a system of technologies and business processes that sense and respond to real-time demand across a network of customers, suppliers, and employees."[10] A DDSN consists of the following elements.

- *System*—a DDSN requires both technologies and organizations that are not only sensitive to customer demand triggers, but also enable supply chain constituents to collectively deliver customized solutions to the marketplace; engage suppliers, delivery capabilities, and customers in collaborative value-creating relationships; build responsive networks that are agile and scalable to leverage new sources of demand; capable of fast-flow, reliable delivery; and deploy technology tools like the Internet to link and coordinate customers, suppliers, and delivery networks in real time.
- *Demand*—the fundamental characteristics of a DDSN reside in its ability to rapidly recognize all forms of demand arising from the marketplace. Demand can come from channel forecasts, booked orders, or emerging opportunities. By using monitoring tools like customer analytics and demand-event notification, supply chains can not only understand demand, but even be able to shape it. Knowing what drives the customer purchase and requirements for product features, price points, and buying habits keeps supply chains focused on real-time demand. In the end, being demand sensitive is more than just filling orders: it is using demand signals to scale processes and resources quickly across the entire supply network.
- *Network*—unlike the traditional pipeline concept of the supply chain where products and services are pushed serially to the marketplace, a DDSN starts with the flow of requirements into the demand channel and proceeds upward to the supply source. Quickly and effectively responding to demand, in turn, requires that network supply nodes possess the ability to rapidly reconfigure internal processes and external channel points of delivery by tapping into the competencies found in outsourced manufacturers, federated partners engaged in sourcing and collaborative product design, and third-party logistics providers. The goal of executing demand-pull systems is realized by channel supply points capable of aligning demand with the network's array of providers and their capacity to service the unique needs and priorities of the customer.[11]

To summarize, AMR Research characterizes a DDSN as "a supply chain driven by the voice of the customer," constructed to serve "the downstream source of demand rather than the upstream supply constraints of factories and distribution systems." A DDSN enables supply and delivery channel nodes to understand and adapt to demand anywhere in the supply chain as it is actually occurring.

6.2.2.2 Strategies for Becoming Demand Driven

Effective DDSNs require companies to reverse traditional thinking about the mechanics of the supply chain. In product-focused channels, supply and delivery nodes use forecasts and other forms of marketing intelligence to determine what the market will likely do, and then products and services strategies are executed driven by operational efficiencies with resulting inventories pushed down the network to meet expected customer demand. When actual demand does occur, however, it is often independent of what was forecasted with the result that gaps between availability and the ordering event can and do occur. In contrast, a DDSN turns this process on its head by deploying demand-sensing strategies and demand-shaping processes. These demand transparency and network synchronization strategies enable network partners to transpose their thinking from *product/supply pushing* to *demand/response pulling.*

Case Study 6.5

Elements of Lean DDSNs

Critical to global trade success is the importance of partnering with local businesses to build supply chain expertise in developing nations.

Astec Power, a worldwide supplier of power supplies to OEMs in the computer and telecom industries has been careful to develop its Chinese partners. The Carlsbad, California firm involves its Asian partners in the innovation, product design, and distribution process. To ensure quality, Astec has created a supplier development program where 50 Astec engineers work with suppliers to continuously drive improvement.

According to George Foo, Astec V.P. of operations, the investment has resulted in the company winning "millions of dollars in new business by investing in local supply chain professionals and in development of market intelligence."

In another example, the Walt Disney Co. has determined that to make the new Hong Kong Disneyland a success, local partnering is critical. Overall the company intends to hire and operate locally to become part of the region's cultural fabric.

An essential part is leveraging local resources to keep the supply chain invisible, increase speed, and decrease the risk of disruption. The company intends to send its Hong Kong employees to other Disney facilities around the world for six months to learn the business. The goal is to ensure growth plans don't move faster than supply chain and organizational expertise allow.

Source: Kuehn, Kurt, "Five Universal Business Plan Challenges Driving Supply Chain Alignment in the 21st Century," *Supply & Demand Chain Executive,* December 2005/January, 2006, pp. 50–53.

As illustrated in Figure 6.3, a DDSN attempts to connect and focus the three fundamental components of SCM detailed in chapter 3—the *demand channel,* the

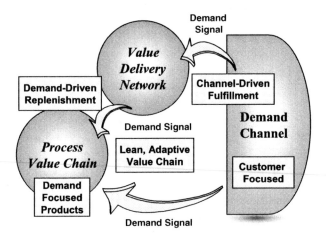

Figure 6.3 Components of a DDSN.

process value chain, and the *value delivery network*—around a demand-driven vision by executing the following five essential cross-functional strategies.[12]

6.2.2.2.1 Customer Focused

A DDSN seeks to understand the content of the actual demand signals it receives from the customer and is the driver of the entire supply and delivery network. The signals transmitted tell suppliers what customers value, the relationships they seek from their supply partners, the transactional vehicles they prefer to use to communicate requirements, and the intensity of the experience they expect to receive with their purchase. DDSNs deploy tools like RFID (radio frequency identification), *point of sales* (POS), Internet connectivity, *sales and operations planning* (S&OP), market segmenting analytics, and demand signaling systems to provide real-time visibility of purchasing and marketing data across the breadth of the supply chain. This data can in turn be used to respond to and shape demand through targeted promotion, pricing, and rebate strategies, identifying opportunities for cross-selling, executing effective product-customer segmenting, and building integrated supply networks designed to respond to each customer's individual solution. In a DDSN the *demand channel* powers the supply chain.

6.2.2.2.2 Channel-Driven Fulfillment

This strategy links customer demand with the *value delivery network*. The driver of this component is the transmission and timely receipt of customer demand signals by channel delivery nodes. These signals seek to link marketplace requirements with supply chain production and delivery resources in real time. By deploying demand visibility technologies that integrate demand data from a wide range of visibility enablers, including POS, EDI (electronic data interchange), Web, RFID, VMI (vendor managed inventory), and ERP (enterprise resource planning) order-promising mechanisms, supply networks can translate and pass customer demand simultaneously to manufacturing, supply network, and distribution functions.

DDSNs utilize these tools to design demand-pull systems that trigger supply commencing at the point of sale, and then pulling the requirement from upstream delivery nodes, point by point, all the way back to the producer. The goal is to provide advanced warning of demand and the channel's collective ability to respond effectively. Demand-pull management increases velocity by reducing channel uncertainty, variability in fulfillment processes, and supply lead time, while linking channel partners together into networks capable of responding to emerging marketplace opportunities. A successful DDSN clearly aligns demand signal and order execution functions with fulfillment strategies designed to foster agility in pull-based logistics, synchronization of orders at every level of the supply network, and the empowerment of cross-channel teams dedicated to using sell-side analytics that keep the entire channel agile and flexible while exposing bottlenecks that inhibit performance.

Case Study 6.6

 **Activating Customer-Driven Fulfillment**

The ability to capture and transmit customer demand-driven signals is essential to an effective DDSN. For example, when a customer buys a package of Folgers coffee at Target, the planners at Proctor & Gamble who manage the product are provided with the demand signal. The data on the purchase, including store location date, and time, is recorded and passed on to P&G within minutes or hours by Target's POS system. The information enables P&G to start planning the replenishment process almost immediately.

Event-driven demand is not just for consumables. Finisar, a manufacturer of fiber-optic and test and measurement solutions for high-speed data networks, depends on demand visibility in the supply chain. This visibility has reduced planning cycles from months to days and enabled Finisar to react quickly to market demand.

For example, a new sales order entered into Finisar's system is quickly made visible to multiple factories worldwide as well as across its supplier network. Knowledge of demand has helped the company to shorten lead times while decreasing inventories. This is accomplished by sharing planning and forecasting information with suppliers. This permits planners to communicate to suppliers exactly how much inventory is being consumed in production. This visibility to critical demand and supply information enables Finisar to deliver higher service levels, shorter lead times, and lower costs.

Source: Muzumdar, Maha, "Supply Chain Makeover," *APICS Magazine,* January 2007, pp. 34–38.

6.2.2.2.3 Demand-Driven Replenishment

For DDSNs to effectively respond to the customer, demand signals must closely link fulfillment with channel replenishment. This means that network players must have the ability to not only sense but also to translate this demand into replenishment signals so that products can be made available as demand actually occurs. The goal of this component of a DDSN is to synchronize the production and distribution of goods and services with the demand drumbeat of the marketplace. Instead of building to a forecast, production and delivery channel nodes base upstream channel replenishment processes on actual demand and understanding of customer priorities.

Activating demand-driven replenishment requires that channel nodes focus replenishment functions on lean, pull-based principles. The goal is to link local lean execution with global planning processes, thereby enabling the establishment of agile procurement and logistics networks. These flexible assets can then leverage Theory of Constraint (TOC) and lean techniques to ensure short process changeovers, strategic sourcing, optimized transportation, and targeted inventory buffers that are aligned exactly to customer solutions and delivery requirements. Operations performance is monitored through the use of scorecards and metrics that measure both demand-fulfillment and well as demand-shaping activities.

6.2.2.2.4 Demand-Focused Products

In addition to delivery, demand-driven networks must be able to quickly design and bring to market those products and supporting services that are in high demand. Innovation that is demand-driven begins by basing development not only on past sales and projected market attributes, but also on actual feedback as to the brand experience customers want to receive, the buying interfaces they would like to work with, and the supporting services that increase product availability, satisfaction, and convenience. The timing and rollout of new product introductions, in turn, need to be integrated with supply network capabilities and tracked at the supply chain level through the demand visibility signal. Finally, design excellence is bound up with the application of lean supply chain principles that fine tune process and delivery node resources. Critical to this objective is the utilization of supplier partner design and participation to both reduce total cost while optimizing quality conformance, delivery, and commercial appeal. The delivery network participates in this process by executing postponement strategies and using intermediaries to activate high levels of supply network flexibility to meet actual demand signals when they occur.

6.2.2.2.5 Lean, Adaptive Value Chain

A DDSN competes by leveraging lean and adaptive supply chain principles and practices to align the *process value chains* and the *value delivery networks* with the signals driven by the *demand channel*. A DDSN is not the result of the efforts of a single company but rather requires the close collaboration and support of all channel partners. Critical to DDSN are channel organizational designs that closely couple product development, forecasting, and supply sourcing teams that can keep the entire network focused on those pull strategies and inventory buffers that provide optimum performance regardless of market conditions. DDSNs seek to realize wider transparency of actual demand conditions so that channel resources can be rapidly realigned to optimize a needed process or shorted material. Finally, a DDSN seeks to reduce possible channel variation by reducing the number of channel nodes so that only the best performers remain.

6.2.2.3 Advantages of a DDSN

A DDSN seeks to reduce risk and respond directly to the threat of marketplace variability by combining lean toolsets and adaptive processes to synchronize *supply flexibility* with demand-pull systems, which in turn optimizes *delivery flexibility*. Based on SAP benchmark data,[13] supply chains guided by a DDSN have increased fill rates and reduced stock outs by 3 to 10 percent, reduced inventories by 7 to 15 percent, improved asset utilization by 10 to 15 percent, decreased cash-to-cash cycles by 10 to 30 percent, and reduced waste and obsolescence by 35 to 50 percent. In addition, DDSN leaders have a higher percentage of perfect order fills, more accurate and timely marketing information, faster response to changes in demand, and execute faster, more effective product introductions and phaseouts.

An effective DDSN helps everyone in the supply chain to create greater value for the customer, forge closer relationships with network partners, and reduce costs. For *value delivery network* intermediaries, demand-driven strategies enable companies to escape the tyranny of the bullwhip effect. Besides reductions in nonprofitable inventories, channel distributors and retailers can also fine tune stocks so that they can concentrate on stocking exactly what the marketplace wants to buy. Increased agility ensures that delivery nodes can create deeper customer relationships while increasing inventories of full-margin stocks, maximizing revenues and profits. Finally, the demand-driven delivery network is able to drastically reduce transportation costs by minimizing channel transfers caused by stocking imbalances and overstock returns.

For *process value chains,* DDSN strategies assist manufacturers to become more agile so they can operate with shorter production runs, develop more flexible response times and planning cycles, and better manage capacities. By converting production functions from a dependence on long-term plans based on forecasts to pull-based models, manufacturers can focus on making what customers actually want instead of just pushing products into the delivery channel, which so often results in obsolescence, excess carrying costs, and price markdowns. Finally, demand-driven strategies enable producers to focus on product innovation, create close linkages to customers and suppliers in the development life cycle, and synchronize product introductions with channel marketing efforts that highlight brand differentiation and enhance customer loyalty.

6.3 Competencies of the Adaptive, Demand-Driven Network

Adaptive DDSNs have emerged in response to the significant risks facing today's supply chain. While the litany of issues—transportation infrastructure and capacity troubles, increasing demand/supply variability, outsourcing, and shrinking product life cycles—has become common parlance, the real difference is the level of *speed* by which supply and delivery channels are expected to respond. The application of lean practices helps to cut wastes and fat, which decrease supply chain velocities. However, increased velocities require more than being efficient: increased flexibilities involve knowing the pulse of actual customer demand and the capabilities of supply replenishment response. Adaptive DDSNs increase supply chain velocities by executing the competencies illustrated in Figure 6.4.

6.3.1 Customer Driven

Perhaps the most important competency of an adaptive, demand-driven network is the ability of channel ecosystems to combine real-time market intelligence with flexible, nimble productive and delivery capabilities to create deep collaborative partnerships with customers and suppliers, which provides real competitive differentiation. Supply chains that can quickly react to customer needs, present

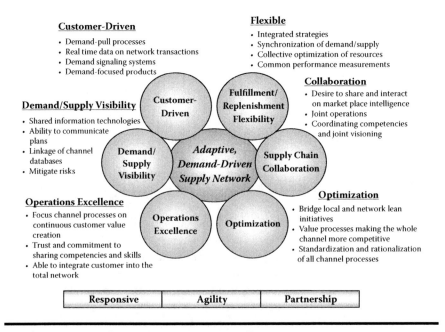

Figure 6.4 Adaptive, demand-driven supply networks.

unique buying experiences, and continuously provide the innovative product/solution mixes that lock in brand awareness, create an exceptional customer service benchmark, and are recognized as the supplier of choice among peers.

Adaptive DDSNs succeed by creating *value* for their customers, their network partners, and their own companies. Such an objective is achieved by viewing the supply and delivery channel not simply as a pipeline for the transfer of standardized goods and services, but as an integrated network capable of quickly locating and adapting resources that treat each customer requirement as unique. Putting the customer at the center of the supply chain can occur only when actual demand can be captured and transmitted in real time to the entire channel. Knowledge of actual demand enables clear pathways for the fast-flow alignment of goods and information, which matches customer service needs and product solutions. The speed and accuracy of response to each channel customer touch point presents channel players with the opportunity to expand and deepen the customer experience and additional value-creating relationships.

6.3.2 Demand/Supply Visibility

In the adaptive DDSN the number one priority is improving *visibility*. As illustrated in Figure 6.5, according to an Aberdeen Group survey, companies are deploying visibility solutions to help them primarily with enhancing the customer experience, and then with improving operational efficiency, agility, and conformance to regulatory and performance standards.[14] Agile supply networks excel in deploying demand-gathering, planning, and execution technologies that reveal events as they actually occur, and then enabling them to rapidly adapt and synchronize supply and delivery resources to capitalize on new opportunities before the competition.

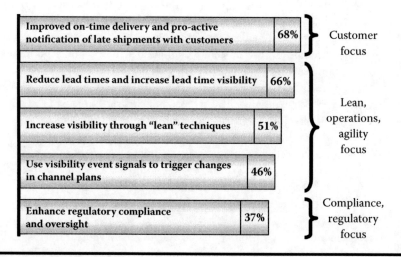

Figure 6.5   Drivers of supply chain visibility.

Visibility tools also activate the capability of the entire network to increase supply and delivery velocity and timeliness by illuminating the intimate needs of the customer and the solutions they value from their suppliers. With respect to performance, companies with highly visible supply chains have customer service levels of at least 96 percent, reduced inventory levels of 20 to 30 percent, and are twice as likely as their competitors to have an on-time delivery rate of 95 percent or higher.[15]

At the heart of supply chain visibility are technology tools that *connect* supply network partners and focus them on customer value delivery. Connectivity here can refer to a wide range of data transfer processes. In its ideal form, connectivity would consist of a single electronic communications hub linking individual ERP, CRM (customer relations management), S&OP, warehouse management, and transportation systems. These technologies would provide for the merger, harvesting, and analysis of supply chain data intelligence, which renders effective business decision-making possible. Regardless of the technology, effective connectivity requires the application of the following enablers:[16]

- *Demand Forecasting.* The ability to utilize forecasts to predict future requirements is at the center of the adaptive DDSN. Although actual demand signals provide critical data driving the demand pull, effective forecasting is still needed for long-term planning. Today's forecasting tools can draw upon simple models or complex algorithms, which attempt to project the future demand of product families or SKUs (stock-keeping unit) driven by data from sales, invoice, POS, lost sales, and promotion histories.
- *Demand Collaboration.* This enabler draws on event messaging to link the various constituents of the supply chain, such as producers, distributors, and retailers, so that demand data can be broadcast and used as a medium for the collective synchronization of forecasts and subsequent scaling of supply and delivery operations to meet expected demand.
- *Demand Shaping.* This enabler permits supply chain nodes to simulate demand intensity through the use of sales techniques such as channel promotions, bonus and incentives, pricing, and advertising and marketing strategies.
- *Alert Signal Management.* The identification of channel supply and demand abnormalities occurring anywhere in the supply chain is the focus of this enabler. Examples of alert-driven signals are unplanned product shortages (or excesses), emergency plant shutdowns, process failures, unexpected outlier demand, and evidence of wide variance of actual demand and supply against the plan.
- *Predictive Analytics and Simulation.* The ability to capture, analyze, and simulate actual supply chain performance is essential to providing visibility of the health of the customer value channel.

Effective demand/supply visibility management can have a dramatic impact on the ability of the supply chain to thrive in today's dynamic business conditions. According to the Aberdeen Group,[17] the above connectivity tools reduce inventories while increasing sales, improving all levels of forecast accuracy, improving service levels, reducing price markdowns due to decreased obsolescence and overstocks, and enhancing production and operations planning for channel producers.

6.3.3 Operations Excellence

The adaptive DDSN is founded on a firm commitment to continuous operations excellence. Supply chains cannot hope to provide the level of service and the type of buying experience customers desire without having the agile infrastructures, scalable resources, and speed of information transfer necessary to activate capabilities that differentiate them from the competition. Such objectives can be achieved only when supply ecosystems continuously clear away constraints, collapse processing times, remove redundant operations steps, even eliminate entire supply chain levels. By applying lean principles, companies can effectively pursue *waste reduction* at all supply chain levels, leverage supply chain partnerships and technology tools to continuously build and sustain a high-velocity *stream of value* to the customer, and finally, deploy cross-channel metrics for effective quality, change management, and collaboration to maintain a focus on network *continuous improvement*.

The competencies adaptive DDSNs must possess to achieve operations excellence begin with the pursuit of strategies designed to realize best practices across the length of the supply chain, while simultaneously achieving superior capabilities in product/service delivery flow, inventory management, and cycle times. To this competency must be added a proficiency in the use of the lean tool kit for continuous improvement. The lean supply chain is dedicated to the elimination of all wastes, root-cause problem resolution, and people empowerment everywhere in the supply network. A companion to lean is the pursuit of quality. This process begins with an assessment of existing conformance to quality targets, delivery performance, and total cost, then proceeds to quality approaches that link lean, Six Sigma, and other toolsets, and concludes with the application of quality targets to the entire supply chain. The final competency is found in the capability of supply chain players to effectively employ outsourcing to continuously match capabilities and resources with expected and demonstrated performance. The goal of these competencies is to keep the entire supply chain lean and focused on total customer satisfaction.

6.3.4 Fulfillment/Replenishment Flexibility

The ability to quickly sense and rapidly respond to an environment of ceaseless change, to be, in short, flexible, is an essential feature of the adaptive DDSN. The word *flexible* refers to the capability of an organization to easily move from one task to another. Being flexible implies that a process can be easily redirected to a limited set of situations that have been predefined. To become *agile*, however, a process must also be capable of continuously evolving to meet *unpredicted* challenges and opportunities regardless of the degree of operational interference. To be agile also implies a comprehensive view of how a company and the supply chain community in which it is a participant acts in the marketplace, how it creates, produces, and distributes goods and services that enrich customer value.

Briefly, the agile supply chain possesses the following key attributes.

- *Customer value enhancement.* An agile supply chain is perceived by its customers as providing them continuous, unique sources of value. The products and services of an agile supply chain offer customized, individual solutions to solve customers' problems.
- *Utilization of channel resources.* The foundation of supply chain agility rests on the ability of companies to utilize the competencies and resources of network partners to assemble rapid response capabilities to meet marketplace needs. The objective is to engineer processes that can create, produce, and deliver new products to market as rapidly and cost-effectively as possible.
- *Event-driven.* Rendering the supply chain sensitive to changing circumstances requires that channel work activities be driven by the synchronization of real-time multitier process events. Once demand/supply events are known, agile, scalable supply chains can realign the supplier network as well as production, distribution, and information to respond effectively to changes in demand, new product launch, or unexpected growth.
- *Increased supplier flexibility.* A critical driver for improving supply chain agility is improvement of supplier relations. Suppliers that are seamlessly integrated into the channel system can continuously work on reducing lead times, possess knowledge of and are capable of quickly responding to product changes, and are committed to transparency and openness.
- *Increased delivery flexibility.* Delivery flexibility requires operations functions that are lean and agile. The application of the toolbox of lean techniques permits managers to attack wastes anywhere in the company or in the supply chain. The goal is the removal of non-value-added functions that simply elongate lead times and increase supply chain volatility.
- *Technology enabled.* The application of technology tools to make visible supply and delivery events is at the core of agility. Technology applications can improve everything from on-time delivery and self-service order configuration, to delivery synchronization and status visibility. Technology tools can be separated into those that improve operational efficiency and channel visibility (ERP, EDI, web, and RFID); those that provide connectivity, information sharing, event tracking, exception management, and dynamic optimization to reduce lead times, wastes, and increase supply chain agility (CPFR, APS (advanced planning and scheduling), and S&OP); those that focus on customer experience enhancement, customer order, and service management solutions; and shipment tracking, channel disruption management, supply chain improvement, and regulatory functions.

6.3.5 Supply Chain Collaboration

Collaboration is perhaps one of the most overused and underexecuted management concepts to be found in today's business literature. Although today's supply chains need to be more synchronized than ever, in reality the ability to share real-time demand and supply information with network partners has dramatically inhibited the construction of truly agile, demand-driven supply chains. However, as companies become more global and are increasingly dependent on outsourcing, the need for closer collaboration between network partners has grown more urgent. According to Moore, Manrodt, and Holcomb,[18] collaboration is needed to

- increase the level of real-time information sharing, particularly in an environment of globalization,
- reduce the degree of complexity inhibiting information sharing and coordination as the population of the supply chain community increases,
- accelerate successful product life cycle management for new and existing products.
- increase the reliability and accuracy of the execution of supply chain "optimized" plans.

For supply chains to achieve the level of collaboration necessary to be adaptive and demand driven, they must be capable of executing several critical steps. To begin with, they must master collaboration *internally*. This step can be achieved through the application of processes such as S&OP, the use of supporting metrics, and the presence of technology tools that can be easily and intuitively used by everyone in the business. Outside the business, another issue is *trust*. Corporate culture issues surrounding collaboration continue to be a barrier. However, the presence of workable, long-term relationships builds the kind of cooperation essential to leveraging visibility and efficiency across channel markets. Another essential step is technology. Integration platforms can be accessed through providers such as E2open, Inovis, Sterling Commerce, and others that eliminate the need for companies to implement separate one-to-one integration with each trading partner. Whether third-party or direct connectivity, information illuminating channel events provides collaborating partners with a chance to react to fresh marketplace opportunities.

Finally, once preliminaries are in place, supply chains can advance to full *integration* where true collaboration can occur. Two approaches are possible. Companies can create customized, individual structures with suppliers and customers, constructed around specific needs and data requirements. However, the long-term goal is to move to the second, and advanced, stage of collaboration. Here, collaboration is centered on the creation of a single virtual industry structure comprised of several supply chains capable of acting as a single, seamless entity. In either case, collaboration provides the supply chain with the ability to quickly align people and organizations around common goals.

6.3.6 *Optimization*

At the heart of the adaptive DDSN is the requirement that channel participants not only seek to optimize internal processes to become more lean and agile, but that they also optimize their relationships with their supply and delivery partners. While optimization requires the standardization and rationalization of all channel processes, it cannot be successful without the end-to-end visibility of supply and demand events so necessary to fostering organizations that are flexible and agile enough to respond quickly and efficiently to the demand pull of the customer. Optimization and visibility, in turn, enable companies to tightly synchronize critical supply chain flows (information, transportation, goods, and services) that maximize customer value.

Supply chain optimization is driven by three major attributes.[19]

- *Optimized strategy.* The first attribute is focused on aligning the corporate vision and direction of each channel player with the overall logistics and supply chain strategy of the supply network. An optimal strategy is based on lean supply chain principles, yet is flexible enough to respond effectively to new opportunities for growth under conditions of marketplace uncertainty. Channel synchronization and visibility to demand/supply dynamics form the optimal approach to countering the growing complexity caused by increased globalization, outsourcing, product proliferation, and the accelerating velocity of marketplace change.
- *Optimized planning.* The second attribute centers around deploying planning tools, such as ERP, APS, SCP (supply chain planning), EDI, web, e-mail, transportation/warehousing software, and POS, to provide the channel ecosystem with access to real-time, end-to-end information flows. The target is to leverage this knowledge to optimize channel forecasting/sales operations, inventory, supply network design, manufacturing planning, and delivery.
- *Optimized execution.* The versatility and strength of the supply chain's ability to optimize demand and replenishment can be measured and assessed in its performance. Some of the prime metrics can be found in the efficiency and cost management arising from channel shipment and warehousing. Another is the impact of postponement, safety stock pooling, and strategic storage of inventories. Finally, other measurements focus on lead time reduction, speed of response, a host of customer service targets centered on order fulfillment, and funds exchange. Collectively, supply chain optimization enables network partners to remove barriers to high levels of channel efficiency and effectiveness and increase their ability to be adaptive to successfully respond to marketplace risk. Finally, optimization energizes supply chains to succeed in an increasingly volatile global market by fostering increased levels of visibility necessary for the increased collaboration that outpaces the competition.

Adaptive DDSNs succeed by relentlessly pursuing the above six critical competencies. Effective execution of these competencies provides companies with the three critical drivers shown at the bottom of Figure 6.4. To begin with, customer-focused, demand/supply technologies provide the depth of visibility necessary for companies to receive real-time information about demand and supply events, which in turn enables them to be *responsive* to demand as it occurs at each node along the channel network continuum. Operations excellence and fulfillment/replenishment flexibility promote *agility* by endowing supply chains with nimbleness, simplicity, and speed to rapidly execute adjustments to demand and supply capabilities as demand shifts over time. Finally, collaboration and optimization intensify visibility and agility and help foster effective supply chain *partnership*, which can enhance and optimize the channel network's competitiveness and profitability.

6.4 Summary and Transition

Although SCM and lean supply chain concepts have enabled companies to construct operating strategies that permit them to accelerate the velocity of supply and delivery throughput while ensuring high levels of efficiency and continuous improvement, the risks presented by today's political events, natural disasters, and increasing globalization of commerce have rendered dependence on these concepts and practices problematical. In fact, it had become starkly evident that a singular focus on waste and cycle-time reduction, process optimization, and outsourcing has resulted in supply and delivery chains that threaten to be too brittle and stretched too thin to withstand the shocks caused by disruptive natural, political, and market-based events. To effectively meet this challenge, companies must realize that they need to move beyond lean to the next stage of SCM: they need to embrace the concepts of *adaptive, demand-driven supply chain management*.

Firmly based on the principles of SCM and lean, operationally agile and customer-centered supply networks constitute the prime drivers of today's supply chain. The concept of a *network* is critical. In a supply network all channel participants are integrated together. This integration permits them to sense, analyze, transmit, and react to changes in real time, whether a shift in customer tastes or major supply disruptions, as a unified supply and delivery community. Furthermore, interactive networking enables companies to merge their competencies and resources into a virtual, seamless supply and delivery engine capable of rapidly adapting to absorb risk and drive profit from any marketplace opportunity. Supply networks by definition enable cross-channel demand identification and adaptability to be designed in and leveraged across the supply chain; they are capable of interpreting event intelligence so that inventories and capabilities available anywhere in the supply and delivery network can be quickly accessed and adapted to respond to both challenges and opportunities.

The *adaptive supply chain* can be defined as a virtual networked community capable of sensing change as it occurs anywhere in the supply and delivery channel, and then communicating through interactive information sharing the critical intelligence necessary to enable channel partners to rapidly adapt their businesses to meet new challenges as they occur. Adaptive supply chains are *demand-driven*, composed of networked federations of suppliers that provide *supply flexibility*, centered on providing visibility to channel events that increase *delivery velocities*, and possessed of *agile organizations* capable of rapidly adapting resources, competencies, and outsourced partners to dampen risk and grow market share. The ability to leverage demand/supply event management, provide visibility of variation, and enable collaborative decision making empowers whole supply chains to focus on sources of disruption, resolve event exceptions, and respond rapidly with solutions that minimize fracturing supply network process continuity.

The term *demand-driven supply network* (DDSN) was introduced in 2003 by AMR Research. DDSN is defined as "a system of technologies and business processes that sense and respond to real-time demand across a network of customers, suppliers, and employees." At the heart of the DDSN is a fundamental shift in the way supply chains are run. Instead of a product focus, a DDSN requires supply chains to be customer centered by deploying demand-sensing strategies and demand-shaping processes. Such a strategy enables network partners to transpose their thinking from product/supply pushing to demand-response pulling. Through the pursuit of lean, agile, customer-responsive concepts and the deployment of a wide range of visibility enablers, including POS, EDI, web, RFID, and others, the DDSN is capable of translating and passing customer demand to all network partners in real time so that manufacturing, supply network, and distribution functions can be adapted and synchronized as rapidly as possible.

Adaptive demand-driven networks provide market leaders with new ways to be customer driven, gain greater visibility of channel demand and supply events, pursue new levels of operations excellence, attain new mechanisms for fulfillment and replenishment agility, and explore fresh opportunities for supply chain collaboration. As we shall see in the next chapter, however, competitive advantage today will go to those supply chains that are not only lean, adaptive, and demand driven, but that also cultivate intimacy with the customer. Customer intimacy opens up an entirely new region of supply chain management by seeking to manage the customer's *experience* with a company and its products. Customer intimacy seeks to build rich relations with customers at every network touchpoint by delivering information, service, innovative products, and interactions that result in compelling experiences that build loyalty and add value to the network community.

Endnotes

1. Robert J. Bowman, "Snake Eyes!!! The Failure to Manage Risk in Supply Chain Can Be Catastrophic," *Global Logistics and Supply Chain Strategies* 11, no. 8 (August 2007): 32.
2. James Kiser and George Cantrell, "Six Steps to Managing Risk," *Supply Chain Management Review* 10, no. 3 (April 2006): 13–14.

3. Beth Enslow, *Global Supply Chain Benchmark Report*, Aberdeen Group White Paper, (Boston, MA: Aberdeen Group, June 2006), 1–4.
4. Vinod R. Singhal and Kevin Hendricks, "The Effect of Supply Chain Glitches on Shareholder Wealth," *Journal of Operations Management* 21 (Dec. 2003), 501–522.
5. For more details on the SMART methodology, see Dirk De Waart, "Getting Smart About Risk Management," *Supply Chain Management Review* 10, no. 8 (November 2006): 27–33.
6. Kish Khemani, "Bringing Rigor to Risk Management," *Supply Chain Management Review* 11, no. 2 (March 2007): 67–68.
7. Some excellent resources on supply chain risk management can be found in Yossi Sheffi, *The Resilient Enterprise* (Boston: MIT Press, 2005); Thomas A. Foster, "Risky Business: The True Cost of Supply Chain Disruption," *Global Logistics & Supply Chain Strategies* (May 2005): 58–68; Mark Crone, "Are Global Supply Chains Too Risky," *Supply Chain Management Review* 10, no. 4 (May/June 2006): 28–35; Beth Enslow, *Global Supply Chain Benchmark Report*, Aberdeen Group White Paper (Boston, MA: June 2006); and Debra Elkins, Robert B. Handfield, Jennifer Blackhurst, and Christopher Craighead, "18 Ways to Guard against Disruption," *Supply Chain Management Review* 9, no. 1 (January/February 2005): 46–53.
8. The sources available on adaptive supply chain management are very sparse. Among the sources used in this text are Claus Heinrich, *Adapt or Die: Transforming Your Supply Chain into an Adaptive Business Network* (Hoboken, NJ: John Wiley & Sons, 2002); Christopher Martin, "Creating the Agile Supply Chain," in *Achieving Supply Chain Excellence through Technology*, vol. 1 (San Francisco, CA: Montgomery Research, 1999), 28–32; *Adaptive Supply Chain Networks*, SAP White Paper (City, State: SAP, 2002); and William T. Walker, "Supply Chain Flexibility," in *Achieving Supply Chain Excellence through Technology*, vol. 6 (San Francisco, CA: Montgomery Research, 2004), 44–47.
9. This summary has been adapted from Richard Howells and Sandy Markin, "Adaptive Business Networks: A Strategy for Change and Efficiency in Manufacturing," in *Achieving Supply Chain Excellence through Technology*, vol. 7. (San Francisco, CA: Montgomery Research, 2005), 152–154.
10. Lora Cecere, Debra Hofman, Roddy Martin, and Laura Preslan, *The Handbook for Becoming Demand Driven*, AMR Research White Paper (City, State: AMR Research, July 2005), 1.
11. These points have been taken from Kevin O'Marah, "Rebuilding the 21st Century on Demand," in *Achieving Supply Chain Excellence through Technology*, vol. 7 (San Francisco, CA: Montgomery Research, 2005), 180–181.
12. These points have been adapted from Cecere et al., *The Handbook for Becoming Demand Driven*, 3–23.
13. These figures are found in Mark Panley and Setfan Boerner, *Demand-Driven Supply Networks*, SAP White Paper (City, State: SAP, 2006), 1.
14. This analysis can be found in *The Supply Chain Visibility Roadmap*, Aberdeen Group White Paper (City, State: Aberdeen Group, November 2006), 2.
15. Ibid., 4.

16. These enablers have been summarized from *Demand Management in Consumer Industries*, Aberdeen Group White Paper (Boston, MA: Aberdeen Group, December 2006), 15–19.
17. Ibid., 4–5.
18. Peter Moore, Karl B. Manrodt, and Mary C. Holcomb, *Collaboration: Enabling Synchronized Supply Chains*, Capgemini White Paper (City, State, Capgemini, 2005), 5.
19. These attributes have been summarized from Peter D. Moore, Karl B. Manrodt, Mary C. Holcomb, and Mike Riegler, *The Power of O3: Optimized Strategy, Planning and Execution*, Capgemini/Oracle White Paper (City, State: Capgemini/Oracle, 2006).

Chapter 7

The Intimate
Supply Chain

Using the Supply Chain to Manage the Customer Experience

There can be little doubt that the application of lean principles and the concept of the adaptive demand-driven supply network (DDSN) have revolutionized the theory and practice of supply chain management (SCM). These enhancements have enabled SCM to focus supply- and demand-side management processes squarely on continuous improvement, and permitted companies to minimize costs and inventories while maximizing revenues and margins. They have also enabled enterprises to exploit the dramatic changes brought about by outsourcing and networking technologies and tap into the competencies and resources of partners anywhere on the globe to engineer the rapid development and distribution of products that optimize inventory availability while reducing investment risk. By enabling the construction of *quick-change* and *migratory* supply chains, which can rapidly adapt and synchronize channel productive and distributive resources in response to changing demand circumstances, today's agile supply chain is superbly positioned to respond to customers' product/service needs and delivery preferences.[1]

Despite the flexibility to cope with the complexity and volatility of today's business environment, it has become evident, however, that supply chains are lacking in the ability to be truly customer centric. In fact, after spending the better part of the new century engineering lean organizations and processes, supply chains have now found that while they are operationally efficient, they are not oriented around the customer. While they can sense and respond to demand as it occurs anywhere in the supply network, they do not understand today's highly dynamic customer, are not organized around making customers and what they value as the number one priority, and are too centered on achieving cost efficiencies at the expense of customer experiences and relationships.

Now that supply chains have become as lean and efficient as they can, the next stage for SCM is to focus on providing value to customers by building sustainable and enriching long-term relationships and loyalties—in short, to be *intimate* with the customer. Becoming intimate means knowing the customers—who they are, what they have purchased, what they value. It is true that such information has long been part of the focus of every marketing department. But being intimate with the customer means not only knowing the basics, but also taking the next step to determine what customers really want from the brands they purchase and the suppliers with whom they do business. Customer intimacy means understanding why customers buy from a company and what value they expect to receive. Tomorrow's winning supply chains will be those that make a special connection, that provide an *experience* for the customer that transcends the simple exchange of value. This experiential differentiator is the key to competitive advantage today. As the Rogers and Peppers Group has stated, "the customer experience is now the battleground for competitive advantage."[1]

This chapter explores the concept of *customer experience management* (CEM) and how to use it to build truly customer-focused supply chains. In place of a strategy based on selling products and optimizing operational efficiencies, CEM understands that the *quality* of a customer's interactions with a supplier is as important as the quality of the actual products and services received. In essence, CEM seeks to generate sustainable profits and growth by engaging customers in activities they find intrinsically rewarding, that deliver the experiences today's customers value. In this view, the purpose of the supply chain shifts from being simply a pipeline for the flow of products and information to a community of suppliers where customers can receive unique, personalized value triggered by emotional responses to experiences that *connect* them to the supplier. The goal is to migrate customers from being dispassionate one-time buyers searching for the lowest price, to long-term customers focused on engendering collaborative relationships with their suppliers to continuously find meaningful solutions to their needs and aspirations.

7.1 Basics of Customer Experience Management

In chapter 2 it was stated that supply chains that expect to thrive in the twenty-first century will be those that understand that it is the customer and not the producer and distributor who determine marketplace direction. It is the customer who has assumed the power to direct the design of product and service content, pricing, transaction management, and information transfer. Rather than simply a marketing category, today's customers expect to be treated as an individual, and require suppliers to provide them with configurable, solutions-oriented bundles of products, services, and information custom designed to meet their unique wants and needs. Finally, today's customer is simply demanding more control over the buying experience, easy-to-use order management tools that empower them to design their own solutions, flawless and speedy fulfillment, robust information content, ease of search, ordering, self-service follow-up, and effortless methods for financial settlement.

Many companies feel that they are effectively responding to today's customer-driven marketplace by structuring their organizations so they can be more customer centered. But while hard components of customer interaction, such as the deployment of *customer relations management* (CRM) systems, web-based transaction management and information transfer, and brand identification reinforcement are crucial, they constitute only a part of the customer relationship story. Of equal, if not greater importance, are the perceptions and attitudes customers come away with from a buying experience that demonstrates a supplier's value to them. In a word, customers have come to base equal value on both the products and services they receive and on the feelings and expectations, tangible and intangible, which surround their interaction with a supplier, its organization, and its processes. Today's best supply chains are succeeding by unearthing and nurturing this special intimacy with their customers aimed at capturing their loyalty, as well as unmistakable competitive advantage, by focusing on managing the customer experience.

7.1.1 Defining Customer Experience Management

For the most part, supply chains have been constructed to facilitate the traditional product/sales approaches to marketing. The primary role of the supply chain is to perform the function of a pipeline for the efficient delivery of products and services to the marketplace. Although the stated marketing objective is to serve the customer, the resulting marketplace strategy is actually focused narrowly on analytically grouping customer segments according to functional features and product benefits with the expectation that customers will rationally select the optimal choice based on differentiating alternatives governed by the Four P's (product, price, promotion, and place). Ultimately, success is gauged by determining the value customers bring to the company and strength of brand loyalty. Products that perform to specification, possess winning functions and features, and are delivered and priced at customer expectations are considered successful and will warrant continued investment.

A closer examination of such marketing approaches reveals, however, that the concepts and models used by most companies are not, after all, really that customer centered. In an expanding and very accessible global economy, the familiar methods for gaining and sustaining competitive advantage, such as product innovation, brand awareness, rebates and reduced pricing, and competitive differentiation, can no longer guarantee customer loyalty. In the past, customers were willing to accept tradeoffs when dealing with their supply chains. For example, when quality was the locus of value, customers acquiesced in the inevitability of high prices and limited selection. On the other hand, inexpensive commodities were expected to be available on demand, but at a lower quality. Stated simply, yesterday's customer was willing to compromise critical values, such as customization and timeliness of service, in exchange for product/service availability.

Case Study 7.1

 **A New Business Paradigm**

According to research done by the Strativity Group, a global research firm, customers' refusals to compromise on all aspects of what they consider as providing value to them is driven by the following trends.

- *Commoditization acceleration* – the shrinking of product life cycles, proliferation of alternatives, and short release cycle are driving increasing commoditization.
- *Customer impatience* – customers have become bored with traditional marketing and are demanding emotionally engaging solutions that are innovative and personalized.
- *Low switching barriers* – product proliferation and almost ubiquitous availability from stores, dealers Web sites, etc. have made switching suppliers easier and cost free.

- *Immediate gratification* – driven by virtually instantaneous availability through the Internet, customers now expect to execute buys and speed of service at the time of their choosing.
- *Abundance of choices* – the seemingly endless array of goods and services has conditioned customers to search for the next best thing, thereby heightening their expectations.
- *Accelerated ROI* – as product life cycles shrink and sales windows of opportunity quickly close, investors are expecting ROI measured in months not years.

Source: Strativity Group, "Doing Business Right Now – Your Customers Won't Wait," *Strativity White Paper,* 2007, pp. 3–4.

Today's customer is most unwilling to accept such tradeoffs. In a marketplace characterized by increasing product commoditization and web-driven global reach that sinks prices, expands the availability of sourcing alternatives, and enables businesses and consumers to quickly and easily switch to competitors, customers are demanding not only dazzling products and superior service, but also innovative experiences that are expanding the meaning of product and service value. What customers are expecting is to receive superlative products and ease of transaction *plus* all aspects surrounding the search, decision, purchase, and receipt process—the depth of service, the advertising, packaging, ease of product configurability, after-sales service, ease of use, reliability, and the sense of being treated as a special individual.

Companies today simply *must* refocus their traditional marketing campaigns and performance metrics to respond to what can be described as the real truth about the customer (who is really you and me).

- They want to be treated as unique, very special individuals; on every occasion that they shop at your site they want to feel that the products, service, and ambience surrounding the experience have been created just for them.
- They simply do not care about your problems or your process policies, especially when they pose a hindrance to their purchasing experience.
- They want *complete* solutions to their wants and needs, attainable with as little cost, time, and effort on their part as possible.
- They want solutions to be available when *they* want them and where *they* expect to find them.
- They have choices and they are ready to use them!

The bottom line is that companies must wear their game face each day, as if they were playing the last inning for the championship and there is no tomorrow—the scary truth is that they really are!

7.1.1.1 Shaping Customer Experience-Centered Organizations

Everyone who purchases a product or service cannot help but consider the overall experience in which the transaction is encapsulated. Often the experience associated with the purchase shapes our attitudes toward the value of the product or service itself; sometimes it is the most memorable part of the buy and it strongly determines how we approach future purchases from the same company. Unfortunately, most companies fail to seriously consider the value of the customer experience. Product development defers to marketing, which focuses on product features and life cycles. Production and delivery are concerned essentially with efficiencies, cycle times, quality, and cost. Even customer service, despite all the rhetoric of customer centeredness, is wholly absorbed in making the sale and garnering favorable statistics.

Despite the overwhelming requirement to surround their product/service offerings with customer-winning experiences, most companies today are not focused on enhancing the customer experience. Some simply do not care. Others have good intentions, collect meaningful data, and create great slogans, but do little to actually follow through. In a 2005 study by the Strativity Group it was reported that 76 percent of the senior executives considered customer experience strategies to be critical. However, only 33 percent said they had the tools to service customers and resolve problems, and only 46 percent felt their company deserved the customer's loyalty.[3] From the customer's point of view, a recent Bain & Company report demonstrated the same lack of realistic understanding of the importance of managing the customer experience. In a survey referencing over 362 companies, 80 percent of the companies believed they were providing superior experiences to their customers. At the same time, the study also found that only 30 percent of the companies had been organized to deliver the promised results and only 30 percent had constructed effective feedback loops. It was little wonder, then, that only 8 percent of the customers who dealt with these companies agreed they were receiving a "superior experience."[4]

Perhaps the gap in what actually provides a winning experience and the array of performance measurements describing it are in fact the measurements themselves. Instead of a tidy metric, the favorable (or unfavorable) experience a customer comes away with is the culmination of a chain of touchpoints, expectations, and opportunities that arise each time the customer shops at a store, hits a web site, phones in to a contact center, or enters an IVR (interactive voice response) menu. And at each instance customers are evaluating the experience; at each occasion customers' relationships with their suppliers can be strengthened or they can be provided with a reason to switch to the competition. Closing this gap between what is recorded and what customers perceive was their experience is difficult since the experience is often not related to the brand's messages or the company's actual offerings. What is needed, according to Meyer and Schwager, is an examination of the "customers themselves—that is, the full range and unvarnished reality of their prior experiences, and then the expectations, warm or harsh, those have conjured up—must be monitored and probed."[5]

Being able to identify and deliver an *intimate experience* is the challenge before today's supply chain. Achieving an intimate experience consists of a range of processes. To begin with, supply chains must be lean, adaptive, and constructed so as to receive and react in real time to the customer's demand signal. These supply chain attributes, covered in detail in past chapters, enable supply and delivery network nodes to be able to develop, produce, and distribute those goods and services customers want at the lowest cost and highest efficiency. Secondly, the *process value chain* and the *value delivery network* must be transformed from a product/service orientation to one where deepening the customer's experience is the central objective. Finally, supply chains must be capable of identifying and monitoring how effectively they are matching the level of intimate experience each customer expects and actually is receiving.

7.1.1.2 Defining Customer Experience Management

The idea that the agreeableness of a buying experience is not only important, but can also be the major contributing factor in future purchasing decisions, has always been known by marketers. The conventional envelope of sourcing, transaction, and

Table 7.1

How important are the following factors in determining customer loyalty?

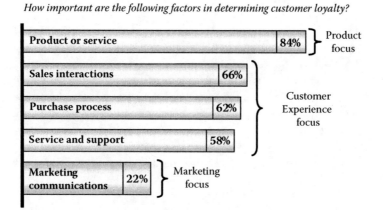

Source: Bob Thompson, *Customer Experience Management: The Value of "Moments of Truth,"* Customer Think Corporation White Paper (City, State: Customer Think, 2006), 3–4.

post-sales functions are saturated with a range of emotional experiences that directly or subliminally impact customers' perceptions of the exchange and the likelihood that they will engage in the process in the future. This is not to say that the primary factor in earning customer loyalty is not the product or service. However, as can been seen in Table 7.1, in a survey on customer loyalty conducted by Right Now Technologies, the quality of the sales, purchasing, and service/support activities (all customer experience oriented) received high rankings. The simple truth is, the survey showed that customers rated the "quality of their *interactions* with an organization as equally important to the quality of the *goods or services* purchased."[6] Now that the importance of *customer experience management* (CEM) has been established, what does it mean and how can it be used to grow competitive advantage?

According to Bernd H. Schmitt, CEM is defined simply as "the process of strategically managing a customer's entire experience with a product or a company."[7] The definition offered by Thompson, "Managing customer interactions to build brand equity and improve long-term profitability," provides a similar slant.[8] A more comprehensive definition has been formulated by the Peppers and Rogers Group.

> [CEM is the] totality of an individual customer's interactions with a company and its brand over time. It essentially ensures that each department and touchpoint—from sales to billing to returns—act collectively in the customer's best interests to generate long-term loyalty. It requires starting from the customer's view first (not the company's), then aligning people,

processes, and technology to ensure that interactions are valuable from the customer's vantage point.[9]

Perhaps the best definition of why CEM is the single most important driver of business today is expressed by Todor in his book *Addicted Customers* (2007).

> Commitment and loyalty to a vendor have their roots, not in the product, but in the experience the customer has associated with the product. Experiences are defined by their emotional and psychological consequences. Therefore, businesses that seek sustainable profits and growth must deliver the customer experiences today's customers value. To do so they must understand what motivates customers, what creates desire and what leads to trusting and valued relationships.[10]

Simply, customers have come to expect the highest quality and the lowest prices available from a wide range of market channel alternatives—the product has dropped into second place in the buying decision. What customers really value and will reward with loyalty in today's hypercompetitive marketplace has shifted to how closely the buying experience resonates with their personal psychological and emotional needs.

Case Study 7.2

Fulfilling Customer Expectations

Perhaps the secret to a successful business resides in providing customers with an array of very special values that actually exceed the nature of the product and services being offered to the marketplace. These companies have figured out how to impart to the customer a unique, and always repeatable experience, that while centered on a quality or unique product/service envelope, produce in the customer a craving, a psychological need that drives them to the brand even if a clearly better alternative is available.

A perfect example is the almost cult-like devotion of customers to the 'Starbucks experience.' Why people would dutifully stand in line to purchase a very expensive cup of coffee has become a much envied proposition. But it is true that customers' pulse rates climb and their sense of anticipation becomes almost unbearable as they are approaching the shop and is only consummated with the actual purchase, the smell and feel of the warm cup, and sitting down in the atmosphere of the shop among other caffeine addicts. Similar attitudes can be recognized by Wal-Mart, Target, and other bargain shoppers who cannot wait to enter their favorite store.

CEM is a business management strategy and not a marketing concept. CEM is about how companies and their partners can use their products and services to provide their customers with exceptional and fulfilling life experiences, rather than just an endless parade of features, options, and brand proliferation. CEM seeks to build loyalty and grow the business by making an emotional connection with the customer that transcends the value of the goods and services they offer. Finally, CEM provides a realistic, measurable approach to creating value built on the strong identification and conscious preference of the customer for a brand based on long-term experience and expectation at the "moment of truth" when the transaction occurs. It is the premise of this book that to be able to effectively respond to the *experiential marketplace* companies will have to transform their supply chains from product delivery pipelines to customer value creation engines capable not only of superlative service but also of identifying and enriching the customer experience whenever the customer is faced with a buying decision at any channel network touchpoint.

7.1.2 CEM and the Supply Chain

There can be little doubt that the evolution of SCM into the lean, adaptive, customer-driven mechanism it has become is essential to survival and growth in today's global economy. These models of SCM have enabled whole supply networks to be collaborative, lean, agile, scalable, fast flow, and demand driven. Such high-velocity supply chains are capable of effectively and decisively responding to any marketplace challenge and avoiding risk by ensuring the right product can be configured, the right solution delivered, and the best service provided when the customer wants it at the minimum cost.

Yet while it is true that these methods have indeed activated superb networked organizations capable of near-flawless execution, they are, nevertheless, squarely focused on pursuing marketplace value from the perspective of the *supplier* and not the customer. Although each SCM model professes to have the customer as the objective, in reality, lean, adaptive, demand-driven concepts actually have as their prime goal the realization of company-focused performance measurements driven by processes capable of delivering the lowest cost and high delivery flow-through. The problem is that despite the success of these SCM methods, they all treat the customer as a passive player in the supply chain process. The concept is simple: marketing and sales shape and capture demand, production makes the products ordered, and distribution delivers the goods as quickly and cost-effectively as possible. Evolving to the next step in SCM, however, requires companies to construct their supply chains not only around efficiency, adaptability, and visibility, but also around the customer's perspective.

Case Study 7.3

 **Nikon's Search for CEM**

Nikon Corporation, a global provider of imaging technology, from digital cameras to film scanners, found itself searching for a way to differentiate its brand in a very competitive marketplace. As the company moved into the digital camera market, it realized that its strategy of selling through specialized dealers had left it without a clear understanding of its customers and their specific needs. In addition, Nikon had also recognized the decreasing brand loyalty of the marketplace as customers utilized the Internet to search for ever-lower price points.

The solution was to use customer service to deliver a superior experience that would provide Nikon with a competitive edge. The goal was to use the CEM philosophy as a basis for revamping a host of service processes targeted at providing customers with a positive view of the brand and the company.

According to David Gentry, Nikon's technical support GM, CEM meant "having ongoing conversations with customers to keep them satisfied and loyal for the long term. We needed to know data that would help inform those conversations, such as how we learned about them, how they learned about us, our mutual interaction history, and the kinds of products they are looking for."

The service initiative represents only the beginning step in Nikon's CEM journey. The goal is to improve the customer experience across all customer-facing touchpoints. By maintaining its focus on delivering a best-in-class customer experience Nikon hopes to keep its recognized marketplace leadership.

Source: Peppers & Rogers Group, "Turning Customer Experiences into Competitive Edge: Nikon's Journey to Leadership." White Paper, 2006.

7.1.2.1 Problem with Lean, Adaptive DDSN Concept[11]

Lean, adaptive, demand-driven SCM was created to address the critical issues facing today's supply chain. These include pressures to improve operational performance and profits, simultaneously reduce prices and enhance service, compress lead times, and deliver low-priced, superior-quality goods and services in the wake of global competition. The object of lean is to reduce waste found anywhere in the channel network, standardize processes across traditional vertical organizational structures, and optimize core resources. Lean supply chains also seek to create customer-winning value at the lowest cost through the real-time synchronization of product/service needs with the optimal supplier found anywhere in the channel, use of outsourcing to support internal process weaknesses, and deployment of technologies to ensure vital marketplace information capture. Finally, lean supply chains are dedicated to the continuous improvement of people and processes throughout the extended supply chain.

The role of adaptive, demand-driven SCM is to build upon lean's ability to deliver cost efficiencies and increased channel velocities to construct supply chains resilient enough to sustain competitive advantage in a business environment threatened by a host of risks, from shrinking product life cycles to disruptions driven by social, political, and environmental factors. The keynote of adaptive supply chains is their ability to rapidly reconfigure themselves in response to market events, such as the introduction of a disruptive product or service, regulatory and environmental changes, financial uncertainty, and massive market restructuring. In addition, adaptive operations and processes enable supply networks to be more capable of sensing and responding in real time to demand across a network of customers and suppliers.

Although many businesses have leveraged lean, adaptive, DDSN principles to achieve dramatic benefits in costs and efficiencies, the focus of these initiatives has all to often been squarely focused on improving *internal* productivity and profitability. The goal is to deploy these concepts to build organizations that facilitate company-level flexibility, process velocities, cost reductions, and the use of technologies, providing visibility and connectivity to local planning and execution value generators. While there is a growing awareness that much of the total cost of a product is directly dependent on the effective management of supply chain processes, companies have been inconsistent in their efforts to apply lean, adaptive, demand-driven network solutions in a systematic way to the entire supply chain.

Such a perspective has produced several outcomes. First and foremost, the focus is on creating value *for the individual supplier* and not for the supply chain and the customer. Despite their best intentions, these concepts are used to quantify company-level competitive values so that managers can improve the efficiency of their firms' product/service strategies. For the most part, companies are not very concerned with understanding customers' needs, the richness of the experiences they want, or how the customer really perceives marketing's value propositions. Furthermore, such a perspective directly supports organizations that are product/service- and sales-centered. The goal of this marketing strategy is to narrowly focus concepts and tools on promoting product functional features and benefits. This view understands competition to consist purely in product/service capabilities, where analytical tools are deployed to measure how customers rationally make tradeoff decisions between cost and feature. The mantra is to pursue "differentiation" and to ensure internal operations can achieve superiority in production, packaging, pricing, advertising, and distribution of goods.[12]

Finally, despite all the talk about the synergies to be realized by SCM, most companies today rarely extend lean, demand-driven initiatives outside their organizations. In fact, such businesses view information and customers as belonging to linear, sequential supply chains where product and intelligence is passed serially from one network node to another. The result is that the customer occupies a secondhand role as the target and passive recipient of the goods and services that have been forecasted for them by marketers up and down the supply chain network. In the end, lean, adaptive, DDSNs are really about promoting product-focused strategies with the goal of increasing company value disguised as customer-centered approaches.

7.1.2.2 Viewing Supply Chain from Customer's Perspective

It has long been known to retailers and consumer goods manufacturers that the most critical point when dealing with the customer occurs at the "moment of truth" when the transaction occurs. For example, Procter and Gamble has broken down this moment into two separate, yet integrated events: "the moment when a consumer stands in front of a store shelf and decides whether to buy a product and the moment when he or she uses the product and decides whether it meets expectations."[13] For such moments to successfully occur, however, it is necessary that supply chains not only be functioning at maximum efficiency, but that they are also intimate with what each node in the supply chain, ending with the consumer, experiences when a transaction occurs across multiple channels. The goal, according to Danny Edsall from IBM, is to be able to gain insight into what customers really want. "It's about getting behind the demand patterns so we can understand not just what a customer bought, but what he really wanted to buy. Then start using that to drive the supply chain."[14]

Getting in touch with the customer's experience, whether it is the consumer or a channel intermediary, requires a new perspective. When viewed through the eyes of the customer, the purpose of the supply chain becomes quite different. Instead of a pipeline mechanism for the delivery of value for the benefit of the supplier, an intimate supply chain provides for the continuous delivery of what the *customer* perceives as value. According to Peppers and Rogers, "Such an effort will manifest itself as a constant, unrelenting, and pervasive need for you to get into the customer's own head, to see things through the customer's eyes, to put yourself in the customer's position, and to treat the customer the same way you'd want to be treated."[15] The customer views the supply value chain from the following key perspectives:

- *Receiving total value.* Customers want value and *WOW!* experiences from their *value delivery networks.* Value for the customer can be defined as a brand, a service, a complete solution to an immediate or ongoing need, a feeling of dealing with a winner, a product that elicits a feeling of total satisfaction—all delivered exactly when wanted, without having to merge disconnected sources, with a minimum number of decisions, and with ease of effort.
- *Finding the ultimate buying experience.* As it becomes progressively harder to compete based on price, product functionality, standardized demographics, and passive customers loyal to entrenched brands, the content and intensity of

the customer's buying experience has become the top priority. More than ever, customers have the power to make decisions about what they buy, how they are going to order, how products are going to be delivered, and from whom they are buying. In a word, customers have come to measure value based not only on the quality and completeness of the product/service solution, but equally on the experiences they receive when they interact with their suppliers.

■ *Building supplier relationships.* Despite the wide range of multichannel opportunities available, customers are more than ever searching to build intimate relationships with their supply partners. Increasingly brand loyalty is being transferred from the feature–function composite constituting the product or service itself to the depth of the experience they actually receive at each buying occasion. This perception is even more important in an environment where the manufacturer's brand often passes through a network of intermediaries before it reaches the customer. A failure at any channel node provides the customer with a reason to switch to an alternative. For example, Wal-Mart customers are fully aware that their shopping experience is directly dependent on a chain of suppliers. Long-standing experiential relationships make customers feel that they will consistently receive an expected level of value, that they are in control of the purchasing experience, and that they are confident that the products and services received will provide the solution they seek.

■ *Conditions of loyalty.* Customers expect world-class products and services each and every time they make a buying decision. However, gaining customer loyalty is more than features and options. Today's multichannel business environment enables customers to acquire the same or like products at similar prices from an array of local or global sources. What makes customers loyal consists of a matrix of feelings and attitudes that compel them to stay or leave a supply relationship. Customer loyalties are primarily driven, first of all, by the *past experiences* they have had with products, purchasing processes, and support. Second, loyalty is driven by *attitudes about brands* such as emotional ties, trustworthy assurance, image, and innovativeness. Finally, loyalty is founded in, and reinforced by, the *conscious and unconscious beliefs* customers form over time about a brand and the type of experiences that they can expect when dealing with a product or service. In fact, loyalty experts say, "emotion plays a much higher role than quality and price in the decision to defect. And poor customer service is the most likely culprit in creating negative feelings that will motivate a customer to bolt."[16]

■ *Alignment of channel offerings and customer expectations.* Customers will always remain loyal to those supply points that are continuously reconfiguring themselves to remain in alignment with their changing requirements and expectations. Alignment can take place on many levels. To begin with, customers expect that the demand messages about product, service, and support they send to the marketplace will be in alignment with actual supply. This means that the pricing, product, and service standards developed by a company will meet expectations and open new avenues for customer intimacy and are not just a management statement founded on operational expediency. Simply, the advertised experiences customers can expect are the ones they actually receive. Finally, the whole supply chain must be flexible so that it can be constantly realigned to create and exploit unique competencies that simultaneously deliver the promised customer experience.

In the end, customers are increasingly coming to understand that the level of satisfaction they seek is the result not solely of the retailer or distributor they buy directly from, but is rather the culmination of a chain of supply network partners who are focused on creating the type of loyalty-building experience that can be achieved only when they are intimate with what makes each transaction occurring anywhere truly memorable for the customer. For suppliers the ability of their supply chains to pursue intimacy with the customer will determine their success or failure.

7.1.2.3 Defining Intimate Supply Chain

The ability of entire supply networks to provide absolutely the best experience for the customer that continuously wins customer loyalty while building highly profitable customer equity is the ultimate objective of the intimate supply chain. As discussed, supply chains were historically built to leverage mechanisms that efficiently deployed capital and productive assets to produce and distribute the best product/service bundle that maximized financial return. In contrast, today's marketplace is demanding that supply chains be organized around the *customer*, that they possess at each node the knowledge necessary to interact with, anticipate, and respond to each customer's individual wants and needs.

As illustrated in Figure 7.1, building a truly intimate supply chain requires organizations to progress through three distinct, yet cumulative, stages. The journey begins with the adoption of lean principles and practices built on top of SCM fundamentals. The goal of the first stage is to *supply the right product at the right time with as little waste as possible.* Lean, responsive organizations centered on continuous process improvement provide the gateway for the pursuit of adaptive, demand-driven supply chains. The goal of the second stage is the creation of *lean, networked supply chains possessing real-time, interactive information sharing and synchronized functions that enable rapid channel adaptation to meet marketplace changes.* Collectively, these two stages provide companies with the capability to be as lean, agile, and adaptive as possible to leverage internal product and service innovation, channel partner collaboration, and the synchronization of planning, logistics, and channel execution to rapidly respond to customer demand and market intelligence as it occurs anywhere in the supply chain.

Lean Supply Chain	Adaptive, Demand-Driven Supply Chain	Intimate Supply Chain
Characteristics	**Characteristics**	**Characteristics**
"Supply the right product at the right time with as little waste as possible"	*"Lean, networked supply chains possessing real-time, interactive information sharing and synchronized functions that enable rapid channel adaptation to meet marketplace changes"*	*"Lean, adaptive, customer-centered supply networks capable of proactively managing the totality of a customer's experience with a company and its brand at each supply channel touchpoint"*
• Value focused on cost/ waste reduction • Product/service centered organizations • Use of forecasting to determine demand • Outsourced functions • Continuous improvement of processes • Linear supply chains and sequential processes • Internally flexible and responsive • All customers created equal • CRM perspective	• Responsive, flexible, adaptive supply chain networks • Metrics focused on speed, predictability, constraints, and quality • Channel network collaboration and integration • Synchronization of planning, logistics, and channel execution • Use of technology for real-time network realignment, visibility, connectivity, optimization, and analytics • Demand-driven supply networks	• Customers the only source of competitive value • Buying experience as important as product/service acquired • CEM channel perspective • Understanding customers' individual experiences and behavior central to revenue and profits • Customer experienced-centered service culture • Succeeding at the "moment of truth" • Customer experience data as critical as operational data

Figure 7.1   The journey towards customer intimacy.

As companies master the management dynamics of the first two stages, they can then progress to the final stage—*the intimate supply chain.* The intimate supply chain can be defined as the deployment of *lean, adaptive, customer-centered supply networks capable of proactively managing the totality of a customer's experience with a company and its brand at each supply channel touchpoint.* Intimate supply chains are today's most potent weapon because they are:

■ focused on understanding not only the product and service needs of the customer, but also the totality of the customer's experience and how it can be used to provide distinct competitive differentiation

■ focused on ensuring that not just the customer-facing supplier, but the entire supply chain can collectively provide for the very best customer experience at the moment of truth when a buying opportunity occurs

■ focused on how the capabilities of the entire supply chain ecosystem can be synchronized to produce the generation of not only superior value for the customer, but also a superior experience that cements their loyalty and renders them "addicted" to the supplier and its brands.

7.1.2.4 Contrasting Lean, Adaptive, DDSN SCM with Intimate Supply Chain

The evolution from a lean, adaptive, demand-driven supply chain to an intimate supply chain requires companies to transfigure their organizations and their marketplace objectives. As illustrated in Table 7.2, the repeating motif is the conversion of marketing strategies from being product centric to customer centric. Instead of a focus on product life cycles, product portfolios, and product/asset/distribution channel P&Ls (profit and loss), companies pursuing customer intimacy perceive the intensity of the customer experience to be the centerpiece of their strategies. In addition, customer experience–centered organizations abandon cost-versus-service tradeoff thinking where the customer's experience is narrowly channeled to fit standardized marketing paradigms, and look to create organizations that strive to provide the customer with a truly unique experience by being motivated, competent, and innovative in continuously generating a winning experience.

Finally, of equal importance in the migration of companies toward customer intimacy is their perception of the function of the supply chain. Traditional supply chains are consumed with the pursuit of cost reduction and efficiency objectives.

Table 7.2 Intimate Versus Lean/Adaptive/Demand-Driven Supply Chains

Lean/Adaptive/Demand-Driven	Intimate
Product/service portfolio the central objective	Value of the customer's experience the central objective
Product/asset/distribution channel P&L	Customer/customer segment P&L
Product/service mix strategies	Customer value propositions
Focus on managing the product life cycle	Focus on managing the customer life cycle
Employees strive to standardize, channel, and minimize the customer experience	Employees strive to provide each customer with a unique experience
Sell-side channels exist to optimize cost-vs.-service tradeoff	Sell-side channels exist to benefit the customer
Lean, outsourced organization leads to marketplace leadership	Customer-centered organization leads to market leadership
Companies wrestle with channel conflict that drives pricing and margin pressures	Supply channels provide a unique occasion to provide additional value to the customer
Channel partners often assume control over customer relationships and break the producer-customer linkage	Channel partners are integrated and focused on providing a seamless supply engine for customers

The goal is to outsource peripheral competencies to third parties, reduce the bullwhip effect, and exploit technologies that optimize product and information throughput. Unfortunately, such objectives often provoke discord in the supply chain, as channel nodes wrestle with price, margin, and control pressures that atomize the customer experience and ultimately threaten customer–supply network linkages. Intimate supply chains, on the other hand, are intent on uncovering how they can be an integral component of their customers' buying experience. Intimate supply chains seek to create an emotional connection with the customer at each channel touchpoint. And finally, intimate supply chains build loyalty and add value to themselves and their customers by converging capabilities to form seamless, unified supply channel engines providing customers with a compelling product, service, and information experience.

There are several criteria supply chains must achieve as they make their way to becoming customer centered. To begin with, the supply network as an ecosystem must develop mechanisms to better understand what products, services, and *experiences* win customers and preserve their loyalty. According to Matchette and Lewinski, this "entails clearly identifying the specific customer needs and expectations the company chooses to meet—recognizing the diversity among individual customers and customer segments and the variability in the cost to serve different customer demographics and needs."[17] Pursuing such an objective means more than implementing the newest CRM system, collecting transaction data, and proclaiming a customer-centered strategy. It means moving beyond a single-minded focus on building supply chains built solely on lean concepts, asset utilization, and channel efficiencies to an approach that seeks to uncover what kind of experience compels the customer at the moment of truth when he or she is faced with making the buying decision.

Once companies make the transition from being product centered to customer centered, the next challenge is to focus on building supply chains that are dedicated to customer intimacy. As discussed in chapter 3, the complexity of this task depends on a number of factors including the depth of vertical channel network integration, the impact of a customer-centered orientation on channel costs and margins, the level of customer experience and intimacy desired, and choice of selective versus intensive market penetration. For example, the intensity of the market penetration strategy will govern how deeply individual companies are prepared to go into the value delivery network. If the choice is deep penetration, the company itself will be responsible for managing customer intimacy. On the other hand, the use of multiple network partners will require much greater coordination of customer intelligence and actual service metrics across several layers of channel organizations.

Mapping the variance between traditional and intimate supply chains is the target of performance measurement. Lean, adaptive, demand-driven supply chains measure success on how effectively supply and delivery network engines have been applied to matching channel capabilities and channel demand. The metrics employed (such as channel total cost, customer service, inventory turns, purchase days-to-cash) gauge the performance of supply chain activities necessary to promote profitable growth while seeking to optimize channel functions to promote total supply chain performance. In the end these metrics enable executives to determine the overall performance of the organization and the financial health of the business.

Although there is no argument about the importance of how standard performance metrics enable companies to be more profitable by being able to know how quickly and effectively they have serviced the customer, such metrics are, however, focused on the pursuit of one goal: *how to grow value for the organization by increasing return on customer.* The problem is that marketers are focused on amassing and quantifying data about what customers want so that they can improve the firm's bottom line. But while customers are sincerely interested in their suppliers remaining successful, responsive, and innovative, the metric *they* are most interested in is how their suppliers can increase *value to them.*

The radical difference between traditional and intimate supply chains is that the latter is focused on retaining competitive leadership by understanding what is important about the firm from the customer's point of view. Marketers in an intimate supply chain are, of course, interested in profits: they are also, however, focused on metrics that provide a window into long-term customer relationships and customer experience. Customer relationship metrics include such elements as customer attrition rate, annual customer value, and lifetime customer value. Customer experience metrics include level and types of complaints, perceived value of customer service, existence of sources of customer frustration and aggravation, quality and timeliness of information, consistency of corporate policies, and the ability of the customer to receive a personalized experience. Collectively, these metrics enable the drafting of an effective customer-centric scoreboard that can be shared with supply chain partners and used as a driver of continuous innovation targeted at retaining competitive differentiation and engendering new sources of customer delight.

7.2 Intimate Supply Chain Competencies

Just a few years ago a successful supply chain was measured by its ability to produce ever-expanding product lines at lowest cost, distributed through complex sales channels that emphasized low prices and incentives to capitalize on short-term gains and operational efficiencies. Today, leading supply networks recognize that they must excel not only at managing the supply chain flow-through by deploying lean, adaptive, demand-driven techniques, but they must also be capable of identifying what customers value and will reward with long-term loyalty. By providing

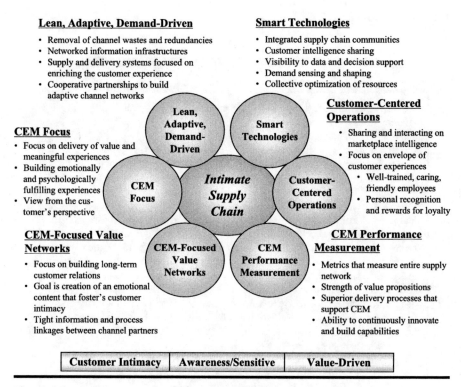

Lean, Adaptive, Demand-Driven
- Removal of channel wastes and redundancies
- Networked information infrastructures
- Supply and delivery systems focused on enriching the customer experience
- Cooperative partnerships to build adaptive channel networks

Smart Technologies
- Integrated supply chain communities
- Customer intelligence sharing
- Visibility to data and decision support
- Demand sensing and shaping
- Collective optimization of resources

CEM Focus
- Focus on delivery of value and meaningful experiences
- Building emotionally and psychologically fulfilling experiences
- View from the customer's perspective

Customer-Centered Operations
- Sharing and interacting on marketplace intelligence
- Focus on envelope of customer experiences
- Well-trained, caring, friendly employees
- Personal recognition and rewards for loyalty

CEM-Focused Value Networks
- Focus on building long-term customer relations
- Goal is creation of an emotional content that foster's customer intimacy
- Tight information and process linkages between channel partners

CEM Performance Measurement
- Metrics that measure entire supply network
- Strength of value propositions
- Superior delivery processes that support CEM
- Ability to continuously innovate and build capabilities

| Customer Intimacy | Awareness/Sensitive | Value-Driven |

Figure 7.2   Intimate supply chain competencies.

customers with unique opportunities to receive unique experiences that surround and permeate the moment of truth, intimate supply chains can build effective long-term partnerships that lead to dedicated customers and sustainable profits and growth.

Building intimate supply chains requires companies to move beyond the competencies associated with the standard supply chain management techniques available today. This is not to say that the attributes associated with waste and cost reduction, increased organizational agility, and the ability to sense and rapidly respond to customer demand is unimportant. What it does mean is that to be truly "intimate" with the customer, a supply chain must possess the competencies displayed in Figure 7.2. As illustrated at the bottom of the diagram, these competencies provide companies with the intelligence as to why customers feel they are an indispensable resource. They enable companies to be sensitive to the long-term needs and satisfaction their customers expect. And finally they are capable of providing a level of value that causes their customers to be addicted to their organizations and brands through differentiation on the customer's experience. The six competencies of intimate supply chains are described as the follows.

Case Study 7.4

Losing Customer Intimacy

We have all had occasions when a favorite store or product has lost its commitment to the customer in the search for greater profits and somehow the buying experience is just not the same.

Even a customer-centered icon like Starbucks can lose its way – and quickly! When Starbucks decided to switch from making its espresso drinks from scratch in favor of automated espresso machines, customers noticed that a former personal touch had now been eliminated. Regrettably, the new process objectified the buying experience – baristas were less involved with the customer, there were fewer smiles, and employees were less engaged. Apparently, someone at corporate had noticed that the machine saved time and time is money!

The moral is that as companies begin to drift from delighting their customers to taking advantage of them, they lose their corporate soul. One commentator felt Starbucks used to "be a delight, and now is a source of substandard, overpriced coffee cranked up with sugar and frills, not to mention snippy baristas with an inflated sense of their own importance. Unrestrained greed, believing your own hype, forgetting who it is that makes you a successful business, the Dark Side are they. Beware the dark side."

Source: Lager, Marshall, "The Devilish Drift," *CRM Magazine,* January 2007, p. 50.

7.2.1 Lean, Adaptive, Demand-Driven Operations

There can be little doubt that the capability to effectively and efficiently manage supply and delivery operations is at the center of the intimate supply chain. Lean, adaptive, demand-driven concepts and practices provide companies with critical toolsets that enable them to gain and maintain competitive leadership by continuously removing cost and waste from every corner of the supply chain, providing the mechanisms to remain as agile, focused, and free of noncore competencies as possible, and utilizing networked technologies that draw each supply chain node into a linked community capable of sensing, transmitting, and receiving real-time data about customers and markets. These toolsets provide companies with demand management databases so that the needs of the marketplace can be clearly understood. They provide the necessary visibility into the structure and type of supply chain necessary to respond to specific customers or market segments. And they illuminate the most effective methods for deploying supply and delivery assets responsive enough to meet customer expectations regarding product, service, and value.

Although these strategies are indeed pertinent and valuable, they are, nevertheless, efforts centered on how supply chain communities can do a better job of what they basically have always been doing: providing superior products and services. Intimate supply chains, on the other hand, view these operations strategies from a radically different perspective. *They require that the development, production, and delivery of the goods and services driven by lean/agile processes be centered on the continuous delivery of value the way the customer expects to experience it.* This objective is very different from being demand-driven or customer centered. Intimate supply chains use these operations performance and marketplace sensing models to discover not only the best products, but also the content of loyalty-winning emotional experiences present at the critical moment of customer decision making.

Intimate supply chains require companies to take the next step in the evolutionary process by designing supply and delivery systems focused on enriching the customer. Three critical processes come to mind. First, an agile, demand-driven supply chain is involved in continuously rethinking how products can cement customer loyalties, how they should be made and distributed, and how the buying experience can be personalized so that relationships with customers can survive marketplace change. Second, intimate supply chains view design, production, and delivery processes as an integrated whole in which everyone has a stake and participates in to ensure solutions that can be easily adapted through agile processes to meet individual needs while remaining cost-effective. Finally, customer intimacy is dependent on cooperative partnerships that can provide entire supply chain communities with the ability to network demand and supply events, shorten product cycle times, facilitate technology transfer and cross-functional resource participation, and enable information and knowledge-based infrastructures capable of being rapidly adapted to provide each customer with a unique buying experience.

Companies like IKEA are succeeding because they are serious about shaping their businesses and their supply chains to deepen customers' experience with their brands. IKEA, the world's largest furniture retailer, focuses on providing a superior customer experience in part from its integrated vision of supply chain and product design. Furniture is designed by cross-functional teams with an eye not only to customer tastes but also to channel logistics. By designing products to fit in easily stored, standardized packaging that is also easy for customers to transport and assemble, IKEA's strategy and operations are merged to optimize store delivery and customer carry-home. By encouraging customers to shop in their megastores versus online, IKEA can provide customers with a personalized shopping experience while pursuing low cost with an accompanying element of fashion and style.[18]

7.2.2 CEM Focus

Today's customer is presented with a marketplace characterized by globalization, product proliferation, and hypercompetition. What is more, customers have had to deal with ever-shortening product life cycles, the lure of low-cost multichannel sources, and an often bewildering range of choices that seem to push even the most sophisticated products into the status of a commodity. As previously argued, the convergence of these factors has caused a fundamental transformation in what customers value.[19] Although it is true that over 70 percent of products on the market are considered by customers to be undifferentiated commodities dominated by the utilities of price and convenience, today's customer is increasingly choosing suppliers based solely on the fact that they offer experiences that are meaningful and of value. The ability of customers to find the products and services they need at a desirable price has become easy. What has become of greater importance, however, is not the *things* but the *experience* surrounding the buying occasion.

According to Todor, customers have come to demand that the mechanisms surrounding a purchase event be permeated with opportunities to provide satisfying experiences, and they are prepared to pay a premium for the chance.

> Increasingly, customers value opportunities to reduce stress in their lives; moreover, they want to become engaged in meaningful experiences and to become immersed in authentic relationships. When a business offers an emotionally and psychologically fulfilling experience, customers will scrimp elsewhere to enable them to splurge on the desired offering. They do so because of the total experience, not just the product.[20]

Starbucks, for example, has built a global empire on serving customers a commodity product in a fast-food environment. As everyone knows, it is not for the coffee, per se, that they are willing to wait in long lines and pay a premium price, but the *experience* people anticipate and feel when they deal with the baristas who process the order, the coffee aroma permeating the shop, and the inviting atmosphere of relaxation promised by the décor. Other fast food shops, such as Panera and Corner Bakery, attempt to create the same mood by offering fresh, made-to-order products presented in an upscale environment complete with wireless Internet.

This growing emphasis on experiential value is perhaps one of the reasons for Wal-Mart's recently flagging sales. According to Fishman's provoking study on Wal-Mart (and as everybody has experienced who has shopped there), the retail mega-giant's unwavering dedication to low cost has produced a buying experience that is anything but delightful: "it is," states Fishman, "often work, and it can easily descend to drudgery and frustration." The vastness of the parking lot, the overwhelming size of the stores, the noise, the clutter of merchandise, "requires concentration and discipline and energy to stay on course." And as the prices come down, the delightfulness of the shopping experience declines also—"Wal-Mart isn't just cheap, it's joyless, when it's not downright vexing."[21] Discount stores like Target and Penny's have recently exploited this hole in Wal-Mart's strategy by offering more upscale products (at a higher price) accompanied by personal service and a more attractive store ambience.

Leveraging CEM to enhance the customer's engagement with the buying process, while increasing customer lifetime value, requires firms to undergo a fundamental shift from competing on price, commoditization, and standardization to competing by enabling customers to have meaningful experiences that build long-term relationships. This can occur only when businesses understand value *from the customer's perspective.* The goal is to uncover what needs to be done to get customers emotionally and psychologically involved in the shopping experience. When customers are excited about and immersed in the activities and experiences surrounding a buying event, they become emotionally involved, are willing to forgo the lure of price and convenience, and become vocal advocates for those companies that provide an unbeatable experience.

7.2.3 CEM-Focused Value Networks

Being able to create the level of continuous value and experience customers expect from the suppliers they have become involved with can occur only when companies have created a supportive and highly integrated supply network community. Traditional supply chains are characterized by disconnected data about the reciprocal dialogues that occur between supply points and customers concerning value and experiential involvement. As marketplace intelligence streams up and down the supply chain, information is used to chart how well companies are performing with their immediate trading partners versus how experiential learning events illuminate how the entire supply ecosystem is impacting customers at any point along the supply network continuum.

What is even worse, a company's decision to compete purely on price and convenience is antithetical to the intimate supply chain. In this strategy the primary objective is increased operational efficiency. Whether it means applying lean techniques inside the organization or the utilization of outsourcing to gain efficiencies through third-party capabilities, the quest is to beat the competition by always having the lowest price, "always." The impact on the supply chain and on the customer is the same: buyers are constantly on the lookout to shop as conveniently and as cheaply as possible, have minimal to no loyalty to the companies they do business with, and treat their suppliers in an adversarial manner. These dynamics encourage both intermediate and end-customers to shop around for a lower bid or a deeper incentive. Each purchasing touchpoint is merely an isolated and often non-repeated event where each product is considered an undifferentiated commodity, as good as the offerings of any other company.

In contrast, intimate supply chains are constructed to support the customer's desire to be engaged in the shopping experience. They must be able to continuously provide the environment for the emotional and psychological affirmation the customer has come to expect from the relationship he or she has formed with the supplier over the long run. Of course the customer is buying to obtain a concrete product or service. The difference is that intimate supply chains seek to build a loyal and engaged customer base, not by bidding for the customer's business, but by charging the buying experience with an emotional and psychological content that produces an intimate connection and becomes the foundation for a desire to repeat the experience.

The impact of an intimate strategy on a supply chain is dramatic. Instead of an adversarial environment where companies vie with one another over price and incentives and are subject (like Wal-Mart's suppliers) to continuous pressures to reduce cost and increase efficiencies or face expulsion, an intimate supply chain is truly a unified ecosystem where each supplier partner is an integral part of the whole. In place of short-term, cost-based objectives, the need for collaborative, long-term partnerships is paramount. Maturing such relationships can be a difficult task indeed as conflict can easily arise over decisions to change the channel structure or to embark on a new brand or pricing strategy that blurs existing channel roles and rights. Realizing intimate supply chains requires the presence of an effective channel master or steward who is continuously revising the supply chain's approach to customer intimacy, and then rapidly sharing the intelligence and integrating processes and metrics with the channel community in order to both continuously renew and deepen the customer's buying experience as well as enhance the performance of the supply and delivery network.

Case Study 7.5

When Wal-Mart Talks . . .

In June 2003 Wal-Mart issued its now famous RFID mandate and its suppliers quickly fell into line. Shortly afterward, they began shipping products with RFID tags, inaugurating the era of RFID.

At the end of 2006, Wal-Mart hoped to execute a similar strategy for environmentally friendly packaging. The five year program is aimed at pushing its 60,000 suppliers to reduce the amount of packaging they use by at least 5 percent while increasing their use of recyclable materials.

In November 2006 Wal-Mart kicked-off the initiative by rolling out its online "green" packaging scorecard to its 2,000-plus private-label suppliers. The scorecard consists of 7 key metrics of packaging: *remove, reduce, reuse, recycle, renew, revenue* (reduce without raising costs), and *read* (education).

In February 2007 Wal-mart voluntarily rolled out the scorecard to the rest of its global suppliers. During a one-year trial period suppliers will be able to evaluate their progress and benchmark against each other.

In February 2008, Wal-Mart mandated the use of the scorecard for all suppliers. It is intended that each supplier will receive a score relative to other suppliers as well as by category such as waste reduction, efficient usage, and packaging sourcing.

While the "green" initiative will not have the same force of compliance as the RFID project, it is clear Wal-Mart will be factoring-in suppliers' scores with future buying decisions. In the end, Wal-Mart alone stands to save $3.4 billion in waste cost reduction.

Source: Editorial Staff, "When Wal-Mart Talks ...," *DC Velocity*, December, 2006, p. 15.

7.2.4 Smart Technologies

The intimate supply chain requires technology tools that enable the timely accumulation and transfer of critical intelligence about customer needs and expectations. The objective is to close the gap between what customers want and what supply chains are actually providing. Realizing this goal means that all supply chain partners must have the same capabilities to receive and process information. In addition, each member of the supply chain community must be on the same page when it comes to intelligence sharing and owning the customer experience. Building such a technology community is a big order. To begin with, it requires seamlessly integrating a variety of ERP (enterprise resource planning), CRM, and SCM solutions. In addition, intimate supply chains will need to integrate other connectivity tools, such as web-based applications, EDI (electronic data interchange), and RFID (radio-frequency identification), which collect data and provide for personalized self-service. Finally, they will need to understand the impact of toolsets such as smart purchase cards, product life-cycle management applications, dynamic pricing systems, biometrics, and predictive monitoring.

The goal of intimate supply chain technology is to obtain visibility of the data and decision-support priorities necessary to closely integrate the customer and the supply chain, manage complexity, and leverage organizational adaptability and demand-sensing capabilities to meet customer experiential expectations. For example, at Zara, the international apparel manufacturer and retail giant, competitive advantage is based on its ability to electronically link its stores, headquarters, and global production network to design, manufacture, distribute, and retail the latest fashions before the competition. The process begins with the collection and transmission of customer style intelligence. Once styles have been identified, Zara is able to move from design to the store shelf in ten to fifteen days. The lightening speed of the process is made possible by linking fabric acquisition from global sources, and then outsourcing patterns, cutting, color treatment, sewing, and assembly. The key is to provide a source of open sharing of information across the supply network, which enables customer alignment with channel solutions, productive and distributive agility, timely response, and an experience unavailable at competing suppliers.

Today's intimate supply chain is deploying technologies that provide four distinct resources for understanding customer experiential dynamics. The purpose of these technologies is to enable a more cross-functional and cross-enterprise approach to creating the type of experiential value that keeps customers loyal to companies and their brands.[22]

■ *Business enterprise backbones.* The application of technologies to achieve customer intimacy begins with the implementation of business system softwares such as ERP, CRM, and SCM. These applications act as information engines for the establishment of critical base data, transaction management, information collection, financial accounting, and a bridge to web-based connectivity tools. Business engines provide companies with an institutional memory about the customer's lifetime relationship to the organization and its brands. Information technology (IT) systems in this area are used to *consolidate all customer information in databases that are shared across the supply chain network.*

■ *Demand sensing.* The ability to sense demand signals as they occur in the supply chain is critical to the establishment of customer intimacy. Technology applications in this area receive intelligence concerning the flow of customer demands as they occur at any point in the supply network, which in turn is translated and immediately broadcast not only to immediate trading dyads, but also to all levels in the supporting supply chain. Technologies in this space are critical to improving the buying experience by putting the customer in the driver's seat and employing the right CRM programs. IT systems in this area are used to *provide a complete view of customer interactions across all channels.*

■ *Operations optimization.* Once actual demand data is available, supply chains can network their business system backbones to streamline pipeline supply and delivery processes. Besides enabling supply chain partners to link and fine tune their operations to ensure customer expectation fulfillment, these software pieces enable supply points to optimize revenues based on a dynamic assessment of cost-versus-value tradeoffs. IT systems in this area are used to *engage lean concepts and practices to reduce costs and wastes at each channel touchpoint.*

■ *Demand shaping.* As intelligence about demand arising from existing products and services is available anywhere in the supply chain, marketing and pricing software can be used to open new opportunities for cross-selling and up-selling. In addition, as metrics regarding the actual level of experience customers receive is transmitted through the supply pipeline, supply chains can invent entirely new approaches to the product/service envelope that are more closely in alignment with customers' expectations. IT systems in this area are used to *provide customer-facing functions with focused order management tools and information to service the customer.*

7.2.5 Customer-Centered Operations

The ability to continuously deliver the type of experiences that make customers passionate about their favorite suppliers can occur only when supply networks are organizationally aligned across all customer touchpoints. Although products, prices, and delivery are generally perceived as the magnets attracting customers to a company and its brands, increasingly it is the investment in mechanisms enhancing customer experience that are determining today's marketplace winners. Accordingly, companies need to establish organizations that employ customer-focused internal resources and cross-channel functional teams capable of delivering a consistent customer experience.

Increasingly companies have begun to understand that the reason customers buy their products and services is the envelope of experiences they receive at the occasion of the purchase. For example, Starbucks' success is not about selling coffee. Rather, "it's the total experience," states HP's (Hewlett-Packard) research director Kathrine Armstrong, "at a Starbucks outlet: buying, drinking, getting online, etc." that has built an army of fanatically loyal customers. Addicting customers to a brand requires several key organizational attributes. According to a 2006 survey conducted by CRMGuru,[23] the top characteristics providing consistently excellent customer experiences were:

- *Well-trained and helpful employees* who are knowledgeable and passionate advocates of their companies and their products. Organizations driven by customer intimacy are staffed with employees who are challenged, motivated, and compensated to develop a truly rewarding employee experience.
- *Excellent customer service* that begins with a detailed understanding of needs and values from the customer's perspective. Companies committed to customer intimacy are focused on executing at those moments of truth that make or break a customer relationship by fulfilling customer expectations concerning the brand experience, the mechanisms guiding the transactional interface, and the availability of exciting innovations.
- *High-quality goods and services* that can compete when it comes to price, availability, functionality, and appeal. Understanding marketplace winners, however, is more than just quality and price: it requires the capability to deliver on the promises that move customers beyond treating the purchase as acquiring just another commodity to one where they feel personally enriched and connected to the product and the associated services.
- *Personal attention and recognition for loyalty* that rewards customers for their continued relationship with a company. Recognition can take the form of personal recognition when dealing with the customer, special privileges and memberships, or tangible rewards and discounts.

Moving from a strategy that focuses on managing products, transactions, and data to one centered on managing customer experiences based on knowledge, insight, and continuous learning requires a chain of networked organizations capable of continuously evolving to ensure the development of new service components and values to provide the customer with that very special experience. In the end, intimate supply chains are not really dependent on a single company's organizational structure: instead they are closely networked communities of customer-centered *cultures* drawn together by a joint vision of product and service excellence, grassroots entrepreneurship, people with the right skills and knowledge, and a passionate desire to get customers addicted to their companies and their brands.

7.2.6 CEM Performance Measurement

The goal of performance measurement systems is to provide a means of organizational control. Performance metrics detail how efficiently the company has been run, how closely marketplace objectives have been met, and in what direction the business should plan to move. Lean, adaptive, demand-driven companies perceive their performance as consisting of how much value their operations and their marketing efforts contributed to the bottom line. In contrast, intimate supply chains measure their performance by how much value they provided to their customers and in turn how increased customer lifetime value contributes to current and future profitability and growth. Intimate supply chains understand that return on customer is maximized when the customer is engaged in building a relationship with the supplier, when their experiences intensify their desire to buy more, and when they are self-motivated to act as advocates of the company and its products.

Actualizing these performance targets requires that supply chains pursue and effectively measure the impact of four processes. To begin with, perhaps the most critical measurement is how well the supply network is achieving metrics that discourage the optimization of individual players and encourage the joint performance of the entire supply channel community. Metrics should focus on the total cost of supply chain operations, profitability of premier customer segments, transactional cycle times, value of channel pipeline inventories, and purchase material days-to-cash. These measurements detail how effectively the whole supply chain is responding to customers' product and experiential needs, as well as the performance of bottom-line costs and profits.

The second process for measurement is charting how effectively company value propositions have generated the types of experience that enhance loyalty and build customer equity. The goal is to measure the impact of the value propositions developed for each customer segment. Have they attracted more customers into the high-advocacy, high-profit area? Have they fulfilled the experiential value proposition by ensuring the customer received the experience that was promised? In designing value propositions, companies must focus on the third process: engineering delivery processes that focus on the entire customer experience. Market leaders recognize that customers' experiences and attitudes are a result of the interactions they have with each supply chain touchpoint. While CRM systems are adept at providing detailed data, experiential metrics can be gathered only by listening to the voice of each individual customer.

Finally, the last process for measurement is charting how businesses can continuously innovate and build capabilities that grow customer loyalty and enhance their relationships with the product/service envelope. A key tool is customer-based metrics based on immediate customer feedback, which measures both successes and points out gaps for improvement. Operationally, managers need performance audits and monitoring that provide reliable, firsthand information about service execution, including specific service skills and behaviors both within the organization and outside in the supply network.

Perhaps the most critical part of this measurement is leveraging appropriate technology tools that can provide a window into company performance as well as customer perceptions and willingness to remain engaged with a company's products and culture. Available customer analytics solutions can essentially be separated into three categories.[24] The first, *embedded tools*, consists of technologies such as business intelligence, predictive analytics, marketing automation, data warehousing, call center, and outsourced services tools that enable companies to explore and build customer profiles and marketing segments, predictive models, and data sets that illuminate customer attitudes and reveal sources of customer loyalty. The second category of technology, *point solutions*, utilizes marketing automation, customer relationship management (CRM), and web marketing applications to define customer segments and profiles prior to campaign execution and to populate dashboards detailing customer lifetime value metrics. The final technology category, *enterprise platforms*, deploy enterprise resource planning systems (ERP), data warehousing, and financial/accounting systems to capture repositories of customer transactional sales data as well as interactional (behavioral) data. Business intelligence or predictive analytical tools can then be applied to these data sources to build predictive models, scoreboards, and workflows.

7.3 Summary and Transition

Today's hyperactive, global economy, where instantaneous communication and rapid innovation provide customers with an almost limitless ability to search for new suppliers and new goods and services, has shifted the basis of previous marketing objectives and strategies. Although lean, adaptive, demand-driven supply networks provide supply chains with unmistakable opportunities to reduce cost and accelerate the flow of goods and information up and down the supply chain pipeline, increasingly marketplace leadership is being awarded to those companies that can create a unique emotional and psychological connection with the customer that engenders long-term commitment and a strong sense of loyalty. The capability to capture and continuously improve on a customer's commitment to a supplier and drive lifetime customer value requires companies to be *intimate* with their customers; in short, to know who they are, what they purchase, what they value, and how they can be left continuously excited about new products and experiences the company has to offer.

This view of customer management is termed *customer experience management* (CEM) and it can be defined as "the process of strategically managing a customer's entire experience with a product or a company."[25] While the value of acquired products and services is foremost, the fundamental concept of CEM is to develop businesses capable of providing the customer with a unique buying experience that resonates with their personal psychological and emotional needs and expectations. CEM seeks to permeate the envelope of their product and service offerings with processes that provide customers with exceptional and fulfilling life experiences, build loyalty by making a connection with the customer that transcends the value of the offered goods and services, and finally, supply realistic, measurable approaches to creating value founded on the customer's conscious preference for a specific brand based on long-term patterns of expectation fulfillment at the "moment of truth."

Achieving CEM requires a new supply chain perspective. Instead of viewing it purely as a pipeline mechanism that benefits the supplier by driving efficiencies, cost reductions, and increased velocities, CEM attempts to perceive the supply chain from the perspective of the customer. Customers expect to receive value and a "WOW!" experience each time they purchase from their suppliers. Customers want to build relationships with, and are prepared to give their loyalty to, those suppliers that can provide the requisite depth of experience and satisfaction. Intimate experiential relationships make customers feel that they will consistently receive an expected level of value, that they are in control of the purchasing experience, and that they are confident that the products and services received will provide the solution they seek.

Intimate supply chains can be said to possess six critical competencies that enable them to move beyond standard supply chain management objectives and goals. The first enables intimate supply chains to be *lean, adaptive,* and *demand-driven* enough to continuously reshape the supply network to deliver the value the customer expects and wants to experience. Second, intimate supply chains must be *built around CEM principles and practices.* Intimate supply chains understand what needs to be done to get customers emotionally and psychologically involved in the buying experience. Being able to create the level of continuous value and positive experience customers expect can occur only when supply chains pursue the third critical competency: building a *supportive and highly integrated supply network community* capable of enhancing the customer's buying experience as it occurs anywhere along the supply chain continuum.

The fourth competency of intimate supply chains is the deployment of *smart technologies.* These technologies provide a source of open sharing of information across the supply network, which enables customer alignment with channel solutions, productive and distributive agility, timely response, and an experience unavailable at competing suppliers. Customer intimacy is impossible without the fifth competency: *customer-centered operations.* In essence, customer intimacy is driven by closely networked communities of customer-centered cultures drawn together by a joint vision of product and service excellence, entrepreneurship, highly skilled and knowledgeable people, and a passionate desire to get customers addicted to their organizations and brands. The final competency, *CEM performance measurements,* provides the metrics by which networked partners can measure their performance by how much value they delivered to their customers, and in turn, how increased customer lifetime value contributes to profitability and growth.

Migrating from a traditional supply chain strategy focused on managing products, transactions, and costs and efficiencies to one centered on organizations that seek to build long-term relations with their customers based on knowledge, insight, and continuous learning requires the construction of chains of networked organizations consumed with the desire to provide exciting new ways to create very special relationships and experiences that lock in long-term customer loyalty. The next chapter is focused on how to structure and operate an effective intimate supply chain.

Endnotes

1. See the comments in David L. Anderson, "Quick-Change Supply Chains," in *Achieving Supply Chain Excellence through Technology*, vol. 7 (San Francisco, CA: Montgomery Research, 2005), 16–19; and Kenneth B. Ackerman, "The Migratory Supply Chain," *DC Velocity* 4, no. 11 (November 2006): 59–60.
2. Peppers & Rogers Group, *Turning Customer Experiences into Competitive Edge: Nikon's Journey to Leadership*, Carlson Marketing White Paper (Norwalk, CT: Carlson Marketing, 2006), 2.
3. Strativity Group, *2005 Customer Experience Management Study*, Strativity Group White Paper (Rochelle Park, NJ: Strativity Group, 2006), 1–3.
4. Cited in Christopher Meyer and Andre Schwager, "Understanding Customer Experience," *Harvard Business Review* 85, no. 2 (February 2007): 118; and Bob Thompson, *Customer Experience Management: Accelerating Business Performance*, Customer Think Corporation White Paper (Burlingame, CA: Customer Think Corporation, 2006), 5.
5. Ibid.
6. Bob Thompson, *Customer Experience Management: The Value of "Moments of Truth,"* Customer Think Corporation White Paper (Burlingame, CA: Customer Think Corporation, 2006), 3–4.
7. Bernd H. Schmitt, *Customer Experience Management* (Hoboken, NJ: John Wiley & Sons, 2003), 17.
8. Thompson, *Customer Experience Management*, 2.
9. Peppers & Rogers Group, *Turning Customer Experiences into Competitive Edge*, 3.
10. John I. Todor, *Addicted Customers: How to Get Them Hooked on Your Company* (Martinez, CA: Silverado Press, 2007), xv.
11. Parts of this section can be found in David F. Ross, "The Intimate Supply Chain," *Supply Chain Management Review* 10, no. 5 (July/August 2006): 53–54.
12. Some of the ideas in this paragraph can be found in Schmitt, *Customer Experience Management*, 11–12.
13. Jean V. Murphy, "Moments of Truth in the Retail Supply Chain Are All About Return on Inventory," *Global Logistics and Supply Chain Strategies* 11, no. 6 (June 2007): 30.
14. Ibid., 32.
15. Don Peppers and Martha Rogers, *Return on Customer: Creating Maximum Value from Your Scarcest Resources* (New York: Doubleday, 2005), 29.
16. Bob Thompson, *The Loyalty Connection: Secrets to Customer Retention and Increased Profits*, Right Now Technologies White Paper, (Bozeman, MT: Right Now Technologies, 2005), 4.

17. John B. Matchette and Hans von Lewinski, "How to Enable Profitable Growth and High Performance," *Supply Chain Management Review* 10, no. 4 (May/June 2006): 50.

18. Ibid., 51.

19. Todor, *Addicted Customers*, 29.

20. Ibid., 2.

21. Charles Fishman, *The Wal-Mart Effect: How the World's Most Powerful Company Really Works—and How It's Transforming the American Economy* (New York: Penguin Group, 2006), 200–210.

22. Some of these points have been gathered from Mark Hillman and Stephen Hochman, "Supply Chain Technology Landscape Has Radically Changed for Everyone," *Global Logistics & Supply Chain Strategies* 11, no. 1 (January 2007): 12.

23. Thompson, *Customer Experience Management*, 13–14.

24. This analysis is summarized from Aberdeen Group, *Business Intelligence*, Aberdeen Group White Paper (Boston, MA: Aberdeen Group, January 2007), 7.

25. This definition is referenced in note 7.

Chapter 8

Structuring the Intimate Supply Chain

Differentiating Your Supply Chain by Engaging Today's Customer

Surviving the onslaught of globalization and encroaching commoditization has forced today's companies to move beyond dependence on past strategies for managing channel demand. Instead of competitiveness based on cost reduction, low price, and the "leaning-out" of every process, it is being argued that companies need to shift their attention to expanding their relationships with their customers—in short to be "intimate" with what customers really want, with increasing the customer experience, which in turn can lead to enhanced loyalty and commitment. All too often, companies have tried to become more customer focused by installing CRM systems, implementing customer care programs, and promoting campaigns to build customer engagement that merely mask traditional marketing efforts to simply sell more products to customers. Moving to the next level requires companies to focus as intently on involving customers in emotionally and psychologically fulfilling experiences as they do in ensuring operational effectiveness and cost management.

This chapter continues exploring how *customer experience management* (CEM) principles can not only support, but actually lead the way in translating customer engagement strategies into higher lifetime value by leveraging the tremendous capabilities found in the supply chain. It has been pointed out several times in this book that companies cannot hope to provide the levels of value necessary to continuously build customer equity without the enabling power of their supply network partners. The challenge is to build channel strategies that enable managers to navigate through the difficulties of developing an effective intimate supply channel. The goal is to transform supply chains from a loose collection of self-serving entities into a unified, integrated business engine focused on creating superior customer experiences and cementing long-term relationships that benefit the entire network.

The driving force behind constructing such a channel system rests on two components. The first involves the rise of a channel steward capable of concurrently building engaging customer experiences and driving profitability for all channel partners. This is a tall order. Whether by coercion or persuasion, the channel steward must be capable of shaping the channel's evolution and ensuring it is advancing simultaneously the interests of its customers, suppliers, and intermediaries. The second component involves the pursuit of three key drivers: choosing the channel design, aligning value propositions with customer needs, and aligning process value and delivery networks. The channel steward must continuously provide the mechanisms as well as the direction necessary for customers to build trust in the channel touchpoints they deal with, to affirm customers' feelings that they are receiving reciprocal value for the loyalty they keep and the sacrifices in price or service they sometimes must bear.

8.1 Economics of Intimate Supply Chains

There can be little doubt that today's business enterprise is under extreme pressure to provide differentiating value to a customer who is increasingly seizing control of the buying process. The source of this uneasiness has been described as being driven by several key trends:

- radically declining product life cycles
- proliferation of product and service choices available on demand on a global basis
- accelerating commoditization of products
- demand for lower prices, high efficiencies, and fast service velocities
- growing customer impatience toward dysfunctional experiences and lack of personalization
- declining loyalties enabled by diminishing barriers to supplier switching
- reducing the gap between customer desires and gratification
- expectation of faster *return on investment* (ROI) by companies and their shareholders

Up to now, companies and their supply chains have tried to counter these centripetal forces by applying strategies that more effectively manage productive and distributive resources. One method of increasing competitiveness is to apply *lean* concepts and principles that eliminate all forms of waste in the supply chain, while increasing supply channel velocities. Another method seeks to counter risk by building *adaptive* supply chains nimble enough to sense marketplace direction and then to communicate change through synchronized information sharing to network partners that enable rapid decision making and optimal execution. Yet a third strategy, *demand-driven supply networks,* focuses on identifying, broadcasting, and aligning supply chain resources with customers' true demand occurring at any point in the supply chain.

Although these strategies have enabled many of today's top performing companies to steal a competitive advantage, such leadership is doomed to be short lived. The problem is that these strategies are fundamentally driven from the perspective of how products, services, and delivery processes can be engineered to increase value to the company. Despite declarations that they are customer centric, most businesses are, in reality, focused on selling product features and benefits that bring values to them. Marketing campaigns seek to unearth statistics about what customer segments are most likely to buy what product/service bundle. Often these campaigns are accompanied by discounts and incentives designed to undersell the competition and highlight differentiation—that is, until the competition counters with a more aggressive campaign.

In contrast, companies focused on customer intimacy seek to build long-term customer value by centering their efforts on building sustainable and enriching *relationships* with their customers. While the product/service bundle remains the basis of exchange and growth, and profitability is still the ultimate target, these companies perceive their path to competitive leadership as providing customers with a positive buying experience that compels them to want to repeat the activity, despite the fact that competitors can offer a lower price or greater convenience in the transaction. By understanding what provides customers with not only a great product/service, but also a gratifying experience, companies can move beyond marketing based just on features and pricing and offer customers unique, personalized solutions that build what can be called *customer equity,* or the wealth-creating potential a firm can expect from the long-term relationships it has built with its customers.

8.1.1 Shifting Economic Paradigms

The basis of the modern market economy rests on the principle of *value exchange.* Simply put, buyers and sellers come together for the purpose of exchanging what each perceives to be a desired object of value. The conditions of the value exchanged depend on two factors: (1) the value content of the objects themselves, and (2) the experience that surrounds and permeates the process of exchange. The first factor is easy to understand and is normally considered as the basis for all value exchange. In this instance a good or service that is desired or needed by a buyer is acquired by surrendering to the seller another good or service of equally desired value (barter) or a financial instrument with an agreed upon abstract value (money). The exchange is purely a calculative affair, with each party to the transaction receiving fair value. The likelihood of such a transaction occurring in the future is based solely on the opportunity of each party to again enter into a fair value agreement; the buyer seeks the lowest price and the seller is intent on receiving a fair profit.

In contrast, while the second factor of value exchange is more difficult to calculate, the experience that permeates a purchasing occasion is a necessary part of every transaction. Actually, instead of being the most concrete, the first element of value exchange is purely an abstraction. Human beings *never* buy a product or service without the presence of some form of emotional or judgmental driver. Even as a product moves toward undifferentiated commoditization, the decision to purchase is never dispassionate, but always contains some form of psychological content that triggers a predilection for one brand or product over another. Whether based on a conscious selection or performed out of simple habit, emotional triggers, such as company logos, store layouts, or product advertising, can predetermine a buying selection despite the presence of competitors offering lower prices and higher convenience. Simply put, what customers value and will continue to reward with loyalty is autochthonous, not to the product, but to the experience they have associated with the product.

8.1.1.1 Abstract Concept of Exchange Value

Historically, marketing efforts have focused not on the experiential content of the exchange process, but rather on the product/revenue/market share perspective. In essence they assume that the purchasing process is undertaken by a buyer who is motivated purely by the exchange of value. This traditional marketing approach consists of the following points:[1]

- Instead of the customer, the focus is narrowly centered on product functional features and benefits. The value of the experiences customers will receive through the use of products is rarely taken into consideration.
- The content of target markets, pricing, and the threats posed by competitors are narrowly determined by comparing similarities in features and benefits. The goal is to present products/services not currently offered by other market players.

- Customers are perceived fundamentally as rational decision makers who carefully weigh features, benefits, and convenience against price. The exchange process is purely a calculative affair with customers choosing the highest value for the lowest cost.
- Understanding of the marketplace is based purely on analytical data that reveals detailed buying patterns and customer clusters that can be used to drive future product, pricing, promotion, and delivery objectives.
- Although the marketing approach does indeed assemble a rich repository of data about customers, it is transactional only and reveals nothing about what value the customer is really seeking during the buying process and after-sales usage.

The above principles have considerable weight in a market economy marked by scarcity and lack of differentiation in goods and services. In such an environment the seller has the power to determine the conditions of value exchange. Marketing has two objectives. The first is to build a high level of brand and company recognition that locks in customers and profits and isolates them from the narrow range of existing competitors. The second objective is to construct metrics that enable marketers to effectively target new customers and retain existing ones. For the customer, value is received in the exchange process. Issues such as unearthing what solutions the customer really wants, opportunities to explore new experiences with the product, or just looking at things from the customer's perspective are not considered. There is not much room for customer engagement and involvement when the only product available is a Model T and it is always black.

8.1.1.2 Experiential Basis of Exchange Value

In today's supercharged global economy, the concept of the marketplace as driven purely by the abstract exchange of value has been largely exploded. The key is the shift from an economy of scarcity to one of abundance, inexhaustible choice, and rapid change. Simply, companies can no longer count on managing the customer's sense of value by concentrating solely on the product/service bundle. As Todor has so aptly put it, companies competing only through product value

> use price, convenience, and incentives to win customers from their competitors—in essence, bidding for customers' business. Customers, in turn see abundance and choice for virtually all products. When competing businesses vie to win customers, they encourage prospective customers to shop around and to do so every time they need that type of product. There is a mismatch between this strategy and the expectation of loyalty."[2]

The bottom line is that winning in today's marketplace through product-price value exchange only is not sustainable in the long run. As companies lower prices (and profit) and increase incentives to keep customers who have been conditioned to treat the products they buy simply as undifferentiated commodities, they begin a death spiral of head-to-head competition with global suppliers as to who can offer the lowest price to attract an increasingly fickle customer. The death knell quickly approaches as they are submerged in an unwinnable war in Wal-Mart World.

The impact of an economy of abundance has been to place the customer squarely in the driver's seat. Regardless of how intently companies focus on building brand recognition and functional and operational differentiation, success is always short lived as customers gravitate to emerging competitors who can offer a lower price and greater convenience. To hold market positions, companies are forced into ongoing sales (Macy's and Target seem to have one going every week), rebates, interest-free loans, and discounts (Ford and GM), which provide disincentives for customer loyalty. Increasingly customers' perception of what provides value begins to be clouded as products and services slip, one by one, into the status of commodities available from the next lowest price seller.

As some of the best companies, such as Dell, Starbucks, and Target have shown, the path to competitive success is not through continuously leaning-out costs, endless product proliferation, and short-term strategies based on low prices and incentives, but rather through their ability to provide new sources of marketplace value *by building intimate customer relationships and loyalty through the creation of unique, emotionally satisfying experiences that, along with their goods and services, allows them to differentiate themselves from the competition.* Instead of competing on products and prices, these companies seek to cultivate special relationships that reinforce the attitude on the part of their customers that they are providing special value as well as meaningful experiences unattainable from another supplier. This view of experiential value as the basis of exchange fulfills customers' desperate need to find a way out of today's often bewildering world of massive product proliferation, the chaos of guerrilla marketers, and the frustrating feeling of anonymity when dealing with companies that have surrendered customer engagement and loyalty to strategies centered on cost reduction and short-term profits.

8.1.2 Building Customer Intimacy

The critical challenge before today's business is to understand the need to build internal organizations and supply chains centered on value exchange based on enhancing the customer's experience. Whether buying products and services to fulfill utilitarian needs or attain a personal sense of gratification, every buying occasion, even in the business-to-business environment, is charged with emotion and personal choice. The goal is to enhance customers' intrinsic desire to see the products and services they buy as a gateway to expand a person's knowledge and ability to tackle achievement of their own goals and aspirations as well as fulfill basic needs.

8.1.2.1 Emotions Make Experiences Meaningful

Each time we engage in the process of buying a product or contracting a service we are consciously or subliminally influenced by the repository of positive or negative experiences stored in our memories. No transaction is really ever truly emotion-neutral: even the purchase of the most mundane commodity is prompted by at least long-standing habit and inherent resistance to change, even if the outcome promises to be better. In fact, most customers feel stress, even anxiety about deviating from the buying habits they have grown accustomed to, the confidence and trust associated with the companies and brands they prefer, and the sense of satisfaction and accomplishment possession of the goods and services continuously brings them over time. People do not go to their favorite restaurant simply to eat or go to an upscale store just to buy products—they go because they receive a particular experience *surrounding* the exchange that they value higher than the goods and service received.

The power of emotion and sense of relationship customers have with their suppliers can be astounding. As a non-coffee drinker, I have been dumbfounded at the success of Starbucks. Coffee is a *commodity* pure and simple. It is available from a host of sources, often at a much lower price. Yet people across the globe cannot wait each day (often several times a day!) to pay a premium for a product that is just hot water, a little ground coffee, and some milk and sugar. The same people who will search for bargains on utility products will allocate a disproportionately high percentage of their daily allowance for the magic brew. The answer is obvious when you visit a store (we have two in our town, amazingly two blocks away from each other!): Starbucks has succeeded in establishing brand superiority not by advertising, but by building an experience that is part of the normal life of the community and customers' daily lives. The stores have become virtual oases where people can escape from the stress of the day and socialize with friends in a familiar neighborhood environment.

Successful companies like Starbucks, Amazon.com, Dell, and Apple understand that a memorable experience is the gateway to customer loyalty. For example, in a survey conducted by CRMGuru it was shown that memorable experiences build loyalty.[3] For highly loyal customers, almost 90 percent of respondents said a memorable experience left them with positive emotions such as "pleased," "comfortable," and "appreciated." On the other hand, customers with minimal loyalties felt "frustrated," "let down," and "angry." Such positive emotions and a sense of loyalty arise probably more from a supplier's ability to consistently deliver on the expectations set with the customer than executing an isolated "WOW!" experience. Finally, positive experiences occur when not just the product and the delivery mechanisms work, but also when employees treat customers with courtesy and attention to detail. Once on a United Airlines flight I did not receive a hoped-for upgrade. However, right before takeoff a first class seat became vacant. I was very pleasantly asked if I wanted to upgrade from my coach seat, which I quickly agreed to. I was thrilled to see (in an industry marked by significant complaints and hassles) that United recognized my frequent flyer status versus just giving the seat to a stand-by passenger.

8.1.2.2 Steps to Build Customer Intimacy

The basics of building customer intimacy involve shifting focus from instinctively turning to product and service design to improve customer satisfaction to strategies that enhance long-term customer relationships by providing individualized, value-generating experiences. Customer intimacy requires companies to design the right portfolio of products and services for specific customer segments that convert them from passive buyers to engaged promoters. Once designed, businesses must ensure that the internal organization as well as the entire supply chain can deliver their value propositions across the entire customer experience. And finally, intimate supply chains and the companies that populate them must perceive their value propositions and delivery mechanisms as dynamic, where sources of positive customer experience are improved and reinvented as marketplace needs change. To effectively pursue an intimate customer strategy that continuously delivers superior, differentiating experiences, organizations must execute the six elements displayed in Figure 8.1.

8.1.2.2.1 Define an Intimate Customer Strategy

An effective intimate customer strategy consists of three primary components: designing supply and delivery portfolios that provide consistent, relationship-generating value, eliminating sources of negative experiences, and consistently delivering "WOW!" experiences. Building strategies that respond to these three components requires a clear understanding of what the customer values and the relationships required to realize this value. Thompson[4] recommends using customer experience maps to identify positive and negative points of customer contact as a prelude to strategy formulation. For example, a simple map detailing my experience at the service station described in the "Introduction" of this book is provided in Figure 8.2.

The map illustrates the high and low points I experienced during my visit. The service station location was excellent and there was no wait to get to a pump. I was blown away by the pump. Not only was it clean and inviting, it had a TV monitor attached to the top part of the pump that provided an action-packed music video (along with a commercial!) and the price was a lot lower than what I was paying in Chicago. Regrettably, the fun stopped when I found that the pump would not take my credit card and I had to go in to pay. Once inside, my favorite candy bar was out

Define Intimate Customer Strategy
- Mapping customer values
- Identifying positive and negative touchpoints
- Charting economics of long-term relationships
- Charting economics of the customer experience

Align Organizations and Objectives
- Flexible organizations focused on customer value
- Customer-centered corporate culture
- Use of experiential marketing
- Effective employee recruitment and management
- Deployment of proper technology toolsets

Determine Drivers of Loyalty and Defection
- Determining customers' attitudes toward brands and experiences
- Use of analytical tools
- Isolating causes of negative experiences
- Building new ways to gain customer loyalty

Deliver Experiences
- Drawing the customer into the targeted experience
- Involving the customer with a company and its brands
- Providing each customer with a level of personal attention and rewards

Setting Goals and Defining Measurements
- Creating metrics that reveal customer loyalty
- Three critical components:
  - brand experience
  - customer interface
  - customer lifetime value (CLV)

Improve and Re-Invent
- Engineering innovations that deepen customer experiences
- Increase value customer receive
- Increase the intensity of customers' emotional triggers
- Project image of ongoing relevancy
- Involve the customer in experiential improvement projects

Figure 8.1 Elements in building customer intimacy.

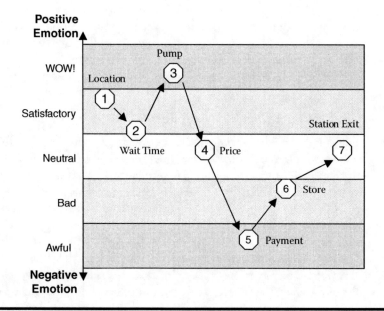

Figure 8.2 Customer experience map: service station fill-up.

of stock, and a gaping absence in alternative choices continued to sour the experience. Exiting the station was fine. In mapping this experience the station needed to accentuate its location and cool pump technology with a company policy that did not penalize me when it came time for payment and a store replenishment system that ensured my craving for the usual goodies could be satiated.

Isolating those touchpoints in the customer experience that provide value from those that encourage defection is essential to effective strategy development. According to the Strativity Group,[5] intimate customer strategies are driven by two financial components: *economics of long-term relationships* and *economics of the customer experience.* Long-term relationships focus on the long-term profitability of the customer relationship and are concerned with such metrics as attrition rate, annual and lifetime customer value, portion of customer's budget captured, and cost of unprofitable customers. Questions to be resolved center on the company's ability to execute strategies using research about what drives customer loyalty, differentiate valuable from unprofitable customers, benchmark customers' experiences versus those provided by competitors, and map what value customers feel they are receiving.

The second financial component, economics of the customer experience, is focused on metrics relating to short-term customer behavior and profitability. The goal is to measure not only the profitability of each customer's transactional interaction, but also the cost of failures in product and delivery that resulted in a negative impact on the customer. Among key operations measurements can be found the cost of help and service desk complaints and resolution management, returns and reshipment management, financial adjustment, and customer triage. Operations questions to be resolved center around value of order management personalization, capability of the customer to customize the transaction experience, capability of manufacturing, delivery, and associated services to meet the needs of each customer segment, and ability to meet customer expectations and requirements to execute the perfect order.

8.1.2.2.2 Determine Drivers of Loyalty and Defection

Loyal customers are the vehicle that delivers company profitability. Loyal customers tend to buy more, cost less to serve, complain less often, and act as a vocal promoter of companies and their products. Studies have shown that customer loyalty is primarily driven by three broad factors. The first is concerned with determining customers' *attitudes* about a company's product and service offerings, delivery record, level of quality, and extent of customer focus. The second factor deploys analytical tools and statistical techniques to uncover the image of the company's *brand* projects: are they best in class, innovative, and trustworthy? The final component driving customer loyalty is driven by the depth of the *experiences* customers have relating to the quality of the emotion they receive from the product and the buying process, how effectively the supplier engages the customer through personalization and participation, and the opportunities for satisfaction the product/service provides.[6]

Case Study 8.1

Jobs Says i-Sorry!

The recklessness with which even the best companies can treat their customers is sometimes dumbfounding. On September 5, 2007 Steve Jobs announced that Apple would cut the price on its iPhone from $599 to $399. Everyone remembers the hype, the long lines—the $599 price tag—that accompanied the release only two months earlier. Jobs was deluged by e-mails from irate customers who had paid full price for their iPhones, and were now complaining that it was too soon for the device to go on sale.

What a direct slap in the face to its very best customers who believe in Apple as a partner! To make things worse, Jobs had a solution: Apple will give each of the early iPhone customers a $100 credit. Jobs's apology letter revealed the real truth. The letter states "First, I am sure that we are making the correct decision to lower the price of the 8GB iPhone from $599 to $399, and that now is the right time to do it. iPhone is a breakthrough product, and we have the chance to 'go for it' this holiday season. iPhone is so far ahead of the competition, and now it will be affordable by even more customers. It benefits both Apple and every iPhone user to get as many new customers as possible in the iPhone 'tent.' We strongly believe the $399 price will help us do just that this holiday season.

"Second, being in technology for 30+ years I can attest to the fact that the technology road is bumpy. There is always change and improvement, and there is always someone who bought a product before a particular cutoff date and misses the new price or the new operating system or the new whatever. This is life in the technology lane."

Next time Apple releases a new product customers are going to give Jobs a taste of "life in the consumer lane" and wait a few months for the price drop! Apple's stock price lost 2.8% the following day.

As important as determining the factors driving positive customer experiences and loyalty, is identifying the causes of why customers defect to the competition. The goal is to pinpoint within the organization and outside in the supply chain, processes that produce negative experiences, frustrating moments, and lack of expected performance. At bottom, customers defect, not simply because they can shop around and get a cup of coffee cheaper at a mini-mart than at Starbucks, but because they feel that they are not treated well, that the buying experience is not customized to their individual tastes, or that the expected intimacy between themselves and the product/service envelope has been replaced by standardization and anonymity.

Maintaining current and identifying new ways to build customer loyalty depend on the execution of the following key drivers:

1. *Communicate with customers.* The best way to prevent defection is to open direct communications channels, which permit monitoring of the effect of intimate customer strategies on loyalty. Human contact can more effectively unearth customers' feelings about the experiences received versus what they

expect to receive, shifts in their wants and needs, and the perceptions of what provides value to them much more effectively than impersonal database analytics. This driver will assist in strengthening existing loyalties while identifying potential defectors.

2. *Eliminate sources of defection.* Diagnostics performed on customers' attitudes will provide an excellent repository for the identification of processes and policies that are diminishing the value of the customer experience. This driver will illuminate sources of disaffection arising from brand quality issues, erosion of trust in a company's leadership, policies, and innovative capabilities, and gaps in service and customer care that spawn negative feelings that motivate a customer to switch to a competitor.

3. *Provide quality and timely information.* The application of information technologies that provide detailed, timely information about the customer help reduce defection by ensuring continuous contact and delivery of experiences that meet customer expectations. Technology tools such as chat rooms, web submission, e-mail, and web collaboration provide methods for customers to interact with supplier organizations. Customers familiar with company brands and processes are more likely to remain loyal.

4. *Cultivate a culture of corporate customer intimacy.* Well-trained employees capable of identifying and delivering a personalized, value-added experience are the torchbearers of an effective intimate customer strategy. Those with frontline exposure to the customer must possess the tools and be empowered to handle exceptions and make decisions that enable the execution of superior customer experiences and sources of recurring value.

5. *Improve exit barriers.* A host of processes designed to strengthen exit barriers can be deployed. Among these tools are using customer information to customize the buying experience, enabling customers to personalize product offerings, reducing risk and increasing trust, deploying loyalty programs, enhancing a brand's "psychic" value through positive affinity, and maintaining a customer's attention through continuous value-added dialogue to retard customer defection by enhancing the customer's experience and overall relationship.

8.1.2.2.3 Setting Goals and Defining Measurements

The fundamental purpose of intimate supply chain metrics is to ensure that companies are providing valuable experiences to their customers and in turn their customers are providing profitable value in return. Product-centered organizations measure marketplace performance by how much value customers create for the business in the short term and how much share of the marketplace they hold. In contrast, customer-centered metrics are quite different from standard metrics, which focus on costs, shareholder value, sales revenues, and return on assets (ROA). Experiential metrics measure how effectively a company is delivering desirable customer experiences and consist of four critical components.

The first, *brand experience,* calculates how effectively company products and services are meeting customer expectations regarding quality, features, availability, aesthetics, and innovation. These measurement attributes can be ascertained only through mechanisms that provide direct contact with the customer. Detailed assessments can be made using communications mediums, such as the Internet, e-mail, and phone, and firsthand contact between the customer and product designers, marketing professionals, and survey teams. Non-personal forms, such as surveys and questionnaires, can also yield additional information. Finally, benchmark information from competitors and other industries about their brand experiences can be used to chart critical gaps.[7]

The second metric, *customer interface,* is concerned with tracking how customers' interaction with the firm impacts the depth of their buying experiences. This metric can be defined as the totality of the experiences customers receive based on all transactions and interactions arising at each supply touchpoint, whether performed in person, over the phone, or online. The interface acts as the vehicle for the dynamic, interactive exchange of experiential communication and value between the supplier's product and the emotional benefits customers anticipate. Whether it is proactive and convenient service, the friendly greeter at Wal-Mart, the luxury of the look and feel of a Macy's store layout, or loyalty programs, the attractiveness of interface exchanges and interactions is a critical determinant of continuing customer loyalty.

The third metric, *customer lifetime value* (CLV), is normally expressed as the present value of all current and future profits from a customer over the life of his or her business with a company. Companies pursuing intimate customer strategies view CLV as detailing not only the value *of* a customer to the firm but also the value of the firm *to* the customer. Instead of focusing on metrics that reveal traditional concerns with sales/share, product profitability, and satisfaction, customer-oriented metrics require marketing teams to concentrate on customer profitability, rate and cost of customer acquisition, profit and growth in customer margins, and cost and success in customer retention.

Goals and measurements driving customer intimacy will need to provide information on the long-term success of relationships and the ability to provide superior value and experiences to customers. Among the questions that must be answered are:

- What are the specific goals, measurements, and objectives necessary to execute superior experience for each customer or customer segment?
- How are these goals to be communicated to every part of the organization and each supply chain partner that impacts the quality of each customer experience?
- How are actual performance measurements to be fed back up the delivery and supply chains to the correct channel partner, company division, and individual company?

- What are the criteria to be used to ascertain the level of positive and negative emotions customers have received during their interactions with marketing, sales, and service?
- How are individual employees and supply chain partners to be rewarded for delivering exemplary experiences, and how can new performance metrics be established that drive new sources of customer value and engagement?

8.1.2.2.4 Aligning Organizations and Objectives

Consistently responding to customer demands for more value-centered experiences requires the existence of flexible, focused organizations capable of continually crafting innovative ways to plan and execute products and services, and deliver exciting new sources of marketplace value. Since the true value a company brings to customers resides in the range of engaging experiences it offers, successful organizations must be constructed around experience management attributes. Organizing for the intimate supply chain includes four tasks (Figure 8.3):

1. *Corporate culture.* All levels of management, as well as those with frontline exposure to the customer, must believe that the continuous creation of differentiated experiences that delight the customer is their primary task. This task is perhaps the most difficult because it entails integrating the experience management strategies of each channel network node so there is a consistent message to intermediate as well as to end-customers. In many cases fulfilling the customer experience will span organizational units and supply chain companies.

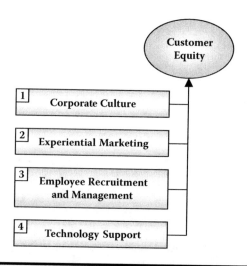

Figure 8.3 Aligning organizations for customer intimacy.

2. *Experiential marketing.*[8] Traditional marketing is narrowly focused on product features and benefits, and perceives the marketplace as a battle for customer share. Although marketers understand that image and emotion are part of some high-ticket items (automobiles, apparel, and jewelry), for the most part, customers are considered price-sensitive, rational purchasers. In contrast, experiential marketing requires a complete transvaluation of past methodologies. In place of brand stewardship, marketers must perceive themselves as engineers of brand experiences. The goal is to promote positive, relationship-building situations and integrate the experiences customers receive at all touchpoints each time they contact a supplier, enter a store, or log in to a website.

3. *Employee recruitment and management.* The focal point of effective intimate customer management occurs where customers encounter the support staff of their suppliers. Unfortunately, the presence of well-trained, genuinely helpful employees has often been forgotten as the prime activating catalyst in the customer encounter. In a study conducted by CRMGuru it was found that a company's employees were the number one attribute customers felt provided a consistently excellent experience, followed by customer service, and quality of goods and services.[9] Building an effective organization requires recruiting, training, motivating, providing meaningful incentives, and measuring employees' behavior so they can be creatively involved in discovering opportunities to deliver a memorable experience for each customer.

4. *Technology support.* Fundamental to assembling winning customer experiences is the deployment of the proper technology tools. To begin with, technology tools enable companies to provide flexible customer order and service interfaces, which enable customers to personalize the buying experience and assume control of the process. Another way technology can assist is to build and make available database repositories that can be used to customize customer contact as well as provide a kind of "memory" about the condition of the customer relationship. Finally, databases also permit the storage of special customer information, such as birthdays, anniversaries, level of loyalty, and special incentives and bonuses, which can be experience focused to provide opportunities to differentiate customers.

8.1.2.2.5   Deliver Experiences

State-of-the-art CRM systems and insightful customer offerings will be stillborn if they are not supported by outstanding execution. Succeeding in intimate customer management means that all parts of the supply chain must have their processes and their information streams synchronized and focused on providing the experiences customers want and value. Lasting customer relationships, the kind that produce sustainable profits, can occur only when customers have a compelling reason to remain loyal to a company and its brand, and these reasons must extend beyond current products, prices, discounts, services, and the newest "thing."

Deepening the customer experience requires the effective execution of the following critical principles. First, companies must design sales and marketing approaches that draw the customer into the experiences devised for the individual customer or customer segment. This process Schmitt calls the *experiential platform* and it consists of a

> dynamic, multisensory, multidimensional depiction of the desired experience (referred to as "experiential positioning"). It also specifies the value that the customer can expect from the product (the "experiential value promise" or EVP). The platform culminates in an overall implementation theme for coordinating subsequent marketing and communications efforts and future innovation.[10]

The goal is to turn passive buyers of undifferentiated commodities into active promoters who are engaged with a company and its brands and excited about telling others of their experiences.

Second, since customer loyalty is really a function of the customer's positive emotional experiences, rather than the mere possession of the product, businesses need to focus their effort on involving the customer with the company and its brand. Locking in today's customer means building gratifying experiences that fulfill their expectations and expand the value context from the physical goods and services they receive. Techniques include such things as:

- Personalizing the exchange process. Personalization permits the customer to use order customization processes to express their uniqueness through the goods and services they purchase by permitting them a voice in their design and creation.
- Mapping the customer experience on an end-to-end basis to identify the "moment of truth" at each touchpoint throughout the supply chain, so that interactions impacting customer loyalty can be continuously improved.
- Detailing what service elements are supportive of fostering customer involvement with the product.
- Enhancing the brand's differentiation and capability to stimulate customer interest to increase the total customer experience.
- Utilizing qualitative input from customers gained through personal contact, surveys, focus groups, etc. that communicate a company's leadership in providing unmatched sources of customer value.

Finally, companies need to provide each customer, whether corporate or consumer, with a level of personal attention and reward for loyalty commensurate with the depth of the relationship and contribution to company profitability. This step begins by truly understanding how customers perceive a firm's brands and the experiences they have come to associate with them. By walking a mile in the shoes of the typical customer, businesses can train and motivate employees and shape sales and service interactions that provide each customer with the human touch, respect, helpfulness, and friendliness that binds them emotionally to the company and its brands. Additionally, customers can be rewarded for their loyalty through bonuses and incentives that make them feel like a special, recognized individual with a unique connection to the companies they do business with.

8.1.2.2.6 Improve and Reinvent

Companies that are organized around an intimate customer strategy know that the experiences provided by their brands and interactive mechanisms are never static. What delights customers today can be assured to be irrelevant tomorrow. In addition, the competition is always waiting in the wings to replicate what may seem to be uncopyable product attributes, services, and engaging environments. Maintaining leadership requires companies to be involved in a continuous cycle of change management and innovation that generates new experiences and opportunities to engage in deeper customer relationships. Firms that fail to evolve or focus too closely on a program of cost efficiencies risk turning once customer-winning experiences into commodities and downward-spiraling irrelevances.

Innovations that enhance customer experience can essentially be divided into three classes. The most radical, but difficult to execute, are "breakthrough" innovations, such as Apple's i-Pod and Sony's Blue-Ray DVD, which dramatically changed everyday lives and spawned whole new industries. Much more commonplace are enhancements to existing brands and services that enrich the customer experience. For example, the addition of wireless service at Starbucks provided patrons with further reason to see the store as an oasis for relaxation and community. Finally, companies may deploy marketing innovations, such as promotions, pricing, and special events, that provide additional dimensions to the customer experience. In any case, it is essential that companies incorporate customer opinions about the experiences they want in any innovation project.

Innovation can contribute to expanding customer experiences in several ways.[11] First, it is essential to note that it is not synonymous with lean continuous improvement. Lean concepts are focused squarely on removing costs and wastes from the process of producing products. Intimate customer improvement, on the other hand, is centered on continuously deepening the experiences the customer receives. Second, experiential innovation increases the *value* customers feel they get when buying a brand or interacting with a company. Third, experiential innovation is focused on intensifying the emotional triggers that draw customers even closer into the buying experience. The goal is to move them from passive buyers to engaged, committed, vocal proponents of the company's offerings. Finally, a commitment to experiential innovation projects the image that the company and its brands are relevant to customers' current and future needs and desires. For example, Sony has had to change its value to customers several times as entertainment technology has migrated from VCR to DVD, video games, Internet services, and now Blue-Ray DVD.

8.2 Intimate Supply Chain Strategies

Succeeding in the twenty-first century requires companies to think beyond the boundaries of their own organizations to the supporting competencies of their supply chain partners if they are to build the kinds of experiences that enhance customer value. Leveraging customer intimacy strategies necessitates supply chain communities collectively providing for the very best customer experience at the moment of truth, wherever it occurs in the supply channel. By aligning capabilities to realize superior value for the customer, supply networks can ensure a superior experience that cements loyalties and keeps customers coming back for more. In the end, the goal is to create supply communities that continuously provide the right products, services, and interfaces that addict customers to a brand and its associated experiences while driving profitability both to channel partners as well as to the customer-facing company.

Intimate supply chain strategy is a detailed planning process that assists companies to transform their supply chains from a loose collection of business partners whose primary focus is on parochial objectives and performance targets to intimate supply chains where creating superior customer experiences and cementing long-term relationships is collectively the critical driving force. Creating an effective intimate supply chain strategy requires two major components. The first is a channel leader capable of continuously focusing and driving the strategy. The second component is the activation of several key drivers that will assist managers in identifying the attributes of effective experiential-based supply chains as well as reveal the barriers that block channel transformation. The components of effective intimate supply chain strategy development are detailed in Figure 8.4.

8.2.1 First Component: Intimate Supply Chain Leadership

Building supply chains that are capable of collectively executing the six elements of customer intimacy described above is an enormous task. While today's information technologies and strategies, such as outsourcing and collaborative planning, have increased integration and mutual dependencies, many supply chains are decentralized and dominated by the channel dyad model[12] where communication and collaboration rarely extend beyond immediate trading relationships. In other cases, supply chains are centralized and held hostage by powerful players, such as a Wal-Mart, that routinely impose their will on weaker members who have no escape. In either case, these channel arrangements poorly serve and reward all participants

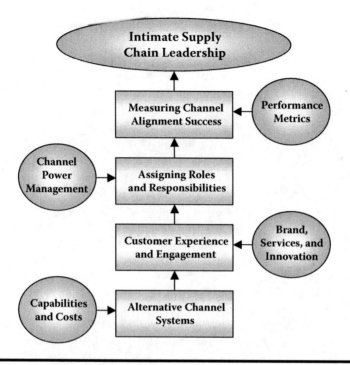

Figure 8.4   Intimate supply chain strategy.

and are incapable of providing the competencies necessary to generate the value-adding experiences that bind customers to companies and their brands. Left to themselves, such centripetal forces simply serve to further splinter supply communities and institutionalize local customer management decisions at the expense of overall channel capabilities to bring an integrated approach to customer intimacy.

Activating the power of supply chain intimacy requires a single supplier or a tightly integrated alliance of a small group of channel players to act as the driving force to engineer a supply network strategy that simultaneously builds engaging customer experiences while driving profitability for all channel partners. Such leadership could be driven from any vantage point in the supply chain: a manufacturer (Sony), a distributor (W. W. Granger), or a retailer (Home Depot). Rangan calls such leaders *channel stewards.*[13] Rather than demanding compliance from channel members for insular programs focused on cost reduction and efficiencies, the goal of the channel steward is to merge individual company goals into a unified strategy that views the entire supply chain from the perspective of the customer.

Practically speaking it is the role of the channel steward to unearth the different components of customer intimacy found in the supply network, devise a comprehensive strategy, and then to advocate change among all participants. When a channel steward can develop such a common purpose, Rangan believes, all participants along the way to the end customer understand, perhaps for the first time, the levers that motivate their partners up and down the line. As a result, all participants are better primed for the give-and-take required to create a value proposition that is as attractive as possible to customers and to the various channel participants.[14]

Stewardship involves carefully building supply chain synergies supportive of high levels of customer intimacy and deepening long-term relationships based on promoting those activities that enhance the customer experience, eliminate weak channel members, and reward channel partners providing discernable value to all supply chain customers.

While fusing each network member into a seamless value channel capable of generating winning customer experiences found anywhere in the supply chain may seem a logical and profitable management step, it must overcome a very strong natural inertia. Getting companies to collaborate on product, price, and service strategies is difficult even for channel masters who can enforce compliance, much less for channels to undertake on a voluntary basis. Even if integrating products and plans is in everyone's best interests and drives profits for all, the risk involved in undertaking a channel transformation may exceed the alternative of simply leaving current working relationships as is.

Still, the advantages of a virtually integrated supply chain are enormous. Whether by coercing or convincing supply network members, the role of the channel steward is to provide the focus necessary to effectively shape a channel's evolution to ensure it is simultaneously advancing the interests of its customers, suppliers, and intermediaries. During the process of aligning and shaping the supply chain to meet the twin challenges of increased customer intimacy and total channel profitability, the channel steward must continuously evaluate the role of each channel touchpoint and possibly require alteration of behavior or even make the decision to eliminate the network node altogether. Success occurs when channel players perceive they are actually part of a single community capable of collectively addressing the needs and desires of all customers.

8.2.2 Second Component: Intimate Supply Chain Drivers

The ultimate goal of the intimate supply chain is the capability of each channel member to leverage the competencies and resources of one another to build virtual communities providing customers with engaging, unique experiences that cannot be copied by the competition. Whether directed by a single channel steward or a channel focus group, the four critical strategic drivers found in Figure 8.5, and detailed below, must be planned and executed.

8.2.2.1 Choice of Channel Design

Architecting an intimate supply chain requires understanding the forces, objectives, and structures that drive a supply channel. Overall, the goal of channel design

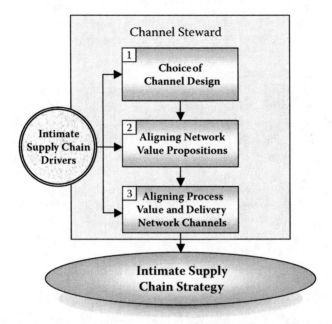

Figure 8.5 Intimate supply chain drivers.

analysis is to reveal gaps and threats and expose opportunities for customer intimacy that often are beyond the horizon of individual companies acting on their own. From the perspective of a channel steward, changes to customer buying habits, efficacy of branding, and challenges posed by competition, technologies, or even regulation that are unforeseen in the immediate marketplace are made plainly visible when viewed from a channel perspective. For example, questions such as "What products are customers buying?" "What channels are they buying from and what types of experiences are they gravitating to?" and "What are the capabilities of existing channels and how adaptive to change are they?" must be analyzed and effective answers formulated. The channel steward then has the ability to communicate or even enforce changes that will enable the entire supply chain to remain customer focused.

The complexity of intimate supply chain management is dependent on the nature of channel design. In a *transactional channel system* where the producer sells directly to the end-customer, the producer is fully responsible for crafting the customer value proposition and intensity of the customer experience. On the other hand, in a *limited channel system* where the producer sells through intermediaries, distributors and retailers are normally responsible for drafting experiential relationships and brand identity with the customer, with the producer performing a strong supporting role. Intimate customer management becomes more difficult, however, as the number of channel intermediaries grows and the end-customer recedes to the far end of the supply chain. This is the case in a *federated network system* where several businesses with equal channel power pool their competencies together and compete as an integrated network. In such channels, members must be sensitive to the experiences and value demanded by both customers and downstream intermediaries.

Choosing a channel configuration depends greatly on the nature of the product (custom or commodity), channel capabilities and costs, distribution of power in the channel, and actions of channel competitors. As the position of the channel steward moves closer to the customer, emphasis will be on superior service and deeply engaging the customer in the buying experience. In contrast, a steward positioned at intermediate or even producer levels will view customer intimacy as facilitating trading partner needs for efficiencies first, and end-customer requirements second. Stewardship in such arrangements can become more difficult with the arrival of a product/service breakthrough or entrance of a new competitor that pushes the need for greater involvement with end-customer experience management further up the delivery and supply networks.

8.2.2.2 Aligning Network Value Propositions

The concept of *customer value propositions* has become a fashionable term in business literature over the past half-decade. A *value proposition* can be defined simply as the portfolio of utility-creating products and services a company offers to its customers.

Unfortunately, value proposition creation has often fallen short because it has been narrowly focused on determining the value of a customer to the company rather than the value the company's brands and services provide to the customer. The bottom line is that companies often devise value propositions without seriously taking the customers' perspective and are unaware of the field of complex motivations that drive a customer to choose one product over another. In contrast, customer intimacy demands that companies become more responsive to customers and incorporate customer insight into their propositions. According to Schmitt, "They need to use customer input when they design the brand experience, customer interface, and when they launch new products. They need to use customer feedback to improve experiences."[15]

Intimate supply chains require channel stewards to construct value propositions on two levels: one that identifies value propositions from a local perspective as the complete experience a company delivers to its customers and the second from a supply chain perspective that is focused around shaping a supply network's total capability to address the needs of the *demand channel*. The intimate supply chain framework acknowledges that a value proposition platform developed in isolation from the channel community is much too narrow to deliver the total value customers now expect from their suppliers. The richness of the experience a company can offer is in reality closely dependent on the ability of each customer touchpoint (whether an intermediate or an end-customer) found along the supply chain continuum.

Building effective customer experience–oriented value propositions on the local level requires the following activities.[16]

- *Customer identification.* Synthesizing customer segment knowledge is the beginning point in value proposition generation. The objective of this step is to identify exactly who the customer is (consumer versus business, new versus established) and the intensity, richness, and variety of experiences expected. Other criteria consider profitability, behavior, attitudes, demographics, and impact of competitors' value propositions.
- *Proposal creation.* This step is concerned with two aspects: identification of the products and services to be offered, and the impact the proposition will have on what Schmitt calls the "experiential world" of the customer. The former is focused on features and benefits and attempts to hypothesize to what extent the proposition will bring in and retain more profitable customers and grow the share of customers' total spending. The latter is concerned with mapping how customer experiences relating to brand, product category, experiences provided by increased usage or consumption of the brand, and engagement with the company, reinforce customers' perceptions of the overall experiential value of the company.
- *Proposition testing and verification.* Before implementation, the value proposition must be verified using concrete tests. One key measurement is substantiating the proposed benefits by demonstrating and documenting findings. *Value word equations,* which assess the differences in functionality/performance between a supplier's offering and the next best alternative, can be used. Another tool is the *value case history,* which documents the cost savings or added value current customers have received from a supplier's offering. The proposition must track the customer experience along each proposed touchpoint. This step attempts to answer questions such as: What are customers doing at each point of the decision process? and How are customers' experiences addressed at each touchpoint? Finally, the value proposition needs to be matched against the value experiences being offered by competitors to ensure value-based differentiation.
- *Value proposition rollout.* After confirmation, the new value proposition can be presented to the customer community. Critical components consist of the anticipated brand experience (the product experience, look and feel, advertising and presentation), customer interface types (Internet, retail, catalog), and level of innovation (new solutions, new experiences, transformed image). In the end the value proposition provides the experiential position (proposition deliverables), the experiential value promise (specific values available), and experiential message (communication of the new proposition experience).[17]
- *Intelligence accumulation and analysis.* After rollout, the impact of the value proposition and possible modification must be tracked. The repository of accumulated customer intelligence provides an effective knowledge base that can be used for the next round of value proposition generation.

As important as local value proposition generation is, it is incomplete without the second level: supply chain value proposition integration. The critical steps at this level consist of the following:

8.2.2.2.1 Viewing the Value Stream from the Customer's Perspective

Intimate supply chain value propositions must begin by understanding customers' demand chain requirements and their perception of the existing value network. Four powerful value propositions come to mind:

1. **Intensity of experience**—exciting products and experiential environments will draw customers into an active mode, deepen their level of engagement, and foster emotional connections and a sense of anticipation that expands the context of what is perceived as providing value.
2. **World-class service**—customer service that provides personalization of contact and recognition for loyalty, along with rapid and reliable product delivery that differentiates companies from the competition.
3. **Convenient solutions**—processes that enable the customer to solve problems, cost-effectively, completely, and in a timely fashion with minimum expenditure of time and effort.
4. **Customization**—enhance product and service value by providing customers with easily configurable choices that permit personalization of the buying process and the composition of the goods and services desired.

The goal of the channel steward is to explore how each channel node can facilitate these general value propositions to drive intimacy at every level in the supply chain.

8.2.2.2.2 Value Chain Mapping

Intimate supply chain management is about extending the anticipated value propositions of each channel member to all customers served by the supply network. The goal is to assemble a supply chain that possesses the competencies and resources capable of serving the demand chain needs of a customer segment. A good example is Dell, which has constructed a unique supply chain capable of delivering the company's proposed experiential value proposition. As anyone who is familiar with the Dell story knows, the supply chain changed as Dell's value proposition shifted from a small PC upgrade business to today's giant provider of customer-configured PC and server equipment. At each transformation, the supply chain was reconfigured to accommodate new forms of marketplace demand and increase its value to the customer.

8.2.2.2.3 Scope of Channel Integration

There are three categories of channel systems that channel stewards can leverage to build the type of supply chain that will optimize their product and service offerings with the necessary value customers desire.[18] In the first type of channel system, *vertically integrated,* the supplier assumes the responsibility for all customer value–creating functions, from demand generation to fulfillment. Examples include Spanish retail giant Zara and Dell. In contrast, in the second type of channel system, *third-party delegated*, the supplier depends on channel members to identify and provide for the portfolio of customer winning experiences and engagement with the firm's brands. Examples include Cisco Systems, Ford, and General Motors. Here outsourcing, partnering, and collaboration are critical mechanisms for success. In the final type of channel system, *composite,* the supplier performs some of the most critical customer value–generating functions and engages network partners to perform the remainder. Examples include Sony and Ralph Lauren Polo.

8.2.2.2.4 Guiding Channel Evolution

If one thing can be said about managing supply chains around optimizing the customer experience and value perception it is that they will change continuously. Effectively stewarding intimate supply chains requires channel strategists to effectively guide channel evolution by focusing on three critical principles.

1. All individual channel member value propositions must be integrated to ensure the maximum value is generated for the customer and that everything from products, availability, and presentation to interfaces and delivery directly increases customers' positive experiences and sense of engagement.
2. Customer loyalty is often gained and retained by a company's ability to offer consistently innovative products, services, and experiences that differentiate it from competitors. Such value propositions require constant analysis of the value offered at each touchpoint to ensure the channel is focused on providing the right combinations of products and services. For example, Sony recently decided to open its own upscale retail outlet as well as sell through the traditional electronics retail channel.
3. Finally, channel stewards need to ensure that value propositions targeted at deepening customer experiences or new innovations are supported by channel capabilities. In addition, it is often the case that superlative channel capabilities can create new dimensions of customer value before the customer actually requires them. A good example is the seemingly never-ending evolution of the cell phone from a communications device to a handheld media center.

8.2.2.3 Aligning Process Value and Delivery Network Channels

The final driver needed to construct effective intimate supply chains is to ensure each participant in the channel community possesses a lean, agile, demand-driven organization flexible enough to enable them to continuously identify new sources of value and exciting experiences that attract and nurture customers into engaging, long-term relationships. Integrating these agile attributes into a single supply chain engine can be a difficult affair. The counterbalance of local versus channel performance targets, channel power struggles, engagement of players outside of the channel community, disruption caused by competitors, and differences in channel player capabilities act as centripetal forces rendering channel stewardship difficult and distract the supply community from their essential objective: *creating the highest value for the customer.*

There are four critical steps channel stewards must take in effectively aligning the supply channel community to achieve customer intimacy. The first step is to map existing and alternative channel configurations. The goal is to gain insight into individual channel partner capabilities and the associated costs of adapting organizations to meet new patterns of customer demand. This step will require realistic assessment of the type and volume of demand, the financial capability of the partner to invest in customer intimacy programs, and the type of pressure to be expected from competitors. Channel stewards can use the results to plan sustainable change based on how the supply chain is actually performing, the level of commitment in the channel to common goals, and what barriers they can expect to encounter.

Once the channel arrangement has been determined, the channel master can embark on the second step: organizing the supply network for customer intimacy. The goal of this step is to grow total customer equity. This means that individual companies must allocate adequate resources in the form of organization and employee skills to provide the right blend of the goods, services, level of experiences, and innovation customers want. The goal is to demonstrate a direct correlation between how improving customer intimacy directly contributes to increased loyalty and, by extension, to individual and supply chain growth and profitability. Saturn, for example, has attempted to provide car buyers with a system that enables them to pick the options they want while using the same information to reduce stocked inventories at the showroom, thereby enabling a make-to-order system at the factory.

The third step is concerned with assigning roles and responsibilities to channel players supportive of the intimate channel strategy. Based on the discovery processes found in the first two steps, this activity is centered on devising the individual functions each channel member must perform for the initiative to be successful. Important considerations must be given to trust and power sharing. Since supply chains are marked by an inherent divergence in goals and objectives, channel stewards must be prepared to enforce or persuade constituents to accept channel-centric strategies. A determining factor is the locus of channel power. For example, an organization like Menards can leverage its access to the market and detailed customer intelligence to command channel power, while a Sony can command compliance centered on its superlative and innovative products. In the end, alignment should provide for the benefit of all by enhancing channel value and total performance.

The final step in the channel alignment process is providing effective measurements that chart the success of efforts to align channel constituents with intimate supply chain needs. Perhaps the most critical function of the channel steward is to collect, evaluate, and report on aggregate channel metrics. Some of the indicators are obvious: gross sales, costs, market share, margins, order volumes, service levels, and so forth. Of greater importance, however, are other metrics relating to growth in customer equity that directly relate to customer intimacy management. In this category can be found growth in retention rates, increased share of existing customer spending, new customer acquisition, satisfaction rates, and identification of which experiences are likely to increase customer equity.

8.2.2.4 Intimate Supply Chain Strategies

The creation of an intimate supply chain requires the development of strategies that move companies past a traditional concern with product life cycles, managing brands and market share, and rating performance based on short-term goals to fresh perspectives that seek to construct buying experiences that are truly customer centric. The goal of the intimate supply chain is the ongoing enhancement of customer equity. Nurturing a loyal army of addicted customers, however, is no small task. In today's global economy no brand is safe, no customer is locked in, no relationship is inviolate. In fact, as products and services increasingly move toward commoditization, customers more and more consider themselves as free agents, bargaining for the best price with a variety of channel format players. This is a game that high-cost producers living in a "lowest price, always" world simply cannot win.

The solution is increased intimacy with the customer: an intimacy that allows vigilant, customer-centered organizations to provide a range of value propositions that commodity-type vendors simply cannot offer. The goal is to convert initial advantages in products and services (that can always be copied) to more personal, emotional, more lasting attitudes about a company and its brands that dramatically exceed the raw calculus of price. Todor has summed the journey toward intimacy by basing it on four processes:[19]

> **ATTRACTING** customers
> **CONNECTING** with customers
> **ENGAGING** customers
> **CONVERTING** the nature of the relationship

The role of the channel steward is to ensure their supply chains promote building customer relationships and accompanying customer equity. The steward must continuously provide the mechanisms as well as the direction necessary for customers to build trust in the channel touchpoints they deal with, to affirm customers' feelings that they are receiving reciprocal value for the money they spend and the recommendations they give, that buying a cup of Starbucks coffee or trans-fat-free pastries from Dunkin' Donuts is more than a transaction and is actually a conscious decision based on a series of past and anticipated future interactions.

In the real world of channel management, where the stresses and strains of blending often divergent network players is primary, customer focus can be lost. In tightly integrated channels dominated by a single channel master, such as a Wal-Mart, supply chain partners are highly focused on providing customers with optimum experiences and tailored processes that consistently deliver on Wal-Mart's value proposition. However, as channels become more segmented, even competitive, the focus on attracting customers and sustaining lifelong loyalties becomes more difficult and requires greater coordination. Regardless of the channel composition, successful strategies will be about how individual companies and their channel supporting partners can search for the right supply community mechanisms that will permit them to leverage their competencies to present their customers with unique experiences and emotional connections that will shield them from the competition.

8.3 Summary and Transition

The intimate supply chain is based on the premise that companies can no longer hope to remain competitive in the long run by focusing their strategies on cost/efficiency-centered tactics that emphasize commoditization, low prices, and incentives to achieve short-term gains. Instead, survival against the continuing onslaught of global competitors marketing low-cost products to an increasingly desensitized marketplace is to be found in an approach that moves away from a focus on *selling* products and services to one that attempts to capture and enrich customer loyalty by providing experiential values unattainable anywhere else in the marketplace. Furthermore, it is believed that this approach cannot be successfully executed by companies acting on their own: in short, what excites customers and draws them into an emotional engagement with a company and its brands depends on the ability of the entire supply chain to act as a unified community capable of stimulating the type of gratifying experiences that build committed, symbiotic relationships and grows customer equity.

The basis for customer intimacy rests on the principle of the *experiential basis of exchange value.* Instead of a purely abstract perception of exchange, where the value a customer receives in a transaction stems from a tradeoff between the price paid and the possession of the features and benefits inherent in the product/service bundle, experiential exchange focuses rather on building intimate customer relationships and loyalty through the creation of unique, emotionally satisfying experiences that, along with their goods and services, allows companies to differentiate themselves from the competition. The bottom line is that experiential exchange value assumes that customers are less interested in the "things" they buy and more interested in the range of value the "things" enable.

Achieving customer intimacy requires two major activities. The first is centered on executing a strategy designed to build customer intimacy. This activity contains six key elements. The first consists of designing supply and delivery portfolios that provide consistent, relationship-generating value, eliminate sources of negative experiences, and continuously deliver "WOW!" experiences. Once these positive and negative points of customer contact have been mapped, the next step is determining the drivers of loyalty and defection that are either winning or losing customers. Statistical and anecdotal output can then be used to drive the third step—setting goals and defining measurements to ensure the value experiences customers want are being offered, and in turn, the appropriate profit is being returned.

The fourth step is engineering flexible, focused organizations capable of continually crafting innovative ways to plan and execute more value-centered experiences for the customer. This step will require restructuring corporate cultures, marketing strategies, employee recruitment and management, and technology support. The fifth step is concerned with the actual delivery of the experiences customers want by synchronizing supply chain processes and information streams. The goal is to turn passive buyers into enthusiastic promoters of the supply chain and its brands. The final step is generating a culture centered on a continuous cycle of change management and innovation that generates new experiences and opportunities to engage in deeper customer relationships.

Once the intimate customer management strategy has been formulated, companies must then turn to building effective supporting supply chains. The text suggests three critical drivers. The first requires channel stewards to map the geography of their supply chains to identify key forces, objectives, and structures. Channel design answers such questions as: "What channels are customers buying from?" and "What are the capabilities of existing channels and how adaptive to change are they?" The second driver, aligning network value propositions, requires matching the channel's portfolio of goods and services with the field of experiences and values demanded by the customer. The final driver, aligning process value and delivery network channels, is focused on ensuring each participant in the channel community possesses a lean, agile, demand-driven organization flexible enough to enable him or her to continuously identify new sources of value and exciting experiences that attract and nurture customers into engaging, long-term relationships.

The creation of an intimate supply chain requires the development of strategies that move companies past a traditional concern with product life cycles, managing brands and market share, and rating performance based on short-term goals to fresh perspectives that seek to construct buying experiences that are truly customer centric. Building an effective intimate supply chain is a multidimensional affair that requires diligent management, supply chain supervision, and effective management tools. The final chapter is concerned with how technology and management toolsets can be deployed to ensure companies are focusing on growing the value of the customer. The proposition is simple: the prime source of value for the firm is building customer equity and this value in turn provides a detailed window into assessing the overall value of the business. As we shall see, building customer intimate organization will require redefinition of charting customer value and how technologies are to be utilized to gain customer lifetime value.

Endnotes

1. These points have been summarized from Bernd H. Schmitt, *Customer Experience Management* (Hoboken, NJ: John Wiley & Sons, 2003), 11–12 and Philip Kotler, *Marketing Management*, 11th ed. (Prentice Hall: Upper Saddle River, NJ, 2003), 20–25.
2. John I. Todor, *Addicted Customers: How to Get Them Hooked on Your Company* (Martinez, CA: Silverado Press, 2007), 16.
3. Bob Thompson, *Customer Experience Management: The Value of "Moments of Truth,"* Customer Think Corporation White Paper (Burlingame, CA: Customer Think Corporation, 2006), 10–12.
4. Bob Thompson, Customer Experience Management: Accelerating Business Performance, Customer Think Corporation White Paper, (Burlingame, CA: Customer Think Corporation, 2006), 8–11.
5. Strativity Group, *Making Customer Experience a Reality—Five Steps from Vision to Execution*, Strativity Group White Paper, (Rochelle Park, NJ: Strativity Group, 2006), 3.
6. See the discussion in Bob Thompson, *The Loyalty Connection: Secrets to Customer Retention and Increased Profits*, Customer Think Corporation White Paper, (Burlingame, CA: Customer Think Corporation, 2005), 4–7.
7. See the discussion in Schmitt, *Customer Experience Management*, 216–217.
8. The term *experiential marketing* was coined by Bernd Schmitt in his book *Experiential Marketing: How to Get Customers to Sense, Feel, Think, Act and Relate to Your Company and Brands* (New York: Free Press, 1999).
9. Found in Thompson, *Customer Experience Management: The Value of "Moments of Truth,"* 13.
10. Schmitt, *Customer Experience Management*, 27.
11. This paragraph is dependent on the comments of Schmitt, *Customer Experience Management*, pp. 166–188 and Todor, pp. 109–135.
12. See the discussion in chapter 5.
13. V. Kasturi Rangan, *Transforming Your Go-to-Market Strategy: The Three Disciplines of Channel Management* (Boston, MA: Harvard Business School Press, 2006), 9–28. The term *channel steward* was coined by Rangan. The choice of *channel steward* is far more preferable than the more commonly used *channel master*. The latter conveys a tone of command and compliance that is out of place in most supply chains, which are often loose confederations rather than monolithic channels as found with big box stores like Wal-Mart, Home Depot, and Target.

14. Ibid., p. 11.
15. Schmitt, *Customer Experience Management*, 46.
16. For these points, see James C. Anderson, James A. Narus, and Wouter Van Rossum, "Customer Value Propositions in Business Markets," *Harvard Business Review* 84, no. 3, (March 2006): 96–99.
17. These themes are explored in significant detail in Schmitt, *Customer Experience Management*, 86–186.
18. These three channel systems have been suggested by Rangan, *Transforming Your Go-to-Market Strategy*, 135–156.
19. Todor, *Addicted Customers*, 194.

Chapter 9

Methods and Technologies
Applying Methods and Technologies to Build Intimate Supply Chains

---

Creating supply chains capable of continuously activating deeper levels of customer intimacy requires the deployment of technologies and demand management modeling techniques that enable companies to concisely identify their customers, define the products, services, and the types of buying experience they want, and effectively measure the results of their marketing efforts. Unfortunately, most businesses develop performance measurements and establish metrics that are one-sided: they view the marketplace only from the perspective of how value propositions are growing revenues and realizing sales targets. While such product-centered measurements are important, it is essential that companies also be able to document how their customer experience management initiatives are growing long-term customer equity and what new opportunities for enhancements have been identified for future rollout.

Investigating how businesses can utilize technologies to assess the success of their customer intimacy measurement programs is the subject of this chapter. Essentially, the creation and utilization of effective intimate customer performance management is a three-part process that seeks to illuminate a customer's entire experience with a company and its brands. The process begins by first identifying exactly who each customer or customer group is and what the nature is of their relationship with the business. This entails developing traditional metrics, such as profitability by customer by brand, which will provide insight into the value of the customer to the firm. This opening process not only reveals what has been going right with the business strategy and illuminates future opportunities, it also provides metrics for measuring the brand experience and the impact of the transaction interface. These metrics will reveal the quality of the experiential features of the product and buying experience as well as the coherence and consistency of the total experience and product attributes emanating from across the supply chain.

Customer and experience identification measurements depend on the effectiveness, completeness, and accessibility of the databases compiled by the technologies and modeling techniques deployed. Although there are several toolsets available, the most common solution is *customer relationship management* (CRM). CRM enables marketers to perform two critical tasks. The first is to provide for the assembling of customer databases, availability of extraction and analytical tools for analysis, and automating sales and marketing processes. However, besides this *calculative* side, CRM also consists of another sphere concerned with identifying and documenting the *human* side— the customer experience that occurred with each transaction, and the corporate culture and the skills, motives, and attitudes of employees and management involved in each opportunity for customer service. Effective CRM metrics reveal both the profitability side of product and service value propositions as well as the capability of the company to engage the customer in long-term relationships that grow customer equity.

The outcome of developing successful customer experience measurements is to use the research to construct new brand-driven customer experiences that actualize core expectations, provide differentiation, and increase customer equity. Activating customer experiential technologies can only occur, however, when companies are dedicated to pursuing a set of *best practices* to ensure the experiential strategy remains focused. These practices begin with leadership to drive the customer-centered supply chain, and progress through the implementation of customer interfaces permitting customers to interact effectively with the business, motivation of employees, utilization of the proper channels of customer feedback, and activation of experiential marketing practices capable of identifying customer-centered goals, metrics, and organizational structures. These best practices must also include developing metrics for measuring the entire supply chain and not just individual companies.

9.1 Quest for Customer Intimacy

The objective of the intimate supply chain can be stated simply as the process of identifying the customer and his or her individual experience with your business, and then seamlessly synchronizing every point in the supply chain where the customer touches products and services to ensure the generation of continuous, unbeatable value and long-term loyalty. Successful companies today do not depend on size, global reach, brand, or even innovativeness. What makes companies like Starbucks, Sony, Apple, Hewlett Packard, and others marketplace leaders is that they have developed a new way of doing business that is profoundly different from their competitors: *they have put customer intimacy at the center of their business proposition.*

It is the contention of this book that sooner or later *every* company will have to reinvent its business to be intimate with its customers. The reasons are overwhelming. Globalization and downward pressures on prices have threatened to reduce every company's competitive advantage to a short-term advantage. Commoditization and competition based on low cost have left customers desensitized to even the most complex product and service as they surf the web for the best price and convenience of delivery and payment. The solution is to build companies that understand that it is the *total experience,* the opportunity to engage in authentic relationships with their customers, which will lock in long-term loyalty and grow profitability. Customers return again and again because the firm delivers what customers value, something they find important to their lives above the utilitarian possession of a good or service.

In an intimate supply chain, companies think of themselves not as the producers and marketers of a portfolio of brands, sales territories, and productive resources, but rather as a "portfolio of customers."[1] It has often been said that a company has no business without its customers. A company focused on customer intimacy not only understands that its customers are the lifeblood of its success, but also understands that the only way to make them more profitable, grow them into bigger customers, and serve them more effectively is to provide them with value propositions that see things from the customer's perspective, that puts the company in the customer's shoes, that demands the company treat customers the way they would like to be treated. In short, an intimate supply chain understands *it can influence customers' behavior by understanding its value to the customer.*

9.1.1 Focusing on Customer

In their article on developing intimate customer strategies, Gulati and Oldroyd have theorized that successful firms consistently embrace three customer-centered disciplines.[2] First, customer intimacy can be gained only by possessing a detailed knowledge of everything there is to know about the customers: their expectations about products and services, past experiences, loyalties, future needs, and how they feel about the competition. Second, businesses know that this comprehensive portrait of the customer is worthless if employees can't or won't share what they have learned about the customer with each other and their supply chain communities. And finally, firms can effectively leverage this insight only when they possess the right technologies, organizations, and people skills to convert this knowledge into seedbeds to grow customer equity. As they become more skilled at tapping into the customer knowledge base, they uncover new and more sophisticated methods of engaging the customer and incorporating new drivers that build extraordinary experiences and lock in long-term loyalties that span the entire supply chain.

9.1.1.1   Three Dimensions of Intimate Customer Management

If there was one thing revolutionary about the dot-com era it was the enormous valuations companies like Amazon.com and E-Bay amassed with the bare minimum of physical assets. What made such companies valuable was their access to massive customer databases. Simply put, customer management has become *the* competitive advantage of today's global economy. Instead of building leadership based on products and prices, companies are quickly realizing that it is about the size and loyalty of their customer base and the ability to give the customers exactly what they want, when, where, and how they want it, and encapsulated in an experience designed just for them that is today's source of value. The businesses that are succeeding today know they must build lean, adaptive, demand-driven organizations capable of eliminating costs, aggregating resources, and tapping into the competencies of channel business partners to produce a complete solution and full-service processes for their customers.

It is a well-known fact that over 75 percent of customers defect to competitors for reasons associated with a poor buying experience.[3] The product features and benefits offered may have been fine; it is just that the *emotional* portion of the experience was so poor the customer decided not to repeat the process. Instead of a single view of what the *average* customer expects from a product/service/price envelope, customer intimacy demands discovering what each *individual* customer wants and expects from a buying experience. In this sense there are three dimensions marketers must analyze in their effort to construct experiences that will retain customer loyalty.

The first dimension consists of understanding *customer valuation*. Compared to the complexities of the other two dimensions, this is a straightforward task. It consists of calculating the metrics needed to determine and segment what value brands and services have had on each customer group. *Customer relationship management* (CRM) systems, data-mining tools, market segmentation analysis, and other techniques enable marketers to slice and dice their databases in an effort to uncover customer stratifications that reveal the most profitable groupings of products and customers. While providing a blueprint for product development, customer care, pricing, advertising, and promotions, this dimension has the drawback that in searching for customer commonality, it misses the mark of considering each customer, one at a time.

The second dimension of intimate customer management is more complex and consists in understanding the *motivations* driving customer loyalties. Customers buy products from a supplier driven by a particular reason. Unearthing that reason and then designing products and experiences that validate and expand on the customer's motive to continue buying is the central focus of this dimension. Motives can run the gamut from pure habit, perceptions of quality, and reputation to status, service, and proven commitment to the customer. For example, an affluent customer may find the purchase of a Lexus to be driven by a desire for quality and comfort, while a less-affluent customer may be focusing on status. The problem is that companies often encounter a wide range of motives from different customer groups; sometimes a customer may buy for multiple motives with the intent of the buying occasion determining which motive is the key driver.

The final dimension, customer *experiences,* is the most difficult to identify and create product and service avenues for fulfillment. Experiences differ from motivations in that the latter is normally the result of a combination of customer desires and learned mechanisms of achieving satisfaction, whereas an experience is always a unique event that occurs with the customer's participation. Motivations are driven by desires that "awaken, seize, titillate, and arouse. Passionate customers are consumed by desire."[4] Desire awakens customers' emotional and mental involvement; it draws them toward a particular product or service. In contrast, an experience is a collection of points during which "a company and its customers exchange sensory stimuli, information, and emotion."[5] The outcome of any experience is always unique and is influenced by a customer's memories, present mood, psychological disposition, life stage, needs, expectations, aspirations, and fears, which may never be present in quite the same way.

9.1.1.2 Stages of Effective Customer Experience Management

Intimate customer management is concerned with a set of interlocking objectives: identifying what customers want, what provides them with value, how businesses can shape product and service offerings that motivate a customer to buy, and that excite and delight at the occasion of the buying transaction. Recognizing these experiential drivers is often a challenge to businesses. They know a lot about their products and services and where they have been sold, but often little about why customers purchased them, the range of experiences they encountered at the moment of transaction, and the connected fulfillment they received when the products were applied to satisfy the motives that spurred their acquisition in the first place. Supply chains can be expected to pass through four stages of intimate customer awareness as illustrated in Figure 9.1.[6]

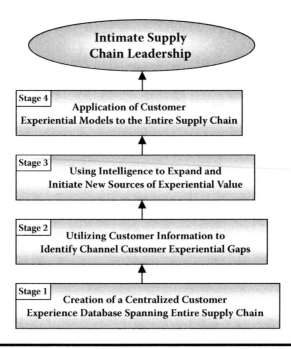

Figure 9.1   Stages of intimate customer awareness.

In the first stage, individual companies and their collective supply chain part-ners are engaged in creating a centralized data repository containing the details of each transaction with each customer. This is a two-part process. In the first part, companies assemble and standardize information about the customer from each channel touchpoint into a single information resource. The creation of such a repository requires a significant effort in time and technologies. Among the issues are overcoming internal and external barriers to information sharing, loss of con-trol, managing the sheer size of the data pool, and devising useful reporting and dashboard access. A critical requirement is to separate normal operational data (sales statistics, territories, sales professionals, etc.) from customer data that can be readily extracted for analytics and modeling.

The second part of creating a centralized customer repository is organizing this information so that meaningful data can be abstracted by individual customer rather than by product, account, or location. Often this will mean aggregating and collating transaction data among several definitions of what constitutes a customer as determined by interrelated channel constituents. The resulting data repository will allow supply network partners to see service to the customer as an end-to-end process, expose gaps in individual supplier processes and channel connective flows, reveal inefficiencies, and illuminate opportunities for cross- and up-selling as customers' real motives and anticipated experiences become visible to the entire channel. Once the databases for intimate customer intelligence have been constructed, supply chains can move to the second stage—customer knowledge sharing.

In the second stage of customer experience management, companies are concerned with utilizing customer information to demarcate channel partner boundaries to isolate sources of customer performance and provide visibility to gaps found in the supply chain. This intelligence can be used in several ways. It can assist individual companies to improve and re-target their product and service bundle. It can illustrate areas where customer motives and experiences are mismatched with the company strategy. Finally, statistical and anecdotal evidence can be used to guide channel recalibration as visibility to downstream partner insufficiencies is documented. The role of the channel steward emerges in this stage. The channel steward is charged with the neutral assemblage of data, correlation into useable analytics and marketing information, communication to channel members, and enforcement/persuasion of findings as a guide to engage in change management with channel members.

In the third stage, supply chain entities not only seek to exploit past intelligence to better match their offerings with what customers are demanding, they also actively search for opportunities to anticipate how they and their channel partners can influence customer motives and get them more engaged in participating in new experiences. This stage contains several key activities. To begin with, businesses must review all processes they control, and identify and eliminate all interactions producing a negative experience. Both employee feedback and transaction metrics can be employed to observe and document negative emotional reactions. Second, companies must develop models that are focused on expanding positive customer behavior. These models should hypothesize how to get customers mentally and emotionally involved by imagining what it is that customers desire and the feeling of experiential fulfillment a successful encounter produces on customer loyalty. The actual product/service received is just the portal to the experience. Finally, the best model should be implemented, the results tracked, and opportunities for enhancements identified to guide future rollouts.

In the final, and most difficult of the four stages, the channel steward, lead company, or channel coalition must apply the customer experiential models developed in stage three to the entire supply chain. Implementers can encounter several barriers. Individual channel partner organizations may be ill-suited for the required coordination, information sharing, and marketing approach. Technology capabilities may be at incompatible levels. Required alterations in product/service bundles, types of customer experiences offered, and integration with channel partners may be antipodal to individual company strategies. Removing impediments to supply chain customer intimacy is definitely influenced by channel power relationships. A channel dominated by a Wal-Mart or a Target is quickly aligned with the customer experiential strategy of the primary player. On the other hand, channels with dispersed power will need the direction of an effective channel steward to keep channel players focused on the experiential marketing objective.

9.2 Working with Customer Management Technologies

The fundamental barrier inhibiting companies from constructing intimate businesses and supply chains is the availability and utilization of technologies enabling them to be intimate with their customers' wants and needs. Marketing departments have long depended on gut feelings, supported by transactional statistics and anecdotal reporting, to determine the direction of company products, resources, and profits. Over the past decade, firms have invested heavily in enabling technologies to provide new insights, techniques, and capabilities to assist in answering the big questions surrounding strategy and growth. *Customer relationship management* (CRM), web analytics, business intelligence platforms, and sales and marketing automation solutions have been widely deployed to meet these challenges. However, while database engines like *enterprise resource planning* (ERP) and CRM have facilitated the ability of companies to derive meaningful information that can be used for statistical analysis and guiding planning and execution of marketing initiatives, they have been unable to provide the levels of intimacy with a customer who today expects a seamless, multichannel, individualized experience at every touchpoint.

Some of this lack of focus is due to the changing historical role of the customer. Managing customers in the past was relatively easy: a company proposed a product or service, and customers came and bought it. Today, we live in a global economy where companies must leverage a supply chain community to provide the right experience and customer information from data repositories scattered across the globe. Much of the reason for the failure of customer management technologies, however, resides in their use. As Arussy[7] points out, humans have a spotty track record of making decisions by applying available and relevant information. The reality is that there is just so much data today that analysis can often be rendered conflicting and confusing. Finally, the objective of technologies can be misdirected into being used primarily to embed current business practices and assumptions versus providing professionals with tools to ask new, disruptive questions and stimulate novel answers focused on radical change and growth.

9.2.1 Defining Today's Customer Management Technologies

The range of technologies grouped around the concept of CRM has, for almost a decade, meant big business. CRM spending was reported as growing as much as 12 percent in 2006 with software revenues rising to $12.6 billion. Looking ahead,

AMR Research expects the CRM industry to expand to $19.2 billion in the next four years.[8] Although this continued interest can be attributed to the requirement for companies to explore the marketplace more fully to better serve the customer, there can be little doubt this growth has been driven by the recognition that CRM is more than just a marketing software platform: in today's global environment it has been identified as an essential part of the suite of modern supply chain technologies.

Despite all the positive signs, CRM has had a bad reputation for payback with a distinctive lack of successful implementation and losses in the billions of dollars. According to a Meta Group 2005 study, 55 to 75 percent of implementation projects were reported as failures; a 2006 Gartner Group reported 55 percent of all CRM projects failed to produce targeted results.[9] And such unfavorable reports extend back, year after year, to the beginning of the new century. What has caused this discrepancy between CRM technologies and a history of broken promises? What is the place of *customer experience management* (CEM) in the CRM suite? And finally, how can CRM provide the structure for the creation of effective intimate supply chains?

9.2.1.1   What Is Wrong with CRM?

Charting the reasons for CRM failure has produced an enormous literature. Among the most common causes cited are:

- too much concentration on the technology and not enough on understanding the customer
- requirement to change entrenched, product-based marketing organizations
- poorly conceived objectives and goals to be attained by the CRM system
- lack of employee and management skills to properly operate the CRM system and deploy functionality to accomplish customer value–generating intelligence
- insufficient budgeting of training and organizational dollars to successfully configure, test, and implement the chosen solution
- minimal to no return-on-investment targets to demonstrate CRM's value to employees, management, shareholders, and customers
- lack of commitment by senior management for the CRM project

Despite the importance of each of the above reasons for CRM failure, perhaps the most important is lack of a concise definition of what CRM means and how it will assist companies to grow customer equity and preserve competitive advantage. For example, Payne and Frow have compiled a list of twelve different definitions of CRM ranging from data-driven marketing to an e-commerce application.[10] Zablah et al. noted definitions describing CRM as a process, a strategy, a philosophy, a capability, and a technology.[11] Newell states that arriving at a commonly accepted definition has been "virtually impossible." Industry analysts and practitioners alike

> think CRM is a matter of technology. Some still believe it's just the process of segmenting customers. Some think it's a matter of selling efficiently. Many marketers still think CRM is just an advanced stage of database marketing—using your customer database to find which customers would be the right ones for a specific product offering.[12]

Unfortunately, this lack of focus has caused the application of CRM to drift from centering on customer relationships to just management of how customers could provide the greatest value for the company. Len Ellis, executive vice president for Wunderman, New York, summed it up best:

> Marketing automation is fine, but it's not about the customer. Most marketing automation is about costs and speed. Selling efficiency is not about the customer, it's just about leveraging your resources. Value maximization, in terms of figuring out which of your customer segments are going to deliver the most top or bottom line, that's not about the customer. So a lot of the benefits that are claimed for CRM are really benefits that accrue to the enterprise, but have nothing to do with the customer.[13]

The problem with CRM has been that companies have lost sight of what Greenberg considers as its three fundamental priorities: (1) provide a mechanism to enhance customer experience to, in effect, market to a "customer-of-one," (2) provide the technological and functional means of identifying, capturing, and retaining customers for life, and (3) provide a unified view of the customer across the entire enterprise.[14] Originally, the purpose of CRM was to record customers' transactions as well as their experiential history so that companies could more effectively shape their brand and service value propositions to attract new customers and engage existing ones in deeper, long-term relationships that locked in their business. Somehow, this side of CRM has been lost and is only now coming to the forefront as the most critical part of the customer management process.

9.2.1.2 Redefining CRM to Achieve Customer Intimacy

CRM is a business technology and a strategy that enables companies to acquire, grow, and retain profitable customer relationships. Unfortunately, instead of developing more meaningful relationships with customers, CRM has been used more as a tool to create databases and automate processes without any real focus on addressing customer experiences. Somehow the real message of CRM's capabilities got lost in the search for profitability and as a support for existing marketing practices. In reality, effectively managing customer experiences is an integral part of CRM. Although some advocates like Bernd H. Schmitt feel that a new method, called *customer experience management* (CEM), should be split off from CRM and given a special status on its own,[15] most professionals see CRM as both a technology and a customer experience management tool. David Rance, managing director of Round Limited (U.K.) has perhaps said it best:

> At its highest level, CRM defines what the company wants from the customer relationship and gathers the information and insight that is analyzed against products and service to find optimum opportunities to sell. CEM is the mechanism by which the customer is engaged to optimize the potential customer loyalty and long-term value that is defined by CRM. The customer experience is the emotional part of any transaction.[16]

In the final analysis, it seems that CRM should actually be considered as consisting of two integrated spheres, both focused on ensuring the highest level of customer equity and the deepest, most enduring relationships between a customer and the companies and brands he or she does business with.

Greenberg has come up with an interesting analogy to describe CRM. He calls it "whole-brained CRM."[17] Similar to the human brain, which is divided into right and left, so, Greenberg feels, CRM should be considered as consisting of two separate but integrated spheres. The left side is described as the "rational" side of the brain and governs language, logic, interpretation, and mathematics. The right side of the brain is described as the "intuitional/emotional" side and governs nonverbal processes, visual pattern recognition, perceptions, and interactions. Most of the problem with CRM is that it has been perceived predominantly as a left-brain tool concerned with mathematical/statistical functions, with using analytical algorithms to improve the value brought to the company by selling things to the right customer segments. The utility of CRM is to be determined on the hard calculus of corporate cost reduction and revenue increase.

The reason why so many CRM implementations have failed can be attributed to ignorance on the part of companies when it comes to the right-brain side of CRM. Organizationally, these issues boil down to a neglect of human-side factors, such as corporate culture, skills and motives of employees, and attitudes of management. When it comes to dealing with the external part of CRM—*the customer*—the situation is often far worse. Although most CRM projects start off as "full-brained" activities, the human side of the customer is often quickly lost. Instead of looking at how the business can provide value to the customer, the focus shifts to how databases and analytics can be leveraged to provide measurements and opportunities for determining how the customer can add value to the company. The left side of CRM looks at customers from the viewpoint of *functional value* while the right side

Table 9.1   CRM Versus CEM

	Focus	Objective	Data	Uses
CRM Customer Relationship Management	Record transaction data and buying habit insights about what customers purchase from the supplier	Provide database for the creation of customer statistics used to chart customers' value to the supplier	Point-of-sale data, market research, customer service feedback, e-business data	Speed time to market, increase bundle penetration, reduce churn, increase profitability, foster flexibility, increase efficiencies
CEM Customer Experience Management	Record attitudes, types of experiences, loyalty, and feelings of engagement customers have about a supplier	Provide database for the creation of better experiences and involvement to increase value of supplier to customers	Experiential marketing, buying experience data capture, customer service feedback, surveys	Optimize customer loyalty and long-term value, align bundle with customer expectation, create new innovative value propositions

views them from the perspective of the *emotional value* the company provides to them. Table 9.1 details the main difference between CRM and CEM.

True CRM attempts to merge both sides—the mathematical and the experiential. And since it is a *people system*, there can be no doubt that it is the human side that should lead the way and not vice versa. While the technical and analytical parts of CRM and the output received from them are important, the central focus should be on the right-brained objectives, which are squarely centered on achieving customer satisfaction and engaging experiences that lock in long-term loyalties. This predisposition can be seen, for example, in the Gartner Group's eight building blocks for CRM success. It is interesting to note that on the list, the customer, people, and strategic elements come first, with the technical resident at the bottom.

- **Vision**: leadership, market position, value proposition
- **Strategy**: objectives, segments, effective interaction
- **Customer experience**: alignment with strategy, feedback
- **Organizational collaboration**: changes to enhance customer experience
- **Processes**: customer life cycle, knowledge management

- **Information**: data, analysis, one view across channels
- **Technology**: applications, architecture, infrastructure
- **Metrics**: retention, satisfaction, loyalty, cost to serve.[18]

The endpoint is to use CRM to provide both a dashboard and a window into what the customer wants and expects from the enterprise—how to turn a company's portfolio of customers into lifetime assets.

9.2.1.3 CRM Definition

When all is said and done, how should CRM be defined? Although there are several definitions, the best has been composed by Greenberg in his massive study of the topic. He states:

> CRM is a philosophy and a business strategy, supported by a system and a technology, designed to improve human interactions in a business environment.
>
> In other words, CRM is a grand strategic business initiative that maps the transformation of business processes to the transformation of a business culture to satisfy the community of customer self-interest. That means it has a definable mission, vision, objectives, and performance criteria that if successful will get an expected result due to the improvement of the individual customer's experience.[19]

Authentic CRM understands that companies thrive when they know the pulse beat of the customer, when they can provide goods and services that anticipate what the customer will want before they know it themselves, and when they provide an experience that makes customers "addicted" to the companies and the brands they come to purchase.

Defining CRM today means starting with the customer's point of view and working backward through the supply chain community. CRM can be described as a:

- *Strategic toolkit* encompassing all parts of the business—marketing, sales, service, distribution, and supporting technologies—focused on forging symbiotic, long-term relationships with channel intermediates and end-customers.
- *Process for facilitating customer fulfillment* enabling marketing, sales, and service to formulate effective customer-enrichment decisions. This element requires the availability of metrics and analytical toolsets that provide a comprehensive, cohesive, and centralized portrait of the customer.
- *Method for optimizing the customer experience* by revealing those product/ service bundles that make customers feel good and personally connected to the supplier.

- *Window into the customer* so that everyone who can influence the customer experience has access to critical information about the customers, what they value most and how to ensure a positive buying experience. Such customer information must be pervasive, integrated, and insightful.
- *Method for companies to measure customer profitability* so that they can determine which customers are the most profitable, what value propositions drive value for each customer, and how to develop processes that consistently deliver to each customer the buying experiences they desire the most.
- *Facilitator of supply chain collaboration.* Customer experience management is never conducted in a vacuum: each transaction is actually an instant in what is often a long chain of events as products and information progress from one entity to the next in the supply chain. Firms that can create integrated, synchronized processes seamlessly across the channel network will be the ones that will have the greatest intimacy with the customer and the most loyal customers, generate the highest revenues, and have sustainable competitive advantage.[20]

9.2.1.4 Detailing CRM Components and Technologies

The promise of CRM is the availability of an array of technologies for marketplace intelligence gathering and decision making that enables conversion of business data into fresh sources of competitive differentiation, customer insight, and high performance. In the past, CRM was perceived purely as a stovepipe, analytical engine assisting marketing to chart and devise strategies to increase customer profitability. Today, the dormant right brain of CRM is being activated to enhance its capability to design and deliver consistent, engaging, and profitable customer experiences that validate brand value propositions and enhance long-term loyalty. "Because organizations can now measure and manage the experience scientifically," states Accenture managing partner for CRM, Woody Driggs, "they can begin looking at their organizations from the outside in and from the front office to the back. This means they can finally see how their businesses are performing from the point of view of the buyer, and shape their business strategies and operations accordingly."[21] The goal of CRM today is to provide a medium to connect to customers, listen to customers, and enable customers to connect to each other.

The components of CRM as a technology and a process for connecting with the customer are illustrated in Figure 9.2. Each represents a critical building block enabling companies to develop a window into what is really relevant to each of their customers and develop strategies to establish new opportunities to grow customer loyalty and customer equity.

9.2.1.4.1 Customer Profitability Scoring

Although charting the current and potential value firms provide to the customer is at the core of CRM, it is also critical that businesses be able to score the profitability

Figure 9.2 CRM components.

of their customers. In an era characterized by globalization, commoditization, and instantaneous supply, it is essential that firms know the profitability levels of their customers. Knowing the customer enables companies to make critical decisions regarding retention/acquisition programs, product/service bundles, innovation, and supply channel structures targeted at growing future profitability and lifetime customer value.

A popular method of charting the relationship between costs and customer profitability in the short and long run is *customer lifetime value* (CLV). The formula for the metric is as follows: the total sales revenue of a customer over the lifetime of the relationship, discounted by interest and inflation. The goal is to unearth what each customer values and from these metrics design products, services, and information structures that will drive increasing loyalty. The process begins by stratifying the customer base. This enables the buying values of the best customers to be contrasted with low CLV or lost customers. Next, qualitative research through surveys, interviews, and other techniques can be conducted to verify and expose strengths and weaknesses in the data. Finally, quantitative research tools can be applied to reveal existing and latent marketplace needs, behaviors, motivations, and attitudes, and how resources and capabilities can be continuously realigned to maximize resources based on the information. The value of customer intimacy is that it can reveal exactly which attributes of individual customer experiences are likely to grow which segments of CLV.

9.2.1.4.2 Customer Segmentation

CRM technology tools have often misled companies into thinking that the immense databases they possess will, by themselves, reveal the most profitable way to segment customers and expose patterns to build deeper value relationships. Possible ways of segmenting customers could be by profitability, or age, or average purchase, or some other dimension. Customer intimacy requires segmenting customers not from the perspective of the company and its products, but how branding, services, value propositions, and innovation provide customers with unique, engaging experiences to increase loyalty.

Selden and Colvin feel that effective customer segmentation consists of three dimensions.[22] The first dimension, determining *customer needs*, centers on documenting what customers value the most from the array of company offerings. This dimension reveals the most critical value proposition available to the customer. The second dimension, *customer behavior*, utilizes technology tools to reveal the experiential world of the customers. The goal is to document how brand and service bundles impact direct as well as usage experiences in both consumer and business-to-business contexts from the perspective of the customer. The final dimension, *customer profitability*, seeks to divide customers into segments by profitability. It is important that this step be concerned with how this information can be used to further long-term customer loyalty and not purely as a way to devise strategies focused on just selling more products.

9.2.1.4.3 Customer Personalization

A critical element in enhancing customers' buying experiences is to ensure they feel that a company's product/service bundle has been specially personalized to appeal to their tastes or is self-configurable to solve a particular problem. The difference between being treated personally and having the ability to customize a buying experience is revealing. *Personalization* is the process of predetermining for customers a range of products based on their historical profile and predictive modeling. *Customization,* on the other hand, involves customers taking an active role in designing the content of their purchase. Today, both these features use a combination of technology and information transfer to convey the substance of the customer experience. When using the Internet, personalization occurs when a supplier uses the web program to design a range of products that would appeal to the customer, whereas customization occurs when customers can configure not only their profile but the features and options of the products they desire.

Personalization provides a company with a chance to achieve genuine customer intimacy. When customers have the ability to actually determine how they want a company to interact with them, what types of products and services they are really concerned about, and how they want to conduct business, companies possess a significant advantage for relationship management. Personalization provides the mechanics and the information to empower customers, enrich their experience, and enhance their connectiveness with their suppliers by eliminating search time and transactional details from their busy schedules.

Some of the basic application functions available for the personalization and customization of online sales can be described as follows:[23]

- *Online catalogs* providing customers with the opportunity to research and compare the array of products, prices, and services offered by a supplier.
- *Online order processing* provides customers with tools to comparison shop, search for desired quality and service requirements, view product/service aggregations, participate in online auctions, and access related product/service mixes through on-screen portals.
- *Online order configurability* enables customers to design their own products and services through special configuration capabilities.
- *Lead capture and profiling* provides detailed repositories of prospect inquiries, customer sales, and profile information that can be used for website personalization and marketing follow-up.
- *Online surveys* enable marketers to quickly test the attitudes and possible behavior of prospects and customers critical for website customization and market segmentation.
- *Literature fulfillment* provides easy access to company and product/service information that can be downloaded or sent via e-mail to qualifying prospects and customers.
- *e-Mail marketing* enables companies to leverage captured customer information to establish customized marketing campaigns communicated to the marketplace via e-mail.
- *Instant messaging* permitting customers and suppliers to be in immediate and continuous contact with each other.

9.2.1.4.4 Employee Effectiveness Scoring

An intimate customer strategy requires companies to hire and train people who are committed to the concept that expanding the customer experience is their single most important role. Charting employee performance, therefore, is as critical as developing customer performance. In reality, all of the touchpoints a company has with its customers should be considered as sources for diagnostic metrics, and that includes employees.

Metrics to chart employee performance in a customer-centric organization can be based on two very different sets of objectives. The first consists of the standard metrics such as customer retention rates, new customers gained, revenue earned, utilization rates, team-based objectives, profitability, cost management, number of complaints resolved, and so forth. These measurements detail how well the employee is managing the customer's value to the organization. The second set of metrics, on the other hand, details how well the employee as an *internal customer* is receiving rewarding levels of experience. Rewarding *employee experiences* provide a new form of professional and personal development that motivates and provides a more satisfying and productive work experience for employees, which directly translates into delivering a great experience to the customer.

How then can high levels of employee satisfaction be gained? The answer, according to Schmitt,[14] is to apply the same process of creating engaged, addicted customers to employees. This means understanding their experiential world, determining what they want from the company, and listening and reacting to the changes they would like to see in their work lives. The firm should seek to get employees involved with the brand, how they can live their daily work lives engaged with the brand, and how they can use this knowledge to get external customers excited about the company. In the past, employee metrics revolved around the *command-and-control* model. In contrast, intimate customer management requires activation of the innovative and value-creating capabilities of a customer experience–focused employee organization.

9.2.1.4.5 Customer Integration Categories

An effective intimate customer strategy should not only provide exciting, engaging experiences, it should also be constructed so as to validate precisely those types of customer behaviors companies have selected as the target of their marketing message and performance measurement systems. Although it is impossible to manage the outcome of every buying experience, it is critical to construct strategies that match the content to the type of experience. Customer experiences can be grouped into three categories of company/customer interaction.

The first category, *stabilizing,* is concerned with retaining new customers. Keys to an effective stabilizing strategy focus on educating customers as to the experiential content they can realistically expect to receive, followed by competence and consistency in delivery. The second category, *critical,* consists of events or encounters that lead to memorable customer experiences. These "WOW!" moments tend to have a powerful effect on long-term customer relationships. The final category, *planned,* is intended to increase both the customer experience and profitability through up-selling and cross-selling opportunities. By matching intelligence about customers' needs with a promotion, companies can construct an appropriate buying message with an anticipated new, enriched customer experience.[25]

Effectively leveraging these interaction categories depends on the technologies used to collect and manage customer information. The most common customer interaction pattern is to view *past transactional experiences.* Intelligence in this category is collected through transaction history analysis, which in turn can provide database metrics detailing customer experience fulfillment, assessment of trends and marketing initiatives, impact on customer categories, and emerging issues.

The second source of intelligence is tracking *present relationships and experiences* to identify performance. The data in this category is collected through electronic surveys, automatically triggered at transaction completion, as well as post-sales studies or focus groups, which provide detailed, immediate feedback as to customer experience fulfillment and strategy validation. The final information is *potential patterns*. This interaction pattern seeks to uncover and test new experience strategies by leveraging forecasting and special-purpose market studies to reveal fresh new approaches to deepen customer loyalties by identifying new opportunities arising from specific customer segments or requirements for unique solutions currently unavailable.[26]

9.2.1.4.6 Metrics and Analytics

It has been stated several times that the fundamental metric in an intimate customer strategy is a customer's lifetime value. Measuring long-term profitability can be determined from a variety of metrics, which include customer retention, acquisition costs, margin, customer satisfaction, market share, and value of the customer base. According to Mengen,[27] metrics used to assess the total customer relationship can be separated into three categories. *Customer-specific metrics* focus on unearthing and categorizing the exact content of what brand solutions customers have been selecting to satisfy their needs and desires. The second category, *diagnostic metrics*, seeks to detail the nature of the customer's experience in selecting a specific supplier. This area may consist of behavioral metrics (for example, selecting a particular channel) or evaluative metrics (satisfaction with product quality, service, or sales channel). Finally, *outcome metrics,* determine the net total value of the relationship (customer profitability, share of spend, cross-sell ratios, and repeat purchase rates).

To be useful, companies need to apply analytical engines that collect, extract, modify, measure, identify, and report on customer information. Analytics can be divided into two types: *descriptive* (dealing with a customer's behavior, organization performance, or customer segment habits), and *predictive* (models used to create "what if" scenarios to gauge a customer's possible behavior). Today's analytical tools not only provide dashboards on past performance, but also predict customer preference and behavior. Among the analytical technologies available today can be found marketing automation tools, online analytical process (OLAP), CRM, web analytics and performance management tools, predictive analytics, and data warehousing/data mining.

While a host of output variables is available from the application of analytics, the most important is measuring success in customer experience domains. Several preliminary steps will have to be performed before customer experience outputs can be detailed. To begin with, the customer will have to be segmented according to the specific attributes and behavior patterns detailed in the above section into meaningful groups. This intelligence will permit marketers to determine the revenue potential and necessary investment for each group. Once this step is completed, companies can apply modeling to fit customers into the various segments based on scoring algorithms that optimize customer revenue and experiential characteristics while minimizing risk.

Once detailed information about customers' interactions with the company has been obtained, marketers can then begin measuring their success in three critical experience domains. Schmitt feels that metrics should be detailed for three essential areas of customer experience: *brand, transaction interface,* and *company innovation*.[28] The content of brand experience can be assessed with models (such as Likert scales or semantic differentials) that measure product/service acceptance with levels of customer expectation. Metrics in this domain can be attained through feedback mechanisms and performance auditing and monitoring. Measuring the experience customers have with the transaction interface tools and perceptions of customer capability for continuous innovation can be achieved using similar methods. In the end, companies need to ask customers to rate the level of coherence and consistency they have experienced from the firm's ability to integrate these three experiential domains.

Each of the CRM components above represents a radical change in direction for most marketing organizations. Customer intimacy management recognizes that customers today demand dialogue with their suppliers as they move from transaction-based to interdependent relationships where trust and a shared win-win approach is the key to success. CRM technologies must be able to facilitate exchange and engagement in an era where customers are increasingly choosing where, when, and how, even which channels they will use to satisfy their needs for meaningful solutions. Customer experience feedback should actually assist companies to reconfigure their businesses and their supply chains in their quest for new solutions and knowledge repositories that activate long-term loyalty and profitability.

9.3 Intimate Customer Management Best Practices

The outcome of developing successful customer experience models is to use the research to construct new brand-driven customer experiences that actualize core expectations, provide differentiation from the competition, and increase customer equity. The resulting strategy will then act as the driver for the application of technologies, processes, and employee training designed to deliver each day the promised experiential envelope. Effective experiential business modeling should enable companies to:

- map customer experience profiles from beginning to end so that the optimal experiences that produce the highest levels of customer value can be implemented;
- gather comprehensive quantitative and qualitative metrics that reveal customer motivations and expectations from the customer's point of view;
- anticipate a customer's needs, develop solutions targeted at customers as individuals, and provide transaction events that succeed in fostering interactive, mutually beneficial relationships;

- build in engaging interactions with product and service bundles that are fully integrated with the total customer experience;
- leverage the supply chain community to broaden and deepen the customer's experience at any touchpoint in the supply network.

Information technology toolsets should provide companies with:

- software that enables businesses from every corner of the supply chain to compile, abstract, analyze, and report on all facets of customer transactional and experiential data
- interactive systems that can easily link supply chain members together so that a complete picture of the customer is available
- flexible applications that permit ease of data mining, reporting, and scoreboard creation that can be shared simultaneously with the entire channel
- visibility to changes and events occurring anywhere in the supply chain
- capability to act swiftly to resolve customer problems occurring anywhere in the supply chain that could endanger positive customer experiences and access to supply chain simulation so that resources and demands can be kept in balance, thereby presenting a single, virtual supply chain response capable of providing superlative experience anywhere along the supply chain continuum

Leveraging intimate supply chain modeling and technology tools requires companies to establish a series of best practices as illustrated in Figure 9.3. The purpose of

Figure 9.3 Intimate supply chain best "practice".

these best practices is to ensure understanding of the right performance attributes so that the customer experiential strategy remains focused.

- *Leadership.* Realizing the competitive advantages possible through the implementation of intimate supply chain management requires effective leadership on both company and channel network levels. Developing the necessary experiential relationships with customers is a long-term commitment that requires the ongoing participation of each participant in the supply chain. Success inside the organization is a top–down affair driven by a powerful executive sponsor responsible for project management. On the other hand, supply chain success depends on the skills and power of the channel steward. In each case the initiative will be stillborn if it is not treated seriously by line, sales, and management staff members, who will unfortunately perceive it as just another temporary improvement project destined to failure.

- *Customer Interface.* This best practice is concerned with the nature of the exchange of information and service that occurs between the customer and the company. According to Schmitt,[29] there are three general types of customer exchange: *face-to-face* (where the customer interaction occurs in person), *personal-but-distant* (interactions occur between people, but remotely via e-mail, phone, or fax), and *electronic* (disconnected interactions occurring via e-commerce or EDI [electronic data interchange]). Regardless of medium, the goal is to ensure the customer's wants, needs, and expectations are satisfied at each touchpoint, personalization of interaction that fosters relationship building, access to experiences that highlight brand and supporting services, and application of knowledge, analytics, and technologies that enable a superior buying experience to occur.

- *Employees.* Customer intimacy requires organizations staffed by people who have been recruited, trained, and motivated with the right incentives to align their behavior with the customer-focused strategies of the organization. Of critical importance are effective measurements that chart employee behavior against a customer experience management standard. The results should be shared with each employee and used as a springboard to deepen employee involvement in not only enabling the customer to receive a memorable experience, but also recording customer feedback data.

- *Customer Feedback.* An intimate supply chain can succeed only when customers provide authentic responses to their buying experiences. Several key principles can be used. To begin with, actionable feedback should be based on customers' viewpoints and not on predetermined expectations centered on company strategies. Next, a methodology should be devised that will effectively gather feedback, complete with monitoring triggers. Following, the customer base should be segmented to avoid skewing of results. Goals for response rates and incentives for participation should be developed by segment. Finally, redefine feedback content so that frequency, medium of data capture, and respondent targeting can be customized to reach any market segment.

■ *Process Reconstruction.* Without the timely reconstruction of customer experiential interfaces, an intimate customer management program is destined for failure. CRM technologies provide companies with applications containing response mechanisms alerting staffs to out-of-bounds conditions. Whether stemming from a survey or an online transaction, the software should provide guidelines on the correct response, including responsible employee, timing, and how proper action should be taken. Strategically, response systems should enable analysts to pinpoint changes to supporting supply chain touchpoints. Criticality of the channel process reconstruction can be demonstrated by assembling costs-versus-benefits statements. The goal of the problem/response channel distribution is:

- Timeliness (speedy compilation and release of information)
- Context (completeness of data)
- Process (identifying correct solution)
- Ease of use (information detail facilitates process reconstruction).[30]

■ *Experiential Marketing.* Customer intimacy management requires companies to drastically change their practice of marketing. According to Schmitt, "experiential marketing focuses on the usage and consumption situation (instead of products), on types of experiences (instead of product features), and on bringing together and integrating the stimuli that customers receive at all touchpoints."[31] Experiential marketing attempts to view product/service bundles in the experiential context in which they are purchased by investigating and documenting the motives, attitudes, and personal drivers that influence the customer's buying decision.

■ *Goals and Metrics.* The primary output of today's CRM application suites is the recording of all elements of the customer transaction and analytical tools for data management and output reporting. The range of goals established should support targeted customer experience objectives, be specific to each business segment, and capable of being summarized to provide channel-level performance. Although metrics detailing customer satisfaction and loyalty are important, analysts should focus on measurements that link customer retention to profitability or operations improvement key performance indicators (KPIs). Finally, goals and metrics should be comprehensive, yet transparent enough to provide the entire supply chain with statistics that serve to validate existing channel structures and act as a guide to new regions of performance improvement and operations reconstruction.

■ *Organizational Architecture.* It is one of the main themes of this book that companies cannot achieve the necessary levels of customer-winning intimacy without effective supply chain support. While many CRM systems will provide each individual company with the data and toolsets to manage their own customers, they are rarely scaled to meet a supply chain environment. An effective CRM system must possess an information architecture capable of managing transactional data and customer intelligence across all supply chain entities. Robust CRM architectures enable analysts to then construct a unified view of the total experience and value received from the perspective of the customer across multiple brands and touchpoints.

The tasks of identifying and improving on customer experiences on the company level, much less in the supply chain, is an enormous task that most companies are just beginning to tackle. Monolithic supply chains (like a Wal-Mart, Home Depot, or Best Buy) have the power to enforce their customer-centered best practices on the supply channels they have come to dominate. The real challenge will be for channels without masters to engineer, behind the guidance of an effective channel steward, mutually agreed upon standards and practices that will focus on providing the best experience to customers wherever they are found rather than simply on local parochial interests and objectives.

9.4 Summary

Companies that expect to be today's market leaders know that they must not only have superior products with the highest quality, but that they also must be focused on becoming as intimate as possible with their customers. Such a strategy requires firms to embrace three customer-centered disciplines. First, they must gather detailed knowledge of everything there is to know about their customer. Second, they need to have organizations that nurture and communicate this intelligence between employees and with their supply chain partners. And finally, this insight cannot be effectively leveraged unless they possess the technologies that permit them to develop the performance measurements and metrics necessary to build extraordinary customer experiences and lock in long-term loyalties that span the entire supply network.

Preparing effective intimate customer performance measurements is a three-part process that begins with identifying the nature of each individual customer's or customer group's relationship with the business. This process begins by mining company transaction data to properly calculate *customer value.* This will reveal the most profitable groupings of products and customers. This step, however, makes transparent only *what* the customer bought. Intimate customer management goes further in that it seeks to understand the *motivations* of customers by deploying tools such as questionnaires, surveys, and direct contact, to determine exactly *why* customers buy a certain product. The final task is identifying the content of the *experience* a customer encounters at each buying event. Such an experience is always unique to the customer and is influenced by such intangibles as past encounters, present mood, psychological disposition, aspirations, and fears.

The ability to assemble the data to make the above step happen resides in the second step: selection and implementation of the proper technologies and modeling methods. Although there are several toolsets available, ranging from ERP to web analytics, business intelligence platforms, and sales and marketing automation suites, the most common solution is CRM. The purpose of CRM is twofold. On the one hand, CRM is a technology focused on populating customer databases, providing extraction and analytical tools for analysis, and automating sales and marketing processes. However, besides this calculative side, CRM also consists of another sphere concerned with identifying and documenting the human side—the customer experience that occurred with each transaction, and the corporate culture and the skills, motives, and attitudes of employees and management involved in each opportunity for customer service. Effective CRM metrics reveal both the profitability side of product and service value propositions as well as the capability of the company to engage the customer in long-term relationships that grow customer equity.

Once the content of customer measurements has been defined and the technology tools identified, companies can move to the final part of effective intimate customer management: the establishment of best practices to guide ongoing business analysis and innovation. These operations-process attributes ensure that the organization is focused on customer experience–based objectives through effective leadership, implementation of customer interfaces permitting customers to interact effectively with the business, motivation of employees, utilization of the proper channels of customer feedback, and activation of experiential marketing practices capable of identifying customer-centered goals, metrics, and organizational structures. These best practices must also include developing metrics for measuring the entire supply chain and not just individual companies.

Endnotes

1. The phrase "a portfolio of customers" was coined by Larry Seldin and Geoffrey Covin in their book, *Angel Customers and Demon Customers: Discover Which Is Which and Turbo-Charge Your Stock* (New York: Portfolio, 2003), 41–44.
2. Ranjay Gulati, and James B. Oldroyd, "The Quest for Customer Focus," *Harvard Business Review* 83, no. 4 (April 2005): 93–101.
3. See Ginger Colon, "By the Numbers," *CRM Magazine*, November 22, 2002; and Bob Thompson, *The Loyalty Connection: Secrets of Customer Retention and Increased Profits*, Right Now Technologies White Paper (Bozeman, MT: Right Now Technologies, 2005), 4.
4. An excellent exposition of the role of desire in building customer intimacy can be found in John Todor, *Addicted Customers: How to Get Them Hooked on Your Company* (Martinez, CA: Silverado Press, 2007), 73–84.
5. Scott Robinette and Claire Brand with Vicki Lenz, *Emotional Marketing: The Hallmark Way of Winning Customers for Life* (New York; McGraw-Hill, 2001), 60.

6. These steps have been loosely adapted from Gulati and Oldroyd. They speak of a four-stage process for managing customers beginning with what they call "Communal Coordination," which then progresses through "Serial Coordination," "Symbiotic Coordination," and ending with "Integral Coordination."

7. Lior Arussy, *Innovating IT: Transforming IT from Cost Crunchers to Growth Drivers* (Indianapolis, IN: Wiley Publishing Co., 2005), 57–76.

8. These statistics are found in Coreen Bailor, "Sizing up the CRM Situation," *CRM Magazine*, September 2007, 16–17.

9. These reports were found in Richard E. Crandall, "A Fresh Face for CRM," *APICS Magazine*, October 2006, 20–22.

10. Adrian Payne and Pennie Frow, "A Strategic Framework for Customer Relationship Management," *Journal of Marketing* 69, no. 4 (October 2005): 167–177.

11. Alex R. Zablah, Danny N. Bellinger, and Wesley J. Johnston, "An Evaluation of Divergent Perspectives on Customer Relationship Management: Towards a Common Understanding of an Emerging Phenomenon," *Industrial Marketing Management* 33, no. 6 (August 2004): 475–489.

12. Frederick Newell, *Why CRM Doesn't Work: How to Win by Letting Customers Manage the Relationship* (Princeton, NJ: Bloomberg Press, 2003), 4.

13. Len Ellis, "Great Expectations," Annual CRM Roundtable, *Direct*, March 15, 2002, 28.

14. Paul Greenberg, *CRM at the Speed of Light: Capturing and Keeping Customers in Internet Real Time* (Berkley, CA: McGraw-Hill, 2001), xviii.

15. Schmitt, *Customer Experience Management*, 15–17.

16. Quoted in Bob Thompson, *Customer Experience Management: The Value of "Moments of Truth,"* CustomerThink Corp. White Paper (Burlingame, CA: Customer Think Corp., 2006), 3.

17. Paul Greenberg, *CRM at the Speed of Light: Essential Customer Strategies for the 21st Century*, 3rd ed. (New York: McGraw-Hill, 2004), 52–64.

18. Philip Britt, "Eight Building Blocks for CRM Success," *Customer Relationship Magazine*, July 2003, 22.

19. Greenberg, *CRM at the Speed of Light*, 64.

20. See the definition in David F. Ross, *Introduction to e-Supply Chain Management: Engaging Technology to Build Market-Winning Business Partnerships* (Boca Raton, FL: St. Lucie Press, 2003), 167–168.

21. Accenture, *Customer Analytics: Becoming Customer-Centric*, Accenture White Paper (New York, NY: Accenture, September 2006), 2.

22. Selden and Colvin, *Angel Customers and Demon Customers*, 118–138.

23. These points have been summarized from Ross, *Introduction to e-Supply Chain Management*, 179.

24. Schmitt, *Customer Experience Management*, 226–228.

25. For a more in-depth review of these three points, see *Categories of Customer Interaction*, Kinesis White Paper (Seattle, WA: Kinesis, 2001), 1–4.

26. See the discussion in Christopher Meyer and Andre Schwager, "Understanding Customer Experience," *Harvard Business Review* 85, no. 2 (February 2007): 117–126.

27. Found in Paul Greenberg, *CRM at the Speed of Light*, 556–558.

28. Schmitt, Customer Experience Management, 216–217.
29. Bernd H. Schmitt, *Customer Experience Management: A Revolutionary Approach to Connecting with Your Customers* (Hoboken, NJ: John Wiley & Sons, 2003), 142–143.
30. See the discussion in Satmetrix Systems, *Customer Experience Management Best Practices*, Satmetrix Systems, Inc. White Paper (Foster City, CA: Satmetrix Systems, Inc., 2005), 12–13.
31. Schmitt, *Customer Experience Management*, 217–219.

Afterword

Surviving and Prospering in a New Millennium

The underlying theme of this book is that the revolutionary changes occurring today in the production, distribution, and exchange of goods and services on a global basis has forever altered long-standing economic patterns of behavior and revealed radically new avenues of opportunity for listening to and engaging the customer. Globalization has awakened companies to the presence of enormous new markets previously closed behind political and economic iron curtains, activated vast pools of new talent, and diffused innovation among a myriad of nations big and small. It has also enabled producers and distributors to explore new technologies and management methods providing for the transformation of once inwardly focused vertical organizations into efficient, low-cost value networks composed of business partners capable of providing superior customer value anywhere on the globe.

While it has provided radically new sources of opportunity, globalization has also placed tremendous pressure on all companies to remain competitive. The ability to access resources and capabilities on a worldwide basis has driven firms to decouple procurement, production, distribution, services, and information management functions, maximize economies of scale, scope, and location, pursue standardization of processes, and accelerate the dispersion of once proprietary product and process technologies among a fluid community of channel partners. In such an environment companies can no longer depend on advantages in products and services: things are continuously in the process of moving to commoditization as copycats deploy newer methods that lower cost and improve quality and functionality.

For all kinds of customers, globalization, rapid innovation, and hypercompetition have resulted in dramatic shifts in what they value in the marketplace and will reward with their continued loyalty. Today's customer has been provided with an almost limitless access to products and services, rapid change, and the capability to switch to new products and suppliers at will in the search for low cost and availability. Customers have increasingly come to view even the most sophisticated products

257

as commodities and the most satisfying of supplier relationships as permanent only until the next transaction. In such a world, customers now reign supreme as they exert increasing pressure on their suppliers to reduce the cost of products and services while demanding individual attention, complete solutions to their problems, and ease of access and payment with the minimum in hassle and total cost of consumption.

In such a business climate, what makes a company and its brand exciting is no longer the array of product features and associated services it offers, but rather its ability to provide customers with unique sources of value that extend far beyond mere product possession. Increasingly, customers no longer care where they get their products and services, as long as they can get them as cheaply, quickly, and conveniently as possible. What they cannot easily get, however, is the experience and sense of engagement they receive when they do business with their favorite suppliers. Despite the ability of customers to shop around in a variety of formats for the best product at the lowest price, customers more than ever are looking to build strong relationships with their suppliers. A marketplace of continuous change, short product life cycles, the hassles of a self-service environment, perceived loss of control of the process, even the sheer abundance of available products and services has stressed customers to the point where they are seeking suppliers that can provide them with a sense of predictability and control, and where they feel they are special and unique.

The desire on the part of customers to be emotionally and psychologically engaged in the buying experience is a universal component regardless of the type of product or service. Whether shopping for a commodity or an individually configured product, the process is immersed in emotions stemming from past experiences and the positive and negative feelings emanating from the present encounter. Companies that construct processes that enable customers to enrich what they find meaningful and fulfilling in their lives by interacting with the firm's brands and fulfillment functions will be able to strengthen their relationships and expand high customer lifetime value. In contrast, companies that seek to compete solely by offering the best combination of product feature, price, promotion, and convenience are doomed to attract only the indifferent customer who buys as cheaply and easily as possible while remaining loyal to companies providing experiences that are much more meaningful.

Understanding that the goal of today's company is to engage the customer in an ongoing journey toward ever-closer relationships and high customer equity is one thing: building the internal and external organizations capable of actualizing this objective is quite a different matter. Internally, company behavior and values must change from a belief that what the customer values is created by them and is manifested in the products and services they offer, to strategies focused on activating opportunities for customers to realize the values they most desire *through* the business's offerings. Activating such a customer-centered perspective will require migration from a *product-centered* to an *experiential* marketing approach, the allocation of organizational resources to improving customer experiences, enhancement of the employee experience, and the refocusing of databases to be customer experience and not just accounting focused.

While the challenges of building an intimate customer environment are significant enough for an individual company, they are magnified when it comes to the supply chain. It has become a commonly accepted axiom of modern management that businesses compete through the supply chain communities to which they belong. Market leaders today must seek to build lean, agile, demand-driven supply chains capable of adapting their value propositions to effectively respond to the demand-pull of the customer. In addition, as companies like Starbucks, Apple, Sony, Toyota, and others have shown, they must also create a unique emotional and psychological connection with their customers that engenders long-term commitment and a strong sense of loyalty. In short, companies must be *intimate* with customers everywhere in the supply chain. They must know who they are, what they purchase, what they value, and how they can be left continually excited about the products and experiences they receive from their value chains. Supply chain intimacy is not an option: it is the only way to retain and build loyal cohorts of customers immune to the enticements of low-cost competitors who are only a mouse click away.

When the concept of *supply chain management* (SCM) was first introduced, companies saw it as a way to execute the low-cost transfer of products by leveraging the competencies and capacities of channel supplier and logistics partners. Today, companies are beginning to realize that SCM is not just about reducing costs but also activating new avenues of business value by aligning supply chain capabilities with the needs of the customer. Intimate supply chain management requires businesses to take the next step: they must utilize the array of techniques surrounding lean, adaptive, demand-driven SCM to build value networks capable of making a special connection with the customer, of providing an engaging experience with the customer that transcends the simple exchange of value. In this view, the prime role of the supply chain shifts from being simply a pipeline for the flow of products and information and becomes instead a community of networked suppliers where customers can receive unique, personalized value triggered by emotional responses to experiences that *connect* them through deep, meaningful relations with their suppliers.

Enabling supply chains to make the leap to customer intimacy, however, requires them to significantly transcend their approaches to SCM by effectively responding to the following dimensions to experience-based channel management.

1. *Channel leadership.* Ensuring the optimal customer experience will require the presence of a channel leader or steward. The content of this role is to ensure the integration and adherence to the customer experience strategies found at each level of the supply chain. In channels governed by a channel master, such as Wal-Mart, Home Depot, and Starbucks, leadership is easily determined by the dominant player who controls all aspects of product and pricing as well as the buying experience. The greater challenge is for supply chains that are not driven by a dominant player. Here a single or confederacy of channel players must shoulder the responsibility of using a combination of persuasion and cohesion to articulate the experiential strategy for the value network as a whole.

2. *Adaptive supply chain architectures.* As the power of the customer expands and competition increases, intimate supply chains must possess a fluid structure that enables them to be rapidly reconfigured to respond to a rapidly changing marketplace. Continuous realignment of channel capabilities and players is made all the more difficult by the fact that there are many types of players that have to be assembled into a contiguous supply engine. Supply chain leaders must possess the skill to reconfigure the structure of material suppliers and producers found in the *process value chain* and the variety of intermediaries constituting the *value delivery network.* Gaps in supply chain continuity threaten the execution of superior customer experiences at the moment of the buying event.

3. *Trust, collaboration, and mutually beneficial relationships.* The application of lean and its emphasis on cost reduction has often resulted in a lack of trust and aversion to collaboration among supply chain members. This dynamic is particularly evident in supply chains that compete along the lines of price, promotion, and convenience. Supply chains that seek, on the other hand, to compete through offering the customer a superior experience depend on closely knit organizational boundaries and heavily collaborative processes. Activating trust and collaboration requires effective methods of communication, integration of processes across business boundaries, goal congruity, and actual performance across a global background.

4. *Alignment and strategic visibility.* A serious impediment to the intimate supply chain is the inability of all network nodes to have a supply chain perspective. Closing this critical gap requires all network players to understand the impact of intimate customer management on the performance of the entire supply chain. Such measurements extend beyond just charting the metrics associated with existing and new product portfolio profitability, fulfillment agility, and attraction of innovation: they must also measure the impact of strategies for growing long-term customer equity in the face of pressures from globalization and commoditization.

5. *Technologies.* Welding supply chains into seamless value networks requires the availability of integrative technologies that provide all levels of the supply chain with real-time windows into the actual pull of customer demand as it occurs, and the availability of comprehensive and easy to mine databases providing for uniform performance metrics. These technologies span the gamut from ERP and CRM system integration to the deployment of web-based applications that provide access to databases for real-time planning, customer management, and performance metric retrieval and scoreboarding.

6. *Effective performance measurements.* Intimate supply chains depend on the ability of channel members to continuously search for mechanisms that interrelate their business processes. This dimension is very difficult because the performance targets pursued by one channel business do not directly

match the same processes occurring in other channel network organizations. This is especially so as globalization and outsourcing render supporting metrics for correlative touchpoints and linkages more difficult to achieve. The supply chain metrics that evolve must be capable of providing much more than just an evaluation of how well the supply chain is meeting cost reduction and throughput targets. In contrast, intimate supply chain measurements must address not only how well the whole supply network is meeting quantitative objectives, but also how channel collaboration and cooperation is enhancing qualitative performance elements associated with enhancing customers' experiences when they are engaged in the transaction process.

In a business environment increasingly characterized by commoditization, the onslaught of global competition, and pressures on prices and margins, companies today cannot possibly hope to remain profitable for very long without focusing on bonding customers to their brands and business culture by becoming as intimate as possible with their needs and desires. To try to compete on products, price, and promotion (the old marketing trilogy) is sheer suicide and dooms companies to a winless war in Wal-Mart World. Companies in the mature industrialized world have one trump card to play and that is to construct organizations and marketplace approaches that build on the fact that today's customer values the *experience* they have in the consumption of the product more than possession of the product itself. To realize this objective they must understand what motivates the customer, what creates a sense of emotional satisfaction and joy, what leads to trusting and value relationships—in short, how intimacy can build permanent bonds that can weather the tempest of a world flooded by buying processes that are increasingly governed by anonymous companies and commodity products purchased by an increasingly disinterested customer who views companies and their brands as indistinguishable and ultimately interchangeable.

Index

A

Absolute advantage, *vs.* comparative advantage, 35–36
Accelerated ROI, 168
Acceptability of risk, 15
Access, 15
Adaptive demand-driven supply chain, xv, 129–130, 161. *See also* Demand-driven supply networks (DDSN)
  advantages, 146
  advent of, 140–141
  attributes, 142
  channel network fabric, 145
  competencies, 154–161
  components of, 145
  customer demand-driven nature of, 142
  customer-driven competency, 154–155
  customer focus in, 146
  defined, 141–143
  delivery flexibility in, 142–143
  demand-driven supply networks within, 147–153
  event visibility in, 146
  exploitation of new revenue opportunities in, 146
  increased channel collaboration in, 146
  in journey towards customer intimacy, 179
  lean strategies in, 146
  management fundamentals, 141–145, 143–146
  operations excellence in, 157
  optimization of, 160–161
  organizational flexibility of, 143
  supply chain collaboration in, 159
  supply flexibility in, 142
  vs. intimate supply chain, 180–182

Adaptive supply chain management, xv, 112, 125, 141, 161, 199, 260
Adidas, supply chain flexibility, 144
Advanced Micro Devices, Inc. (AMD), 43
Advantaged goods, 36
Advertising agencies, facilitator functions, 88
Aesthetics, and conformance, 15
Agents, 81–82
Agile processes, 63
Agile supply chain, 165
  attributes of, 158
Agile support, 16–17
Agility, xv, 140, 142, 161, 162
  event-driven nature of, 158
  and fulfillment/replenishment flexibility, 157–158
  and supply chain visibility, 155
  through integration and networking, 33
Agricultural marketing, commission houses in, 82
Alert signal management, 144, 156
Alliances, 91
  in value delivery networks, 76
Allied manufacturers, 84
Amazon.com, 5, 43, 203
AMD, 29
Annual customer value, 206
APL Logistics website, 89
Apple Computer, xiii, 231, 259
  customer intimacy faux pas, 207
  iPod, 213
  and memorable experience as gateway to customer loyalty, 203
Asset agility, 112
Asset utilization
  improving with DDSNs, 153
  and operations excellence, 109

Total productive maintenance (TPM), 117
Total Quality Management (TQM), 114
Total value, 176
Toyota Production System, xiii, 114, 117, 259
Trade, as core of civilization, 34
Transaction-based systems, 90, 217
Transaction interface metrics, 248
Transactional cycle times, 192
Transactional mechanics, 11, 16
   and agile/scalable support, 16–17
   and customer-centric value chains, 16
   digitizing sourcing, 18–19
   and fast flow fulfillment, 17–18
   networking and, 18
Transportation flexibility, 139
   with DDSNs, 153
Transportation functions
   creating flexible transportation, 139
   of facilitators, 88
   role in logistics, 98
   value delivery networks, 87
   waste in, 117
Truck wholesalers, 83
Trust building, 109, 260
   and supply chain collaboration, 159

U

Underutilization, of employees' minds/values, 117
University of Chicago, xxi
Unpredictable demand, 131
   and agility, 157–158
Unprofitable customers, cost of, 206
U.S. account deficit, financing by foreign capital, 26
U.S. imports and exports, 27
   dramatic growth with globalization, 26

V

Value, 22
   based on customer intimacy, 41
   of channel pipeline inventories, 192
   continuous delivery from customer perspective, 185
   customer perceptions of, 176
   from customer perspective, 187
   measuring in customer terms, 20
   optimizing from customer perspective, xiv
Value-added resellers, conflicts with, 92–93
Value-added services, 70, 82–83
   as function of value delivery networks, 86
Value-centric strategies, 44

Value chain mapping, 220
Value creation
   with CEM, 173
   by DDSNs, 155
   for suppliers *vs.* individual customers, 175
Value delivery networks, xv, 54, 58, 61, 64, 73, 76–77, 94, 95, 97, 150, 152, 153, 170, 176
   building product assortments via, 86
   bulk breaking functions, 86
   buying functions, 86
   construction of, 60
   decisions, 89–94
   defined, 76–77, 94
   delivery network facilitators, 88–89
   designing structures of, 79–80
   differentiation from demand channel, 58–59
   driving customer intimacy via, 75–77
   functional flows, 70
   functions, 85–87
   intermediaries in, 81–85
   linking customer demand with, 150
   managing channel conflict in, 91–94
   marketing information functions, 87
   merchandising functions, 87
   process method choice and, 67
   rationale for, 77–79
   and reverse flow channels, 87
   role of, 85–89
   selling and promoting functions, 86
   systems choice, 90–91
   transportation functions, 87
   value-added processing function, 86
   warehousing functions, 87
Value dimension, 11–13
Value discovery, in SRM, 71
Value exchange, 199. *See also* Exchange value
   seller *vs.* buyer power to determine, 201
Value-focused global operations, 47
Value networks, 101
Value/price tradeoff, 15
Value production, 114
Value propositions, 103
   aligning for intimate supply chain creation, 198, 218–220, 225
   customer identification for, 219
   from customer's perspective, 220
   in demand management strategy, 59
   intelligence accumulation and analysis, 219–220
   proposal creation, 219
   proposition testing and verification, 219
   requirements for building, 219
   rollout phase, 219